Beyond Hybridity and Fundamentalism

Beyond Hybridity and Fundamentalism

*Emerging Muslim Identity
in Globalized India*

TABASSUM RUHI KHAN

OXFORD
UNIVERSITY PRESS

OXFORD
UNIVERSITY PRESS

Oxford University Press is a department of the University of Oxford.
It furthers the University's objective of excellence in research, scholarship,
and education by publishing worldwide. Oxford is a registered trademark of
Oxford University Press in the UK and in certain other countries

Published in India by
Oxford University Press
YMCA Library Building, 1 Jai Singh Road, New Delhi 110 001, India

First Edition published in 2015

ISBN-13: 978-0-19-945361-0
ISBN-10: 0-19-945361-6

Typeset in Adobe Jenson Pro 10.5/13
by The Graphics Solution, New Delhi 110 092
Printed in India by Rakmo Press, New Delhi 110 020

CONTENTS

ACKNOWLEDGEMENTS

I thank my colleagues and the Dean's office at the University of California, Riverside, for the financial and moral support extended to this project. I am grateful for the fellowship from the Asia Research Institute, National University of Singapore, to revise and edit my manuscript. And I am indebted to my mentors who have made this jouney possible. I address each one of you personally and heartfully for taking me this far, when I had little faith, but was driven only by that urge to speak and to make a difference. Thank you Anwar Jamal Kidwai, Narayani Gupta, Drew McDaniel, S. Y. Quraishi, Ron Hunt, Toby Miller, Peter Moller, Hailey Duschinski, and Vijayluxmi Bose for keeping that flame alive.

I acknowledge the faith and the struggle of my informants. You have inspired me to chart a new direction in my life. I don't know where this journey will take me, but whereever I go I will remember and cherish the confidence that you have placed in me. I hope I have lived up to it. Thank you Rana Khan, Manisha Sethi, Kashif-ul Huda, and all the others whose names I do not mention here, but who know well that I speak of them.

I acknowledge my friends, their love and their warmth, which endures through years, sustains despite distances, and extends across oceans to envelope me.

And mostly I acknowledge the acceptance of my family. Thank you for giving me that space to grow. And thank you Sana and Samreen for being my light burning bright into the future.

INTRODUCTION
Beyond Hybridity and Fundamentalism

In India, an overtly religious country, the dominant view is that Muslims have an unduly strong attachment to their religion and culture (see Ahmed, 1983; Hasan, 2004). The problem with this assumption is that while the Islamic brand of religiosity does not spur the business of packaged tours as does India's famed spirituality, it definitely presents Muslims as less amenable to assimilative trends and more prone to standing apart from mainstream national life (see Hasan, 2002) in a state of calcified inertness. In the context of everyday life in secular democratic India, the markers of our stubborn insistence on maintaining a particular identity are presumably evident everywhere. The most prominent, besides the sartorial choices of the *burkha*[1] and the unkempt beard, are the crowded urban ghettos—residential spaces of most urban Muslims across social and class spectrums where non-Muslims fear to venture. We are also distinguished by our infamous politics of *fatwas*[2] and arcane decrees, and by our persistent resistance to uniform civil code—acts that are seen as stalling the possibilities for peaceful co-existence and assimilation into Indian society.

The Muslim distinctiveness presents a unique problem to nationalistic discourses in a country where differences born of diverse regional, religious, linguistic, and ethnic affiliations have been reconciled in the contradiction of 'unity in diversity'[3] (Nehru, 1951); and despite a thousand years of shared-eclectic history, Muslim presence continues to be seen as disrupting the equanimity of the Indian version of multiculturalism. However, when our cultural politics is perceived to be particularly reprehensible and in negation of secular-democratic ethos and modernity is when it denounces liberal critics of Islam— such as Salman Rushdie—who are otherwise celebrated as ideal hybrid citizens[4]. In secular democratic India, Muslims maintain a precarious hold on their rights as Indians and as citizens because they are also held responsible for the Partition of the subcontinent into India and Pakistan, and are seen as constituting a continuing threat to the integrity of the Indian nation on account of their suspected and divided loyalties.

Therefore, the assaying of a distinct Muslim persona, which is immediately announced even when one is not sporting a beard or a veil with the mere mention of Persian and Arabic names, has its moments of disquiet. In urban middle class milieus inhabited by a privileged few, within a largely impoverished community, remarks such as 'oh, but you don't look like a Muslim,' uttered by well-meaning colleagues and friends are often received with a sigh of relief. This was particularly so for the older generations of middle class Muslims. This is because the power of discriminatory and derogatory discourses to demote an uncertain standing in social and professional realms is infinitely more acute in a state controlled economy with limited employment opportunities; it was also more deeply internalized that many of my generation would breath a little easy on hearing that remark, believing that the threat to social privileges associated with inclusion in mainstream society appeared to have passed for the moment. I remember, as a young adult in New Delhi in the late 1980s and early 1990s, that such a comment was never openly critiqued or challenged for being offensive, though its veiled meaning was that our presence would be welcome in certain settings only if we eschewed all overt identifications (and perhaps even sympathy) with our community. In the current contexts, whence extreme anti-Islamic sentiments prevail, as local antagonisms conflate with fall-outs of global events such as 9/11, it would appear that the pressures to silence the Muslim distinctiveness and have them refrain from challenging the hegemony of the dominant identity would have become even more relentless. However, despite clear indications of the rise of such trends, considering the steady emergence of the most belligerent form of Hindu right-wing nationalism in India since early 1990s; the augmentation of Hindu fundamentalism by aligning with the global war on terror implicating Islam; the mounting evidence of the state's increasing impunity in targeting Muslim youths; and despite the dwindling critique from liberal-socialist quarter of these unsavory developments,[5] Muslim victimization is not the reason why I raise the issue of Muslim identity today.

The Indian Islamic identity has become an issue worth examining at this particular juncture defined by far-reaching changes in the Indian society ushered in by the forces of economic liberalization and revolutionary developments in communication technologies, because despite the overwhelming salience of stereotypes defining Indian Muslims as a monolithic, static, and unchanging, their lives and experiences have become emblematic of the inexorability of globalizing processes. The articulations, especially of Indian Muslim youth's identity, reflect the extent of their implication within cataclysmic restructuring of Indian society, polity, and economy, and thereby present a point of intervention in the ongoing debate and theorization about identity in globalized, multicultural, and increasingly interconnected worlds. I argue that their lived ideologies and current politics have become important, not because of the increasing and relentless persecution by state and other powers that be, but because the complexities of their emerging identities render as irrelevant, the dualities contingent within an either–or dichotomous frameworks conceived as opposition between victims and agents as well as between modernity and tradition. And yet notwithstanding the possibilities for a sizeable minority population's investment in the far-reaching changes in Indian society, the power of dominant stereotypes has prevented any investigation into the Muslim condition within contexts of neoliberal globalization. A large body of scholarship in multi-disciplinary fields[6] is devoted to understanding the nature of change in Indian society following economic liberalization, rapid globalization, and revolutionary growth of communication technologies of satellite television, mobile telephones, and the use of interactive media technologies of the Internet, W.2 applications, chat rooms, and social-networking platforms like Facebook. However, much of the research in these vast annals have analysed the drastically altered socio-economic-cultural environment only from the perspective of the dominant community. But, it is not only the paucity of research or the neglect of Muslim experiences that has set me on my research path (extending over the years 2006 to 2013) to map the Indian Muslim youth's subjectivities.

I am attracted to the issue because of the lived ideologies and experiences of Indian Muslim youth within an evolving Indian society driven by neoliberal globalization, contexts of enhanced interconnectivity, and a veritable explosion of media content that draw attention to the power of new flows and forces operating in a globalized, media saturated, and intricately networked worlds. Their lives and experiences are acutely illustrative of the unpredictability of the processes and the trajectories of globalization, which have been conceived as being driven mostly by exigencies of the Western world, including its imperialist and colonizing ambitions. According to John Gray (1998) 'the thinkers of the Enlightenment, such as Thomas Jefferson, Tom Paine, John Stuart Mill and Karl Marx never doubted that the future for every nation in the world was to accept some version of western institutions and values' (p.1). This inherent arrogance validated the violence involved in the decided and often remorseless missions to enforce the Western Enlightenment ideology in non-Western world. It also underlined notions belittling the East, as Amartya Sen (2006) argues, and condemning it as possessing neither the will nor the ideas, the knowledge, or the ideologies worth proselytizing. Therefore, the ensuing modernities of the non-Western world, it has been assumed, almost always emerge on contact with the West and are inevitably imbedded in Westernized thoughts and ideas. But, expressions of the Muslim youth's identity within urban middle class spheres, which is the focus of my ethnographic research, complicates established notions about what globalization entails and, therefore, how modernity may now be conceived.

Indian youth today live in a world where global influences are not limited to the West, rather they converge from all directions, and blow with equally strong force from the East as from the West. However, much of the scholarship exploring the question of identity in a globalized world order conceptualizes it within an East versus West binary framework and positions the world as being divided between those arrayed against modernity, as stable stalwarts of convention and tradition, and those embracing its possibilities and ambiguities in their heterogeneous composite personas. However, the plurality and diversity of contemporary Indian ideological force-fields make the question of emerging identities so much more complex and beyond the debates between essentialist and the liberal pluralist views of identity, as I will elaborate later. The Muslim youth's experiences and subjectivities not only epitomize this complexity, but they also pose important questions, such as: Does modernity, within post-colonial contexts, always imply the ascendance of ideas emanating in the intellectual upheavals of the Enlightenment period (as reiterated in the postcolonial notion of the hybrid)[7]? And is it modernity's prerogative to consistently announce itself in opposition to or negation and/or denial of established traditions and perspectives within non-Western contexts?

Writing against Culture

The aim of this book is to position Indian Muslim youth's emerging identities within large-scale realignments of Indian socio-economic and political contexts. And, the attempt to firmly locate a population, given up as stagnant and backward-looking, within the cataclysmic transformations of the Indian socio-cultural and political landscape, is defined, to quote Abu-Lughod (1991), as a task of 'writing against culture'. Culture is a term, which has come under express criticism for enforcing differences and solidifying them with deeply hierarchical relationships, which even efforts of interpretive ethnographers, such as Clifford Geertz and his politics of 'thick description' marking cultural differences as a celebration of diversity, have been unable to address.[8] It is also a term that has been effortlessly employed to simplify complex geopolitical dynamics such as in Hungtington's (1993) 'the clash of civilizations argument'.[9] In the case of Indian Muslims, it is their particular cultural norms based on their religious beliefs that offer an uncomplicated explanation for the Muslim community's social and economic impoverishment and their political disempowerment. The evocations of Indian Islamic cultural fallibilities help deny as well as obfuscate the role of political, institutional, legal, and economic discriminatory forces in the construction of their current demoted position in Indian society (see Sachar, 2006). However, a project that explores how Indian Muslims may be implicated within the revolutions in Indian society calls attention to the working of socio-cultural and economic forces, and thereby exposing the entrenched prejudices and inaccuracy of views projecting Muslims as stuck-in-time and stubbornly inward looking—views that impede Muslim participation in public life and delegate them to the margins of Indian society.

Therefore, I seek the narratives of the coming of age of Muslim youth in an era of far-reaching change in the Indian society. The focus here is on 'processes of becoming,' because as Stuart Hall (1996c) argues, identities are more about where we are headed rather than where we originate. Although Hall's theorizations of identity imbued with a 'deep sense of historical and political urgency' may seem idealistic, as Ien Ang (2000, p. 1) contends, they present an important interventionist frame-work to challenge essentialist and determinist views of Muslim identity with the intention of overcoming their pernicious effects. Moreover, as I seek to understand who Muslims are in their everyday and ordinary lives, I approach this task with an ethnographic investigative lens. It is a methodology most suited to understanding how the Muslim youth's social, cultural, and economic life proceeds within the evolving Indian society. It calls for identifying a contained research area and a research community as well as establishing the ethnographer's authority by gaining the trust of the informants to the extent that they allow the researcher to observe and take part in their daily rituals and are willing to share their thoughts and ideas. Engaging in what Abu-Lughod (1991, p. 153) calls 'narrative ethnographies of the particular,' I spent six years (from 2006 to 2013) trying to establish a rapport with my informants in order to understand how the altered contexts may be impinging on their life choices, dreams, and aspirations. I have specifically drawn on experiences and imaginations of Muslim youth inhabitants of the specific socio-cultural landscape of the historically and spatially differ-entiated exclusive Muslim enclave of Jamia Nagar situated in the heart of South Delhi. It is a space redolent with signs, sights, and sounds of the Indian Islamic culture. However, even as I contextualize a specific cultural landscape of a religious minority population, I do not highlight the coherence or the timelessness of religious beliefs and traditions. Rather, in the process of 'writing against culture', I focus on the inter-connections forged between the closed spaces of the Muslim youth's actual residence and the potential spaces of both imaginative as well as real habitation that lie outside.

Jamia Nagar is but one among the many geographically segregated and culturally distinct spaces of Muslim inhabitance existing across urban Indian landscapes, with some variation in the permutation and combination of key factors defining Muslim lives—namely isolation, low income levels, underemployment as well as fear of state persecution.

In Jamia Nagar and its various sub-divisions, life has a distinct flavour markedly different from the rest of the city of Delhi as the sound of *Azan* (Islamic call for prayer) resounds many times a day setting the rhythm of everyday life around definitive obligations of Islam; and here in its narrow criss-crossing lanes and bylanes, the aroma of slow roasting meat and freshly baked *naans* overwhelms the senses, confirming the lore of the 'sensuous Musalman.' However, these quintessential expressions of the Indian Islamic cultural life are also perceived as signs of an emphatic otherness. To the extent that Muslims in urban India have felt free to assert their religious and cultural identity only in such segregated enclaves. However, sympathizers like Sayid Hamid, an eminent Muslim scholar and bureaucrat, view the Muslim community's retraction into physically and cultural differentiated locales, in the face of the majority community's hostility, as being tantamount to suicide. According to Hamid, these closed spaces of Muslim residence visibly confirm Muslim disconnect from India's express destiny ('Education only way out...,' 2006). However, despite contestations around Muslim cultural life and spaces, this is not an attempt to rehabilitate Muslim cultural differences by exploring layers of embedded meaning in any 'thick description' of the Indian Islamic cultural life as interpretative and cultural anthropologists want to propose as a celebration of diversity and reaffirm relativity.[10] This is not an apology for Muslim 'otherness' either by calling attention to them as repositories of distinct cultural norms[11] or as victims of religious-cultural persecution, because both of these scenarios deny ascription of positive transformative and creative agencies to Muslims.

The Communication Revolution and Jamia Enclave

This book aims to explore new dynamics in the Muslim community arising from its involvement in the evolving Indian society, and to analyse the Muslim youth's shifting social, cultural, and ideological life. In the words of Kalb and Tak (2005), this is an ethnography of agency and experience, looking 'up and outward' at the 'critical junctions' or the connections 'in and out of a place/in and out of a group'(p. vii).[12] It is a scenario wherein the Muslim youth may still inhabit the same enclosed spaces where lives of their parents and of other older generations were shaped,[13] but their existence is no longer dictated by the logic

permeating and defining these enclosures. Globalizing narratives ushered in by new communication technologies have effectively breached
the isolation of cloistered, exclusive enclaves such as Jamia Nagar, and
the ubiquitous presence of global satellite television and the impressive
access to mobile phones and Internet ensure a constant implication of
the global within the local contexts. I examine the connections and
interactions between their closed physical and psychological spaces
and the institutions, structures, and socio-economic processes of the
world outside and the manner in which they are impinging on the
Muslim youth's consciousness. Therefore, I do not focus on the meaning invested in the cultural rhythms of religious observations, language,
literature, or food,[14] but the way established meanings and characteristic patterns are being disrupted by other expressions from far away.
I interrogate the creative dissonance, disjunction, and dissensions that
may be laying the foundation for new ideas and ways of being.

In the narrow lanes and bylanes of Jamia enclave, hundreds of cable
wires delivering content off global media platforms crisscross with
electric power lines and dangerously hang over head; while satellite
dishes of all shapes and sizes (indicating connectivity to different satellite transponders) crowd roof-tops, and billboards advertising business
establishments of various communication services (mobile telephones,
Direct to Home TV, Cable, and Internet Cafes) dominate street-level
view. However, the global flows interrupting a distinct way of life are
not just reserved to virtual or mediated spheres, because the forces of
global finance and economy also interject in the community's ecology
and bear down (like the very real cable wires and satellite dishes) on
its aspirations. The narrow lanes of Jamia Nagar's various sub-divisions,
house employment agencies promising jobs in the Middle East, garment
export businesses which cater to Indian disapora populations in various
global centers from Dubai to Durban as well as travel agencies and
courier businesses that employ the local youth. Here, the music videos
playing on satellite channels would be interrupted when the sound of
the *azan* from nearby mosques would resound and even mobile phone
conversations would be suspended in a hurry on hearing the alarm set
for the prayers. The pervasive presence of globalizing impulses entails
that the consciousness of Muslim youth, born after the late eighties,
is formed not only through accretion of forces of tradition and habit,
but shaped through active contention with ideologies and cultural

moorings that undermine stabilities of established customs, habits, and habitus, while allowing them to participate in ways of life far removed from their own. The developments in the reach, spread, and capabilities of communication technologies concomitant with new global financial regimes have embroiled their lives within far-flung turbulences in such a way that it is not the sights, sounds, and smells of their unique Islamic culture that offer them any stability, rather it is the prospect of constant change which has garnered an element of permanence.

The Personal as Political

My focus on a society in transition disrupts the connotations of stagnancy associated with the Muslim population and is a powerful way for 'writing against culture'. The focus on how the Muslim youth's desires, dreams, and expectations are being shaped at the intersections of local realities and the myriad imaginaries, ideologies, lifestyles, and selfhoods presented by global narratives helps demonstrate the Indian Muslim community's investment in India's express destiny (as opposed to their presumed disconnect)and these proofs of engagement help in making a more substantive claim for their rights as equal citizens, which the scholarship mapping Muslim disempowerment and impoverishment has been unable to do. However, my effort to lift the pall of silence suppressing and negating Indian Muslim existence, and to promote critical dialogues countering negative stereotypes, is also a personal journey.

I highlight the personal inspired by the reflexive turn in ethnography, which urges that the ethnographies of contemporary, fragmented, and deeply ambiguous contexts should be constructed with a reflexivity and an acknowledgement of how the strategic positioning and the ensuing proclivities, preferences, and biases of the scholar affect knowledge production (see Fox, 1991).[15] This is in marked contrast to the assumed objectivity of the social scientific research, wherein the personal, the institutional, and the procedural biases inherent in the research process are elided as being unimportant. But, the reflexive turn in ethnography, supported by both the postmodern and the feminist scholarship, has insisted on demarking the personal as a way of acknowledging the limitations, the inbuilt bias as well as the power dynamics of knowledge production (see Abu-Lughod, 1990; Clifford, 1986; Paramsewaran, 2001; Wolf, 1992). However, the personal as a

construct of material contexts, including those of class, access to education, and its attendant privileges of greater mobility, social, and cultural
capital becomes another standpoint in the context of my research from
which to 'write against culture' (see Abu Lughod, 1991), discrediting
monolithic, universalizing narratives of Islam and of Muslims as one
undifferentiated community.

I focus on the community's internal differences and hierarchies
structured by workings of class that some ethnographers argue have
not been adequately attended to (see Narayan, 1993; Ortner, 1991),
because the subtle material and ideological differences created by
class dynamics destabilize the myth of a unified Islamic identity. They
also help support arguments that theoretical frameworks conceptualizing identities must be more attentive to material realms rather than
focusing on discursive spheres or representations as has been the case
in postcolonial and cultural studies, which I will further elaborate in
the next sections. However, even as I evoke the power of personal to
express in tangible and palpable terms the differences in our social and
economic vantage points, (following the lead of scholars like Bell Hooks
and Gloria Anzaldua) I consciously check myself from intoning the
subaltern voice. This is because, I not only critique realist ethnographies
that fail to question authoritative promulgation of the interlocutor's
voice in ethnographic narratives while silencing the very voices it pur-
ports to project, but because I wish to call attention to these very dis-
parities structuring the Muslim experiences. For example, I have never
forgotten an encounter with a very senior civil servant, one of the very
few Muslims ensconced in the haloed precincts of the Government of
India's key ministry, on the eve of BJP's defeat in 2004 parliamentary
elections. The first thing he said on seeing a fellow Muslim was '*Aur
chaar sal ye rehte tu Allah ka khahair nazil hota hum par*' (four more
years of BJP's rule would have wrought God's wrath on us). He was sitting in his office, hence his voice was almost inaudible, but I heard him
clearly though he was speaking under his breath because I concurred
with his views completely, and recognized the release of suppressed
anxiety in his voice. I recount this story recognizing both his standing
in New Delhi's elite 'the corridors of power,' and my own privileges of
education and employment, in order to enunciate the extent of demor-
alization that must have been created by Hindu right-wing politics for
those Muslims at the other end of the social spectrum.

However, as I said earlier, the focus on Indian Muslim identity in transition is not only to rescue it from the discriminatory narratives and practices, which plague its existence, rather, the elaboration of Indian Muslim expressions of selfhood within contemporary neoliberal globalized India. It has become important because they problematized dominant discourses about identity and modernity, at a time when, according to Stuart Hall (1996c), 'there has been a veritable discursive explosion. . .around the concept of identity' (p. 1)—comparable only to deluge of scholarly attention focused on Islam, Islamic societies, and subjectivities in the wake of the events of 9/11.The question of Indian Muslim identity offers an important point of interjection in the ongoing debate, while the exploration of their organic and everyday reality, as attempted in this research, present an opportunity to build theory from the ground up.

Identity and Postcolonialism: Is That All There Is?

The discussions on identity as the core driving force and organizing principle of culture and polity have gained such an overwhelming salience in contemporary times within disciplines like cultural studies, under the influence of emerging fields of postcolonial theory and critical race studies, that it prompts cultural studies scholars like Lawrence Grossberg (1996) to ask, 'Is that all there is?' (p. 87). According to Zygmant Bauman (2001), identity has become the 'prism through which all other topical aspects of contemporary life are spotted, grasped and examined' (p. 121). The question, therefore, is how may an exploration of the Indian Muslim identity further an already rife and extensive debate?

My argument is that despite the multidisciplinary and multifarious nature of the scholarship on identity, the frameworks elucidating the constitution and the politics of identity remain fairly limited. As this investigation of Indian Muslim youth's subjectivities reveals, they are also not inclusive of the experiences of minority and marginalized populations. The dominant theoretical constructs have been deduced by focusing on experiences of certain segments of population, and in such a manner that the elision of realities of vast majorities, are gone unacknowledged.[16] Moreover, dominant theoretical frameworks have been unable to adequately account for the extreme flux in the age of neoliberal globalization as it shapes everyday lives and emergent subjectivities, spawning tendencies to simplify complex realities by containing them within binary frameworks, as reflected in the arguments of hybridity and fundamentalism, which view the world as being divided between those who embrace the flux of new influences and others who withdraw from it or reject it.

Essentialist Frameworks and Islamic Identities

Islamic identities have been particularly restricted by the essentialist conceptualizations of identity, which, according to Hall (1990), stress on the authentic, the original, and the intrinsic as being the core of the self. The arguments for a complete, distinct, as well as unchanging, and stable self also view cultures as hermetic and airtight constructs (see, Huntington,1993). These determinist definitions of cultural and individual identity highlight separateness and antipathy. For example, Islamic identities are condemned as existing in sheer opposition to the project of Western modernity, marked by deep-rooted antagonism to Western civilization's stress on democratic values, liberalism, equality, and free markets, while upholding patriarchal and non-libertarian belief systems (see Huntington, 1993; Rushdie, 2004). Islamic identities are not only perceived 'as a reaction against unreachable modernization (be it capitalist or socialist), the evil consequences of globalization, and the collapse of post-colonial nationalist project' (Castells, 1997, p. 19), but overlooking the diversity in the histories, the politics, and the economic circumstances of the different Islamic societies, this is perceived to be a universal trend. For example, Castells proposes that a primordial nostalgia for a pristine past engulfs the entire Islamic world, and that 'an Islamic fundamentalist project has emerged in all Muslim societies, and among Muslim minorities in non-Muslim nations' (p. 20),wherein the longings for a 'communal heaven' display 'little internal differentiation' (p. 67).

In India, the fault lines between Islam and the rest, which fix Indian Muslim identity as stagnant and regressive can be traced back to the divisive politics of the British colonial rulers (Metcalf, 1995). According to Metcalf, it was in the interest of the colonialists to emphasize the differences and the antagonism between Muslim and Hindus, and to highlight Muslim prosecution of Hindus, because it helped to legitimize

British colonial rule as a comparative blessing. However, the question Metcalf asks is that even if the hostilities were a British creation, why were they not dismantled in independent India? The strained relationships between Hindus and Muslims have erupted into violent conflagrations on many occasions since independence and partition of the subcontinent in 1947.

Scholars have many different opinions as to why Indian Muslims are yet to claim their rightful status within the Indian nation, and why, despite claiming India to be their homeland, they continue to bear the brunt for the creation of Pakistan. According to Shahid Amin (2004), the sense of belonging to a nation is sutured through narratives, stories, and icons, because the coming together of communities as collectives is concomitant with construction of narratives about 'long-existent collectivities' (p. 93). However, Indian Muslims have never been able to insert themselves effectively into the story of the Indian nation, and misconceptions about Muslims as foreigners and as outsiders persist at the highest levels of governance and policy making. Drawing attention to the Indian government's national integration campaign, he points how the Indian Muslim is depicted as wearing a Turkish cap, and this notwithstanding the fact that the possibilities of finding a Turkish cap in a Muslim household are about as remote as arranging for a Shakespearean costume (p. 94). And yet, these skewed impressions display a rare tenacity, because, as he argues, they are essential to the design of fabricating a Hindu nationalist history, claiming an uninterrupted and undiluted Hindu past, and validating Hindu identity's hegemonic status.[17] But, according to Amir Mufti (2000), Muslim alienation from narratives coalescing the nationalist identity has been a reality from the very incipience of the Indian state, given the fact that the Indian Muslim community had an uncomfortable relationship with anti-colonial nationalist discourses which were almost exclusively couched in Hindu iconography and symbology, and not accommodative of alternative Muslim imaginations of nationhood (which were in no way a sign of their disloyalty). The Muslim sense of disconnect from the nationalist identity only seems to have increased following the rise of right-wing Hindu nationalism. The increasing salience of Hindu iconography, symbols, and narratives, which were indeed effectively deployed and circulated in the public sphere to help the BJP come to power, as Rajagopal (2001)[18] argues, would only heighten the Muslim community's identification as a minority population. This is because, as Myron Weiner (1997) argues, a minority population recognizes itself as one through its lack of connect to 'the central symbols of the society' and that 'it is not simply that a community lacks power, but rather that the symbols of authority, the values that are propagated from the centre, and the culture that emanates from the centre are viewed as not theirs' (p. 462).

However, even as divisive historical accounts defining India's people, and drawing the boundaries of citizenship between those who belong and others who must be disenfranchised, are being disseminated with even greater vigour with often violent outcomes (Metcalf, 1995, p. 952), it is indeed ironic that a large body of scholarship which is committed to explaining the nature and cause of these conflicts with the aim of preventing them should be instrumental in augmenting the hegemony of divisive perspectives.[19] This is because this large body of scholarship also studies Islam mainly in the context of discord, and thereby augments the association between Islam and violence. Moreover, the dominant perception about Muslims as being inordinately influenced by their religious doctrines get further entrenched because there is a conspicuous absence of research on Indian Muslims within the ordinary contexts of their everyday lives, and as they go about fulfilling their socio-economic needs (see Ahmed, 1983; Hasan, 2002). Furthermore, according to Hasan, this lack of knowledge about the everyday life of Indian Muslims leads one to believe, 'that the major preoccupation of a Muslim is praying, going on pilgrimage, and observing other religious rituals' and 'that Muslims, more than any other religious entity, attach greater importance and value to their religio-cultural habits and institutions' (p. 8–9). My research addresses this paucity of knowledge about everyday Muslim life as well as the power-knowledge structures that prefer to silence the debates on the Muslim question.[20] Such a scholarship, according to Barbara Metcalf (1995), would not only speak for the Muslim reality, but would also question 'the history that identifies Indian Muslims as aliens, destroyers, and crypto-Pakistanis, with its profound moral and political implications for citizenship and entitlement,' and challenge 'the social and political interests that sustain belief in fundamental difference' (p. 963).

But it is not going to be an easy task because views promoting implacable differences between cultures, (such as Huntington's Clash of Civilizations thesis) predisposed to rage and hatred, also provide a debilitating simple black and white perspective on the world, which underlines foreign policy decisions and steers the global war on terror. These simplifications also obfuscate Indian Muslim realities and how they are being shaped within a globalized world order driven by neo-liberal capitalism. I now turn to the analytical frameworks in disciplines such as cultural studies and postcolonial studies, which are expressly devoted to overcoming tendencies to contain the world within simple binaries, challenging the authority of dichotomous frameworks.

Identities as Fluid and Fragmented

The arguments developed and professed by cultural studies scholars are anti-essentialist because they deny claims of complete and authen-tic identities, as arising from universally shared experiences, beliefs, and worldviews. Instead, they highlight instability and fluidity, which confront the modern self at the level of the everyday, continuously, and incessantly. According to sociologist Anthony Giddens (1991), the 'reflexivity of modernity,' or the dynamism of modern society, marked by a lack of certainties and mutability of all knowledge systems, has extended 'into the core of the self' (p. 33). Hence, unlike the traditional world order, wherein changes and transitions in identity (such as the passage into adulthood) were manifestly ritualized, today 'the altered self has to be explored and constructed' continuously and innovatively (p. 33), within dire and unusual circumstances, as forces of modernity, namely money, modern institutions, and media bring the local and the global together in such a way as to 'propel social life away from the hold of pre-established precepts or practices' and flung it into unknown spheres (p. 20). Therefore, as Hall (1996c) argues, the settled character of many populations and cultures has become disturbed by events of migrations and technological advances, unhinging selfhoods from historical, geographical or racial facts, and propelling them to be actively constructed using 'resources of history, language, and culture,' whereby identities are 'never unified . . . but increasingly fragmented and fractured . . . constructed across different, often intersecting and antagonistic, discourses, practices and positions' (p. 4). Hence, there is a new 'openness of social life' as tradition loses its hold, while the 'plural-ity of contexts of action,' and the lack of absolute authorities force individuals 'to negotiate lifestyle choices among a diversity of options' (Giddens, 1991 p. 5). The stress is on 'becoming' rather than on an inert status of 'being' as identities in contemporary mediated, global- ized environments where societies are 'more fluid, less predictable . . . more dependent on performance and less dependent on . . . inherited tradition' (Hall, 1996b, p. 129); especially when imagination becomes a quotidian of everyday life (and distinct from the world of high art), creating ever increasing and ever 'new resources . . . for the construc- tion of imagined self and imagined worlds' (Appadurai, 1996, p. 3) .

And yet despite the cultural studies' stress on the evolutionary nature of identity, the conceptualizations of identity continue to highlight the centrality of 'difference.' According to Hall (1996c), identities are less a question of 'naturally-constituted unity' and more a 'product of the marking of difference and exclusion' (p. 4), because as Thurlow (2010) argues, 'we make sense of ourselves by defining ourselves in relation to different people' (p. 227); and recognize ourselves through par- ticularities, differentiating characteristics, and other novelties (Jackson and Moshin, 2010). And this according to Laclau (as quoted in Hall, 1996c), is an act of power because 'an objectivity manages to partially affirm itself . . . by repressing that which threatens it' (p. 5), and find internal homogeneity within 'the play of power and exclusion' (Hall, 1996c, p. 5). However, even as cultural studies and postcolonial studies profusely acknowledge that constructions of identities as well as mark- ings of 'otherness' reflect the unfolding of power dynamics, they have been reluctant to address the workings of power within everyday mate- rial realities, and that they prefer to deal with it in largely discursive terms (see, Dirlik, 1999; Eagleton, 1999 & Murphy, 1999).

This criticism also includes the foundational arguments in the field as extended in Edward Said's (1979) text—*Orientalism*. Drawing on Gramsci's analysis of hegemony and Foucaldian discourse theory, Said challenges the meta-narratives of the Orient, and exposes how supe- rior power equations of the subject combining with diffuse function- ing of power at different levels influence the creation of knowledge about the object under scrutiny. He illustrates how the Orient could be Orientalized 'not only because it was discovered to be 'Oriental'. . .but also because it *could* (sic) be' the object of study of the Western missionary, soldier, scientist, bureaucrat (pp. 6–7). Moreover, in offering little resistance to the ruling race's exploratory and controlling gaze, 'the Orient has helped to define Europe (or the West) as its contrast-ing image, idea, personality, experience' (p. 2). He argues that the ontological and epistemological distinction between the Orient and the Occident, predicated upon complex hegemony of the Occident over the Orient, instituted a 'basic distinction' which was accepted as 'the starting point for elaborate theories, epics, novel, social descrip-tions, and political accounts concerning the Orient, its people, customs, 'mind,' destiny, and so on' (p. 2).[21] However, his creative engagements with discursive construction of the Orient have been severely critiqued for positing all knowledge as biased, and for perpetuating simple bina-ries of the powerful West and the subjugated and powerless East. The criticism is positioned within cultural studies itself against the opposi-tional model of oppression, wherein the colonizer/oppressor is rallied against the colonized/oppressed/transgressive subjects, when scholars such as Grossberg (1996), dismiss it as being woefully 'inappropriate to contemporary relations of power' and as 'incapable of creating alli-ances;' because the model makes it impossible to 'involve fractions of the empowered in something other than a masochistic, guilt-ridden way?' (p. 88).

Hyrbidity as the Cultural Logic of Globalization

Cultural studies and postcolonial studies have taken the criticisms lev-elled against Said's argument very seriously and there has been a great deal of attention focused on deflecting these assessments, rather than on taking his critique forward, and turning the attention to dismantling machinations of power and to understanding its operations in every realm of life (see Ahmed, 1996; Dirlik, 1999; Eagleton, 1999; Sarkar, 2002). It is from within these ruminations that hybridity has emerged as a powerful concept countering attacks against Orientalism and presenting encounters between different cultures in terms other than either/or politics and dichotomy of oppressor/colonizer and oppressed/ colonized subjects. Hybridity provides the framework to theorize con-temporary eclectic and dynamic world order and subjectivities, shaped by the coming together of vastly different tendencies and ideologies, within fluid borders made porous by interconnectivities of trade, travel, and media[22] unequivocally announcing that 'a frappe culture is upon us' (Kraidy, 2005, p. 2). The focus within cultural studies and postcolonial studies is on fluidity and ambivalence, and the concept of the hybrid unsettles the fixed nature of either/or narratives, foregrounds the matter of discontinuity and disconnect with history and locality, while highlighting the shifting loci of power. As Bhabha (1994) argues, 'borderline engagement of cultural difference may as often be consensual as conflictual; they may confound our definitions of tradition and modernity; realign the customary boundaries between private and the public, high and low; and challenge normative expectations of development and progress' (p. 2).

Moreover, according to Bhabha, hybrid identities are empowered identities, because their construction through acts of translation and mimicry, displaces the dominant subject's power; considering that 'mimicry is at once resemblance and menace,' bordering on mockery when the 'disciplinary gaze' of the 'disciplinary double' (meaning the colonized subject) threatens the 'civilizing mission' of the colonizer (p. 86). He perceives 'the hybrid' as the site of resistance, and proposes that 'hybridity is heresy' (p. 225), offering a possibility, to quote Turner (1974),'of standing aside not only from one's own social position but from all social positions,' and for formulating 'potentially unlimited series of alternative social arrangements' capable of subverting 'prestigious programs' of control (p. 14). Given the hybrid's potentiality to generate multiple options for undermining of authority, Bhabha upholds it as a creative 'third space.' However, notwithstanding the hybrid's reputation within cultural studies and its potential for undermining authority as a creative 'third space,' the question is, does the concept effectively challenge dichotomous frameworks of identity formed on the underlying equation between identity, modernity, and difference, and does it capture the nuances of emerging subjectivities and consciousness?

The hybrid's potentiality to do either would depend on whether the examples of creative resistance within postcolonial studies as well as cultural studies were identified within material rather than discursive realms. However, according to Bhabha (1994), the practitioners of alterity, liminality, playful mimicry, and other strategic politics of the creative 'third space' are the postcolonial writers writing in English. He refers to Salman Rushdie as the ideal hybrid subject, and a 'man in translation,' who existing in the 'in-between' spaces, expertly balances the tension and the indeterminacy of his existence, while practicing politics of heresy, and effectively challenging tradition, authority, and notions of pure origins (p. 223–9). And eliding all references to postcolonial nations' material realities, Bhabha identifies language, narratives, and literary texts as emblematic sites of cultural hybridity. He also privileges transnational contexts, and experiences of diaspora populations,[23] arguing that it is from a 'hybrid location of cultural value ... that the postcolonial intellectual attempts to elaborate a historical and literary project' (p. 173).[24] However, even if 'specific histories of cultural displacement' and migrancy (including histories of slavery and indenture) have drawn attention to 'the construction of culture and the invention of tradition,' exposing purity of origins and the endemic nature of cultural differences as untenable (see Bhabha, 1994, p. 172), the optimistic conceptualizations of hybridity as playful encounters between cultures without the establishment of hierarchy (p. 4), when one culture does not overwhelm the other are hard put to locate in everyday circumstances.

The conceptualizations of the hybrid, without reference material and lived realities, and the workings of power structures have attracted sharp criticism. For example, Aijaz Ahmed (1996) dismisses liberating discourses of hybridity as being nothing other than 'a carnivalesque collapse and play of identities' (p. 286), which fail to illuminate distinctions of location and politics, and amount to nothing more than an undifferentiated state revealing little other than their own embeddedness in the very structures that they had set out to expose (p. 278). Hence, according to Arif Dirlik (1999), the concept of hybridity as well as postcolonial scholarship represent a verbose rather than a real engagement with politics, and despite the deep concern of postcolonial scholarship's with the issue of identity, there is no clarity about the identity (read politics) of the postcolonial scholar, or of the identity (read politics) of the postcolonial scholarship (p. 149). While historian Sumit Sarkar (2002), decries the influence of excessively discursive postcolonial scholarship on Subaltern Studies, a radical, dissident-Left historical writing endeavour invested in both a critique of orthodox Marxist theory and practice as well as in the renewal of socialist-Marxist ethos. According to Sarkar, the postcolonial studies' association with the Subaltern Studies has reduced a project committed to 'concrete historical research' and writing of 'histories from below' to a mere valorization of 'non-western community consciousness,' which is dismissive of the specific and the contextual workings of domains of power, and disregards a stress on materialism as recourse to reductionist Marxist ideology (pp. 400–3).

Therefore, given the postcolonial scholarship's lack of investment in concrete workings of power, it is not surprising that despite claims about the hybrid's intent and capacity to overcome binaries and dislodge established powers, the hybrid has itself emerged as another point of opposition and even oppression. According to Dirlik (1999), the postcolonial celebrations of 'in-betweenness' countering essentialist assumptions of authentic nationalist identities by including 'the culture of the colonizer as a constituent moment' also reassert the 'cultural priority' of the very groups which have emerged of these encounters, such as the English speaking elites in the Indian context (p. 151). Supporting this view, Tabish Khair (2001) argues that 'the solid state hybrid' in postcolonial contexts has produced its own 'other,' 'outsiders and strangers', becoming 'in its operation (if not in intention) . . . another identity, another devise of exclusion, or appropriation' when 'it leaves out and posits itself against those who are seen as not-hybrid, fundamentalists, essentialist, nationalist, ethnic and so on' (p. 92). For example, Khair argues that even 'a politically aware and polemically anti-imperialist writer' like Rushdie could not avoid positioning 'an Indo-European hybridity against a homogenized rest-of-India in *The Moor's Last Sigh* (p. 93). But the reason why the hybrid has come to oppose the 'other' identities in this iniquitous fashion is because, critics argue, there is no awareness of its own role in polarization, and the concept's articulations fail to account for 'their own location within, and implication with, the formations of modern power' (Grossberg, 1996, p. 89). And indeed the issue of power is obscured when 'only certain identities (such as the westernized postcolonial ones) are perceived as hybrids or more hybrid' to the neglect of other hybridities which emerge as postcolonial societies embrace the dynamics of development creating a new churning of social and cultural contexts (Khair, 2001, p. 80). Khair also posits that the hybrid continues to be limited to an essentially East and West interaction, and evoked in terms of mimicry, appropriation, and nomadism, to the neglect of pertinent issues of 'otherness, conflict, and alienation' because this positionality corresponds with postcolonial scholars' situatedness in Western academia, and their general distaste with regards to dealing with discourses of estrangement for fear of being defined as alienated (p. 93). Therefore, questions of power, which are central to experiences of alienation and conflict, along with their 'ontologically pejorative' associations, are studiously avoided by postcolonial scholars to avoid undermining their own status in Western academia, leaving one 'to account for the improbability of dialogue without opposition (and the improbability of this opposition without alienation in the general sense)' (p. 81).

Therefore, given the postcolonial and cultural studies scholars' discomfort with unraveling the workings of powers within material contexts, the conceptualizations of the hybrid continue to be confined to mostly literary and discursive spheres. However, such is the pervasive influence of ideas delineating cultural contact in terms of appropriation (without referencing either resistance or conflict) that they even inform scholarship, which purport to study the hybrid concept within historical and migratory compulsions, legislative dictates, and economic and technological imperatives of the neoliberal globalizing world.

Hybridity and the Globalized World

Marwan Kraidy's (2005) argument, *Hybridity or the Cultural Logic of Globalization,* is one such noteworthy example. Kraidy lays down a comprehensive account of the hybrid within different historical epochs and geographical locales, and also traces its trajectory within contemporary globalized societies through ethnographic research among Lebanese youth. However, so overwhelming is the discursive force of the idea of the hybrid that Kraidy assumes hybridity to be the defining logic of globalization even before he begins fieldwork and often in the face of evidence from the field pointing to the contrary. For example, Kraidy expressly states that his research purpose is to examine localized experiences of Lebanese youth 'as site of existential and epistemological engagement with a local-to-global continuum culturally manifested in terms of hybridity,' and thereby assigns an umbrella term of 'hybridity' to all the myriad experiences constituted within the local to global continuum (p. 118).

Moreover, despite his avowals to position the hybrid within contemporary power equations, there is no accounting of how the social and cultural capital of his informants, shaped by experiences of class and economic facilities within a highly fractured Lebanese society, influences their ascription of ideas and ideologies from the developed western world. And once again, such is the overwhelming salience of the conciliatory gestures of mimicry, translation, and nomadism and the extent of their numbing effect on research that Kraidy is unable to account for events and subjectivities which fall outside of these neat descriptions. For example, he is silent on the powerful testimony of one of his informants, Antoun, who bitterly complains that the Lebanese youth pretend to be what they are not and that they ape the western styles blindly even as they hold on to their archaic attitudes and beliefs (p. 138). His informant is clearly referring to the tensions which exist between what Arab society is and what it is attempting to project itself as. Antoun's testimony is not to be seen as unusual or one-off considering that the Lebanese society was marred by civil war and is mired in protracted tensions. However, instead of elaborating on the power dynamic and the complex states of simultaneous acceptance and rejection which underlies the encounters with the West, its lifestyles, and ideologies, Kraidy endeavours to explain Maronite youth's lived experiences of hybridity by drawing comparisons with cultural expressions of hybridity as in the music of a Lebanese artist Ziad Rabbani. The assumption of an equation between lived experience and cultural expressions is endemic to postcolonial scholarship as it reflects its favouring of discursive as opposed to materialist spheres. Kraidy, therefore, not only overlooks the working of power in the highly complex and ambivalent interactions between the Arab worlds and the West, but also commits an act of theoretical naiveté when he proposes that Maronite youths' mimicking of westernized lifestyles (which face internal critique from informants like Antoun) are subversive acts capable of challenging sociopolitical contexts (p. 146).

The Hybrid and Neoliberal India

Hybridity has also emerged as the dominant framework to conceptualize emerging identities within the context of neoliberal globalized India. However, the scholarship exploring the hybrid's trajectory in India is in many ways evocative of Khair's (2001) description of the Indian novel in English and of its relationship to Indian realities. According to Khair, the Indian English novel is a product of westernized education and is therefore marked by its accompanying facilities and privileges, while its audiences profess the same privileges of class and education. Therefore, he argues that the Indian novel in English is incapable of translating experiences of the dispossessed and underprivileged populations in India, given its situatedness in middle class socio-economic contexts, without either appropriating them from a position of power or occluding them all together (p. x). Similarly, discussions of cultural hybridity within a globalizing Indian society almost exclusively focus on subjectivities shaped within middle class contexts marked by circulation of consumerist discourses, images, and products emanating from the West (see Mankekar, 2004; Mazarella, 2003; Parameswaran, 2001; Parameshwaran 2004a). Moreover, experiences shaped outside the market and of those incapable of encountering westernized modernity through elite education, employment, or consumption of goods and services do not feature in discourses which posit consumptions as an expression of agency. The implicit privileging of a certain middle-class urban consumerist sensibility, including its capabilities to participate in globalized contexts marks Parameswaran's (2004a) description of the Indian Miss World contestants as ideal hybrid subjects displaying the perfect balance between Indian values of 'respect and humility' and 'bold' glamour of upper-class Western feminity' (p. 362). And though she acknowledges the role of the market—especially in recounting how the capacity to fluidly move between the disparate cultures is acquired at a high cost of intensive English language sessions with celebrity language trainers and by going through a thorough body and face makeover, including intrusive surgical procedures, prescribing to Western standards of beauty, diction, and carriage, Parameswaran fails to critique how this tough act of balancing two vastly different cultures flies in the face of arguments of the hybrid's ability to playfully deflect power. The very presence of Indian women in Miss World contest, whether qualifying as acts of translation, mimicry, or nomadism, not only vouches for the pre-eminence of gendered identities based in celebratory, materialistic, and consumerist discourses emanating from the more developed west, but it also establishes that within postcolonial contexts only those capable of entering global discursive and material spheres through their capacity to consume western modernity can successfully assay a hybrid identity. The sway of upper middle-class experiences in delineations of the hybrid are also evidenced in Mazzarella's (2003) research, which explores the manner in which globalizing and profiteering imperatives of multinational corporations are intercepted and translated by Indian English speaking elite professionals, specifically 'the Churchgate set' of advertising executives, in such a fashion as to ensure their own indispensability. Mazzarella's examination of the intermediary role of English speaking advertising elites in the interest of multinational corporations marks the top down trajectory of hybridity and presents the perspective of those at the helm of neoliberal globalizing Indian society and economy.

The continued focus on experiences of a limited section of middle and upper middle class society presents an incomplete picture of the globalization process, because the pitfalls and opportunities of new economic and social regimes are transforming all sections of society. And given the endemic social and economic inequalities, it is important to understand the differences in translating the processes of globality from the distinct vantage points of those who have access to social and economic capital and others whose lives are defined by a marked lack of it. However, the radical politics of the hybrid only establishes the credibility of those individuals who are able to deal with instabilities of the new order due to their facilities of class, education, social mobility, and financial stability while obfuscating the role of these privileges in favourably situating these hybridities within modern formations of power (Dirlik,1999).[25] The realities of the minority and impoverished populations shaped outside the solidarities of consumption are either ignored or decried as anti-modern. Therefore, Dirlik argues that a renewed investment is required in social, economic, and political conditions of emerging subjectivities, ending the compartmentalization between culture and political economy, and paying heed to the fact that 'the economic is also social, political and cultural, just as the cultural is at once social, political and economic' (p. 163). Supporting this viewpoint Lee and LiPuma (2002) argue, that the extent and rapidity of social transformations wrought by new communication and intertwined economic regimes and defined by the intensity of flows of technology, finance, populations, images, products, and ideologies, overwhelming everyday life with diversity, dissonance, and difference, invalidate the disciplinary boundaries between culture, material, and economic realities.

It becomes important to review the current frameworks that elaborate both identity and culture, because not only do they provide an incomplete picture of the globalization process, being incapable of grasping the full complexities of emerging subjectivities from different socio-economic perspectives, but also because they are unable to challenge dichotomous and essentialist conceptualizations of identity and culture. According to Grossberg (1996), cultural studies' theoretical conceptualizations of identity continue to be predicated on workings of difference within a modernistic logic, wherein the modern itself is an 'adversarial space' which 'constitutes its own identity by differentiating itself from an 'other' (usually tradition as a temporal other or spatial other transformed into temporal others)', while also being fearful of contaminating contact with the retrograde non-modern 'other' (p. 93). Moreover, the lack of attention to power dynamics entails that there is no understanding of how difference or symbolic boundaries of self and community are conceived and maintained, and how valence is ascribed (p. 97). Therefore, the cultural studies' theoretical conceptualizations of identity 'have failed to open up a space of anti- or even counter-modernity' and continue to remain mired 'within the strategic forms of modern logic' while denying in their very essence 'the possibility of an alternative which might escape its logic (the logic of the modern),' and stall all efforts to 'contest the formations of modern power at its deepest level' (p. 93). My research among Muslim youth attempts to address these lacunae by invoking the political, social, and economic correlates and their attendant power dynamics in the construction of identity so as to have a more nuanced as well as complete picture of emerging subjectivities within contexts of neoliberal globalization, beyond the limited perspectives of hybridity and fundamentalism.

Muslim Subjectivities: Neither Hybrids nor Fundamentalists

My ethnographic research among Indian Muslim minority youth seeks compelling evidence from ground-up and from the perspective of marginalized populations in order to understand how material realities situated within specific political, economic, and social power equations shape responses to relentless processes of globalization. It takes a decidedly different approach to the cultural studies' largely discursive exploration of identity in examining Muslim youth's self identifying consciousness within contexts of work, leisure, and other exigencies of everyday life, including limits imposed on their hopes and aspirations by their contested and impoverished position within the Indian society. My research grapples with questions of how to theorize subjectivities, enacted and realized as much 'within the timeless space of flows of global networks and their ancillary locales' (Castells, 1997, p. 11) (such as those created by social networking platforms with unexpected and irregular circulatory pathways and unique opportunities for re-enactions of selfhood), as within the Muslim enclaves with their limits and immobilities. The lived experiences of Muslim youth, though contained within their physically demarcated and exclusive enclave, are equally implicated in contemporary deeply transformative phase of neoliberal globalization, as the unprecedented 'speed, intensity and extent' of social, economic, and technological transformations (Lee and LiPuma, 2002, p. 191) breach the community's isolation.

Presenting a glimpse into the inexorable emergence of a new consciousness among younger generations of Jamia enclave's residents, within contexts created by forces of technology and neoliberal globalization, I argue that the Muslim youth's emergent consciousness marks a break with the consciousness and the politics of older generation Muslim residents, confounding popular stereotypes about Muslims as fundamentalist, inward looking, and backward. I have observed during my fieldwork among the younger generations of Jamia enclave's residents, inklings of new imaginaries of selfhood and new practices of presentation, enabled by protean possibilities for self-creation as circulating in globalized media narratives. Moreover, there is also an increasing salience of virtual spaces in the lives of the Muslim youth, where boundaries between real and imagined, and local and global are blurred, creating a very different relationship with their exclusive Muslim enclave as compared to the older generations of Muslims. While the enclave's older residents express a greater ideological attachment to Indian Islamic cultural heritage and to the *adab, tehzib,* and *aqkhlaq* (etiquettes, mannerisms, and ethos) of the Indian Muslim community, the younger generation's greatest concern is to learn the English language and speak it fluently, so as to find well-paying employment in multinational corporations. The youth are explicitly focused on moving forward, and like a large section of urban Indian youth, they are deeply invested in the idea of consumer citizenship. And many of them are wont to effortlessly declare their life ambitions as 'I want to be rich,' thereby unequivocally expressing their investment in the materialist and consumerist discourses dominating the Indian cultural and social spheres rather in their own shrinking socio-religious and cultural heritage.

I read these new ambitions for economic well-being as revealing the extent to which they are now being pulled into the mainstream Indian society—a space they have been shut out and distanced from. However, Muslim youth's bolstered desires to seek a secure foothold in the economic spheres also reflect their changed socio-economic circumstances as compared to the older generations. The youth's dreams have been particularly buoyed by the culture of meritocracy introduced by multinational corporations that established their presence in India after liberalization of the economy in 1991 (see Varma, 1998). These global enterprises have created a very different environment from the one prevalent in the former state-controlled economy. The state enterprises were hierarchical institutions mired by cronyism, and their recruitment process actively shunned Muslims and stymied their participation in the economic workforce (Sachar Committee, 2006). However, the contexts of neoliberal globalization, even as they open up the Pandora's box of other structured inequalities, have inadvertently created new windows of opportunities, promising some degrees of freedom from discriminatory regimes for the minority Muslim populations, by bringing a greater focus to bear on efficiency within professional work environments as opposed to religious or cultural affiliations.

The other important aspect of the Muslim youth's environment today is the much greater degree of diversity and dissonance defining their social, intellectual, and emotional force-fields. The current phase of neoliberal globalization has not only created opportunities for increased interactions between the backward East and the dynamic and technologically advanced West, but has also led to unprecedented connectivity between different Eastern cultures. This is on no small account due to the fact that open skies policies and privatization of media not only increased the presence of images, products, ideologies, and lifestyles evoking a westernized consumerist modernity (from the glitzy Hollywood perspective peddled by global media conglomerates) but also create a surge in programming in various indigenous Indian languages. The 350 satellite channels and more that are currently broadcasting in the country (FICCI, 2011) offer a great diversity of programming; and some of these satellite channels even address the ignored or vilified Indian Muslim audiences.

Today, there are a number of satellite television channels which are broadcasted and uplinked from various sites in the Middle East and other Indian cities such as Mumbai and Hyderabad, that speak specifically to Muslim audiences, addressing their 'symbolic annihilation' in public and mediated spheres. In my research I discovered that these Islamic channels enjoyed considerable popularity among Muslim youth and are therefore significant interjections awakening a recognition of their Islamic identity, especially as Muslim youths have no access to their rich Indian Islamic cultural and literary heritage due to their inability to read and write in Urdu—a language once spoken by both Muslims and Hindus alike. However, even as state policies ensure Urdu's demise by confining its shared and eclectic history to be the exclusive concern of the Muslim community alone, the Islamic satellite channels and websites, though carefully monitored and policed by the Indian government, help Muslim youth confront their disconnect with their Indian Islamic cultural heritage. However, the point to note about these channels is that they do not specifically evoke the Indian Islamic heritage or its eclectic and encompassing spirit, instead they are important nodes of influence circulating ideas and ideologies about Islam and its varied expressions from Muslim worlds, stretching from Indonesia to the Middle East, in ways that were not possible before the advent of privatized and globalized media. These Islamic satellites channels, while breaking the silence around Islamic identity, ensure that Muslim youth are not only exposed to ideas, ideologies, and identities originating largely from the West, which are often offensive to their cultural and religious mooring, but are also able to apprehend different notions of Islamic identity.

I admit that I was at first most surprised when young Muslim men barely out of their teens confided to me that they spent their time watching either Peace TV or MTV; while Peace TV is an Islamic version of televangelist television, MTV is the global referent for 'cool'; where one evokes the traditions of faith and virtues of community, the other exemplifies extreme individualism and unique pursuits of pleasures mainly through consumption. And yet the Muslim youth effortlessly prescribe to these two widely divergent sensibilities, and I argue that their ascription to the flux of competing ideas and ideologies exemplify the universalizing tendencies of modernization (see, Appadurai, 1996 & Hall, 1996c), but not in the way conceived by postcolonial theorizations of hybridity. Their consciousness represents a confounding juxtaposition of Western consumerist modernity with new ascriptions to Islamic cultures and lifestyles, and pushes the limits of current theoretical frameworks.

My research, which is concerned with understanding how Muslim youth's subjectivities are being constructed at the intersection of many competing, contesting, complimentary, and contradictory discourses, also tests the relevance of current explanatory frameworks of globalized subjectivities. For example it seeks to understand: Can the dominant perceptions of the hybrid accommodate the intersections of consumerist individualism driven by imperatives of neoliberal globalization with an assertive desire to espouse a religious identity? How is the simultaneity of engagements among young men and women with opportunities for education, consumption, and mobility in a neoliberal Indian society and involvement with religious practices, obligations, and identities to be explained? How should a desire for a fashionable but patently Islamic persona incorporating designer brands, celebrity styles, and command over the English language to be conceived? And in an age of strident anti-Islamism, can this eclectic mixing qualify as expressions of agency, symbolizing a creative resurgent space, envisaged by Bhabha (1994) as the creative 'third space,' but situated outside the interactions between the East and the West?

Beyond the West: New Power Centers

These questions and reflections on current theoretical frameworks have become important because the current phase of globalization cannot be adequately captured by the cultural logic of concepts such as the hybrid, which are almost exclusively imagined as arising from interactions between the East and the West (see Kraidy, 2005). Today, the compulsions of economic globalization, in addition to the facilities of satellite and digital communication technologies, have also greatly increased the interconnections between nodal sites within the East. For example, the neoliberal havens of the Middle East (including Dubai, Abu-Dhabi, Kuwait, Oman, and Saudi Arabia) exert a particularly strong pull on South Asian citizens. According to Chad Haines (2011), Dubai, as a consciously manufactured brand, actively interjects in the lives of residents of Asia, Africa, and Middle East and is inter-referenced in their imaginations and everyday life as a new landscape of hope and desire, representing new visions of global success and wealth, as well as new expressions of urbanity. The glamour of brand Dubai, representing dreams of luxury and high-class consumption, is reproduced in a dialogue with self imaginations and national reconstructive projects of people stretching from Africa to Asia to Middle East; because even as urban landscapes of cities like New Delhi, Cairo, and Karachi are being developed (often in partnership with world class contractors from Dubai) for the new rich of these countries, hundreds of thousands of the poor from India, Bangladesh, Afghanistan, Philippines, Pakistan travel to Dubai to build and maintain its Disneyesque landscape. The point to note is that renewed interactions with centers of urban luxury and wealth in locations within the East like Dubai, Abu Dhabi, Kuwait, Doha, as well as Singapore, Kuala Lumpur, Jakarta, and Hong Kong are constructing geographies, which have captured the imaginations of the third world populations in ways which the big cities of London, Paris, or New York were once capable. These new cities vie with power and prestige traditionally associated with Western metropolises.

And what is most important about many of these new centers of influence situated outside the West is that not only do they present alternatives to Western urban modernities, but they also have an intimate relationship with Islam. They are also opening up prospects for employment, growth, and material well-being to Muslim youth, even as Islamophobia within many Western nations is closing the door to opportunities in their face. The neoliberal economies of the Middle East have become implicitly and explicitly involved in shaping and reshaping the aspirations of the large sections of middle classes and lower middle classes among Muslims. Many among my informants either already had relatives who were working in the region or they were themselves eager for prospects of migrating there. How should the desires of Muslim youth to chase employment opportunities in the Middle East and realize their materialist aspirations be conceived? They present a conundrum to contemporary theorizations because their dreams of material well-being are equally implicated with their desire to live freely as Muslims.

Middle Class Aspirations and Religious Identities

The Muslim youth's internalization of the flux created by relentless globalization represents their unique adjustments to modernizing forces, because, according to Hall (1996c), globalization is synonymous with modernization (p. 4). I argue that the Muslim youths' embrace of the Islamic identity is neither a return to tradition nor an answer to yearnings for stability, as claimed by nuanced authors like Castells (1997). It is perhaps an exercise of agency, considering the discriminatory regimes arrayed against Islam, but in contexts wherein Islam is becoming associated with a new modernity and upward mobility. The practices of travel and migration to the global cities of the Middle East and the apprehension of notions of Islam emanating from these spaces through mediated discourses of satellite channels, social networking sites, among others is creating a shift in the Muslim youth's understanding of their Islamic identity, which cannot be accommodated within frameworks of either progressive hybridity or regressive fundamentalism. The connotations of Islam associated with these new sites, which are also consumerist havens, are implicated both in notions of material well-being as well as informed with an aura of authenticity.

Hence, the increasing visibility of Islamic markers of identity—the beard, the veil, and the *hijab* in public spaces of both consumption and leisure has a very different meaning today than when I was growing up in the 1980s. At that point, the *burkha*, or the loose black coat with a face veil, worn by Muslim women was immediately recognizable as a mark of poverty, illiteracy, and even lack of personal hygiene, making an encounter with a *burkha* clad woman in public places was deeply embarrassing for middle class and upper middle class Muslims because it resurrected the entire list of stereotypes from which they so wished to be disassociated. This generation of middle class Indian Muslims, like their counterparts in Pakistan, in the words of Saba Mahmood (2005), expressed a 'profound disease with the appearance of religion outside of the private space of individualized belief', and perceived 'the slightest eruption of religion into the public domain... as a dangerous affront,' one which brought to the surface the potential threat of being subjected to the 'normative morality dictated by mullahs and priests' (p. xi). But today, encountering the veil which has been transformed from the dowdy and unbecoming burkha and reborn with a Middle Eastern flair has a different meaning, which has not been captured in explanations viewing the veil's increased visibility as a sign of Arabization of Indian Islam (see Ghosal 2010).

I would like to recount an encounter with two young veiled Muslim women in a coffee shop in New Friends Colony's community market, an upscale part of New Delhi and in close vicinity of Jamia Enclave. It was surprising to see young Muslim women unescorted in a space evocative of westernized leisure practices. But what truly stood out about them was that in this age of Islamophobia they were not at all self-consciousness about their very Islamic presence. They wore their *hijab*, draped in the Middle Eastern fashion, with a quiet confidence and I noticed its effect in my friend's gaping jaw. But it was his comment, 'gawd ... I love their confidence...and the British School Dubai accent,'' which made me think that even if I may dismiss these encounters as being rare and limited to rarified settings accessible to Muslim diaspora populations with substantial disposal income (because paying an equivalent of three or four dollars for a cup of coffee is not what most Muslims can afford), it was becoming evident that a significant shift was occurring among the younger generations in the way they assayed their Islamic identity. This is because on another occasion, I even came across a slightly older veiled woman having a cup of coffee all by herself, and it was hard for me not to stare.

There is a very prominent presence of signifiers of Islamic identities, especially the veil, in the Indian public spaces now as compared to earlier times when they used to be confined to exclusive Muslim enclaves like Jamia. Today, it is not unusual to find veiled Muslim women in spaces emulating Western leisure and consumption habits, such as the new coffee shops, which have come up all across India indicating globalization of everyday life. Drawing attention to the transformation in the Indian Islamic identity, these women announce their Islamic presence with the least bit of self-consciousness. And if do sometimes standout, it is often for, what my journalist friend noted, their jaw-dropping British School Dubai accent.' One could argue that such a self-assured expressions of Islamic identity would be accessible only to upper middle-class Muslims, but the fact of the matter is that even Muslims with Middle Eastern petro-dollars must also reside in the crowded urban enclaves. Their markers of wealth have yet to secure them accommodation in more cosmopolitan localities. But the fallout is that the presence of the migratory populations from the Middle East in the exclusive Muslim enclave have introduced new modernizing impulses as well as sky-rocketing property prices.

I argue that the veil establishes its presence in the Indian public sphere within aspirations for middle-class modernity, new mobilities, and new interpretations of the Islamic identity. It becomes noticeable not only for the sheer increase in its numbers, but also holds one's attention for its transformation into a version popular in the Middle East, and invites scrutiny for the poise with which it pronounces its particularity. I meet with veiled women in movie theatres, in popular markets and in shopping centers like Lajpat Nagar, Shankar Market, and Connaught place, which are thronged by all classes of Indians. There is a quiet confidence, which is very different from the diffidence that had enveloped veiled Muslim bodies before. Moreover, the veiled women, who are comfortably shopping in Delhi's markets, and whom I have seen even looking through lingerie in Lajpat Nagar with ease, are more middle class and even educated rather than outright poor and illiterate. And their adoption of the Islamic attire is in sheer contrast to the pref-erences of the middle class women of yester years who had expressly shed their *burkhas* before venturing into public arenas. For example, my mother recalls that though she wore a *burkha* to her women's col-lege as her family mandated this, but as soon as she had entered the gates of her elite educational institute she had shed the garment and packed it away, till it was time to go home again. But, wearing a veil today to educational and other training institutes is not uncommon even if the presence of increasing number of young Muslim women in such places is truly uncommon, given the historically low level of education among Muslim women and their lack of representation in the workforce (Sachar Committee, 2006). In Jamia University, I have encountered many more young women wearing the veil as compared to when I was a student more than a decade ago. The veil was an oddity in the eighties and nineties even within the precincts of this Islamic institution. But now it is everywhere, transformed from its earlier drab and dreary Indian style to a more sleek and stylish version resembling the fashions in the Middle East.

However, the prominent presence of Islamic markers of identity cannot be read as declarations of piety. This cultural phenomenon is more complex than the Arabization of Indian Islam. This is because Muslim youth are deeply desirous of participating in the Indian economic and social mainstream, the espousing of an Islamic identity will have the contrary effect of isolating them given the strong anti-Islamic political climate. Their articulations of identity evoke contradictory tendencies wherein ascriptions to religious symbolism and ideology fuse with visions of mobility, social capital, and also a new modernity. And they are very different from the position occupied by older generations of middle class Muslims who clearly distanced themselves from their Islamic roots in order to participate in social and economic life. However, the youth are drawn towards it, and even make an investment in it, which in the light of the discriminatory regimes arrayed against Muslims, seems to defy logic. However, I argue that the Muslim youths' subjectivities and styles of self presentations are indeed a response to multifarious and conflicting visions of selfhood and identity, which engulf their lives in mediated, discursive, and material spheres, enabled by flows created by neoliberal globalization, but which are beyond the scope of current theoretical frameworks of identity. They are also expressions of new facilities acquired through participation in new economic spheres and activities and indicate an agency which confounds articulations of mimicry, translation, or nomadism attributed to the creative regenerative hybrid.

Therefore, to find an explanatory framework that will delineate the Muslim youths' self actualization processes and the conflations of contradictory tendencies in their emergent subjectivities, I am drawn to theorizations of 'alternative modernities' (see Taylor, 2000). In addition, I explore the Muslim youths' experiences to further a debate that perhaps a singular definition of modernity, one that is deeply complicit within Western historical experiences, may not be capable of encompassing the different experiences of other populations implicated in modernity through processes of relentless globalization.

Modernity, Globalization, and Experiences of Alterity

Charles Taylor (2002) defines modernity as 'historically unprecedented amalgam of new practices and institutional forms (science, technology, industrial production, urbanization), of new ways of living (individualism, secularization, instrumental rationality), and of new forms of

malaise (alienation, meaninglessness, a sense of impending social disso-
lution)' (p. 91). It is a definition tied to specific ideologies, moral order,
and social, economic, and technological transformations that have
engulfed the Western world since Enlightenment. And the question
is, can this conceptualization of modernity encompass all its different
trajectories created by other cataclysmic events of conquest, domination, and colonialism? Taylor asks, 'do we need to speak of *multiple* (sic)
modernities, the plural reflecting the fact that non-Western cultures
have modernized in their own way and cannot be properly understood
if we try to grasp them in a general theory that was originally designed
with the Western case in mind?' (p. 91). However, the 'acultural theories'
of modernity conceptualize modernity as involving a set of transformations which any culture can go through, and in such a fashion that at
the end all cultures will emerge looking alike and as mirror images of
Western modernity (Taylor, 2000, pp. 365–66). The acultural theorists
describe transitions to modernity in terms of loss of tradition, religion,
established beliefs, and social ties through operation of scientific reason,
urbanization, mechanization, and rapidity of change.

But opposing this cohesive vision, cultural theories of modernization contend that transformations undergone by different cultures may
share certain similarities but they will not converge into a homogenous
pattern because the adoption of two key institutions of modernity,
namely market-industrial economy and a bureaucratically organized
government, will bear the imprint of the constituting core and defining
characteristics of every culture. Therefore, according to Taylor (2002),
it is necessary to speak of a Japanese modernity, an Indian modernity,
and an Islamic modernity alongside Western modernity. He contends
that, 'a successful transition [to modernity] involves a people finding
resources in their traditional culture, that modified and transposed,
will enable them to take on the new practices' (p. 368). However, he
firmly rejects efforts which profess: 'we will take your technology and
keep our culture' as not modernization at all because he argues creative
adaptation involves profound changes beyond acclimatization to modern institutions of governance, exchange, and technological efficiency.
According to Taylor, it requires the development of a social imaginary
which incorporates 'typically modern understandings of time, of space,
or history. . . which involve a very different temporality from the pre-
modern modes' (p. 373). In Taylor's arguments, the concept of social

imaginary is the key construct underlying the embrace and acceptance of modernizing ethos. Taylor's intent has been to negate assumptions of 'acultural' theorists that societal modernity (paralleling the structural, technological, and organizational aspects of society) and cultural modernity (which indicates the ethos of modernity as expressed in notions of individuality, attitudes of scepticism, persistent realignment of the personal in the social historical contexts) always coexist and that the induction of capitalist mode of production and organization of society coupled with systems of administration and the attendant bureaucracy, inexorably lead towards the creation of a modern outlook marked by rationality, pragmatism, scientific temper, and a secular society of popularly elected governments. However, despite Taylor's valuable contribution, he is not entirely successful in establishing the argument for multiple modernities. This is because he defines the concept of social imaginaries in terms of difference, placing it within the same adversarial relationship of modernity versus tradition. Moreover the concept remains entrenched within western conceptualizations of modernity, even as the author holds forth on his argument for multiple modernities.

On other hand Gaonkar (1999), while concurring with Taylor's arguments, gives us a better handle on how to conceive 'alternative modernities.' According to him, modernity is not culture neutral because its evolution itself is a cultural specific event 'with a distinctive moral and scientific outlook consisting of a constellation of understandings of person, nature, society, reason, and the good that is different from both its predecessor cultures and non-Western cultures' (p. 15). He argues that the philosophical discourse of modernity, inaugurated with the project of Enlightenment, and expounded by critical visionaries of the past two centuries, ranging from Marx, Baudelaire, Nietzche, Weber, Simmel, Benjamin to Foucalt (who have engaged with the societal, scientific, rationalistic, administrative, and cultural manifestations of modernity), concurs on the core definition of modernity as an attitude of engaging with the present. Gaonkar (1999) sums it up as the concentration on 'presentness' with no claims to the past and no bequeaths for the future—as 'a leap in the open air of the present as…history [sic] (p. 7). And as modernity becomes ubiquitous, arriving slowly and awakened over a long period of time through commerce as well as administered by empires and ensuing nationalist struggles, and today propelled by the circulation of global media, finance capital, and manpower (see also Hall, 1996c), Gaonkar is of the opinion that 'modernity is best understood as an attitude of questioning the present' (p. 13). But at the same time he reasons that if the present is to announce itself as the modern at every national and cultural site, then the pervasive attitude of questioning the present makes modernity a deeply embattled concept which 'no longer has a governing center and master-narrative to accompany it' (p. 13). And yet Gaonker urges that this is not to be construed as a call for abandonment of Western discourse on modernity, with its critical reflexivity, moral order of rights, responsibilities, autonomy, and individuality realized in social practices and institutions of the free market and democracy. Rather, it is to be seen as an argument for thinking through and thinking against the grain of Western modernity in order to understand how alternative modernities are formed in various local spaces, which have become inextricably interpolated in the global (p. 14).

The need for theorizations of 'alternative modernities,' which is a matter of understanding how different people of the world make themselves at home before the relentless march of capitalist modernization from which there is no escape for any people or cultures (see Marshall, 1982), has become so potent that *Public Culture* has devoted two special editions entitled *Alternate Modernity* (1999, 11 (1)) and *Social Imaginary* (2002, 14(1)) to the task. Chakrabarty (1999), in his contribution to the debate, delineates the history of the social practices surrounding the '*adda*' (translated as a meeting place) in colonial and postcolonial Bengal. He provides an insight into how collective and individual consciousness are shaped at intersection of inherent/established ways of being with new ideas of sociability. According to Chakrabarty, the shared space of the '*adda*' in the Bengal of the 1950s and 1960s encouraged the 'practice of friends getting together for long, informal, and unrigorous conversations,' and it emerged as a 'dwelling in modernity,' shaped within distinct conditions and contexts of Bengal, including not only the Bengali gentlemen's penchant for conversation and company, but also the soil, climate, and the many months of salubrious evenings so conducive to outdoor meetings that are particular only to Bengal (p. 110). The 'adda' was a modern space, not only because it was intimately associated with youth culture, but also because it broke the strict caste rules and norms of the deeply hierarchical Indian society, by enabling unencumbered mingling of people from different castes and social stratums. It was a different space from the soirees of the elites, which were dedicated to the consumption of high art and culture and were popular in much of the 19th century. The 'adda' was unique, even if the conversations at the 'adda' were still centered mainly around Bengali literature, concerns about its revival and resuscitation, along with local politics. Firstly because it was open to everyone, as opposed to a select few who had gathered in the homes of the elites strictly on invitation. At the 'adda', which was often synonymous with a popular coffee house or restaurant anyone could come uninvited and speak at will instead of respecting hierarchies and protocols so evident at the soirees of the elites. However, according to Chakrabarty, the 'adda' despite its significance in the construction of Bengali modernity, and the Bengali middle class's public life devoted to literary and political pursuits in freewheeling democratic conversations, is not comparable to the Westernized conceptions of the democratic public sphere . The rationality and purpose, which underline the modernity of the public sphere, are deeply antithetical to the spirit of the 'adda,' which would wither away under the utilitarian ethos. And yet, this place of aimless conversation and of purposeless getting togetherness was instrumental in the articulation of ideas of freedom of speech, expression, and association. It aided participation in the cultural and political construction of nation and society. Chakrabarty proposed that the 'adda' symbolized a unique struggle to produce a 'metaphysical identity for oneself—both collectively and individually' in the face of globalizing capitalism which offers no escape, even if 'the control that different groups can exercise on capitalism is at best uneven and subject to global distribution of institutional power' (p. 110).

However, Chakrabarty (1999) in his deliberations on the construction of an alternative modernity does not dwell upon inherent conflicts and contradictions that may also underline appropriations of Western ethos to create a new social practice, especially considering that iniquitous power relationships between the colonized and the British colonizers were realities contextualizing the practice of the 'adda'. The evolution of 'alternate modernity' is presented as an uncomplicated affair almost untouched by strife created by rejection of modernity's precepts. And yet, the 'adda' could qualify as a distinctive expression of modernity only because it was marked by both an acceptance of ideas of freedom of speech, association, and democratization of public spheres as well as an active negation of the spirit of rationality and purpose that define the political nature of conversations in the public sphere. There is a denial of Western modernity in its aim of celebrating freedom of expression as an end in itself. But the author does not excavate this tension. This is also the case with other analyses of construction of modernity in postcolonial contexts. For example, even Appadurai's (1996) investigation of how modernity is experienced and internalized at the site of the highly popular game of cricket (which the Indians learned from the British—first at the behest of various colonial exigencies, and later to enter the spheres of modernity created by legacies of colonialism) makes no mention of how the desire for experiencing modernity is differently calibrated among different social classes, and how ascriptions to modernity are facilitated or denied depending on class affiliations.

The problem that I identify in these discussions of alternative modernities is that they suffer from the same partial-sightedness as the discussions of hybridity. And, even though there is an acceptance that 'modernity is inescapable' (Gaonkar, 1999, p. 1) and a global reality, the analytical approach to understand this ubiquitous phenomenon takes an overwhelmingly Westernized perspective, while being immersed in Enlightenment's deeply optimistic view and boundless enthusiasm for reason's and rationality's potential to create just and progressive societies, these discussions are inattentive to power-inequations, dissensions, and contestations that also define the transitions to modernity. Moreover, in these discussions of 'alternative modernities,' the modernities shaped within new geographies of rapidly globalizing capitalism of cities like Dubai, Singapore, Hong Kong, and Kuala Lumpur would also be rejected as not modernity at all (see Gaonkar, 1999; Taylor, 2000). The cultural and economic geographies of these cities rescind assumptions (especially of 'acultural' theorists) of the harmonious interlinks between the establishment of market-driven industrial economies, bureaucratically administered states, rule of law, urbanization, mass media, literacy, and the emergence of cognitive transformations in terms of growth of scientific consciousness, rationality, secular outlook, and individualist understanding of self. These societies are a construct of rapid appropriation of Western technologies and consumer-capitalism, which has imbued them with the semblance of power and capitalist well-being that once characterized only the West, but without the emergence of values of individual rights and responsibilities, freedom to participate in the construction of political and social life, human rights, free speech, faith in rationalism, and reason that are integral to Western modernities. This scenario, though evocative of Weber's dark vision of modernity, which bemoans the destruction of meaning-making and life-sustaining structures and networks, and their replacement by economic exigencies and bureaucratic norms of efficiency, must be addressed because the dystopias fashioned by neoliberalism's relentless global restructuring exert enormous influence on the national, social, and individual imaginaries of populations across much of Asia, Africa, and Middle East (see Haines, 2011). Moreover, the lack of connection between social and cognitive aspects of modernity is becoming the dominant expression of neoliberal modernization.

The breakdown and disjunctions between the ideological and the material-technological aspects of modernity are becoming evident in the heart of Western modernities too. Scholars like David Harvey (2005) argue that ambivalence is created by neoliberal capitalist regimes in the interest of neoliberal capitalist imperatives, and a discourse of freedom is employed to legitimize the state's denial of its responsibilities towards the poor and the marginalized and to commit the most blatant acts of violence against other nations. The tropes of freedom and human dignity are given salience in an age witnessing the most aggressive suppression of individual freedom and breakdown of collective regenerative politics. Pointing to disjunctions in contemporary political, social, and cultural spheres of Western capitalist societies, McRobbies (2009) notes a 'double entanglement,' indicating a point of existence wherein neoconservative values with regards to gender, sexuality, and family (as seen in the rising hysteria of the pro-life groups with increasing violence directed against pro-choice organizations and individuals) exist concomitantly with greater institutional recognition to and liberalization of policies towards same-sex marriages, diversity, and choice in domestic, sexual, and kinship relations. And in the same phase, struggles for equality adopt the limited vision of 'identity politics' seeking equality for a select few, while ratifying hierarchies of state and capitalist ideologies[26] (Duggan, 2003); even as feminist politics dismantles, and there is a 'disarticulation' of feminism when aggressive individualism replaces collective feminist politics[27](p. 12).

My argument is that such complex fall-outs of new economic and cultural regimes are marking the global-scapes as neoliberal capitalism becomes the global logic. Its compulsions are putting the idea of modernity as situated within Enlightenment debates under crisis. But as argued earlier the dominant theoretical frameworks have not explored the vortex of contradictory discourses and conflicting pulls that beset emergent modernities. They remain content with analyzing unproblematic experiences in comfort zones of middle class Westernized hyrbidity/modernity, while leaving the questions of material correlates of power unexamined (see, Dirlik, 1999). My research seeks to understand as well as to theorize what constitutes modernity within a context marked by social and political inequalities, but enthused by new flows of ideas, images, and also opportunities for self-creation and imagination.

Convoluted Modernities of Muslim Youth

I focus on the Muslim youth's difficult negotiations, given their disadvantaged and marginalized position, with the ambiguities, incongruities, inequalities as well as opportunities within the contexts of neoliberal globalization; because, while it is true that the Muslim youth's aspirations for consumerist materialistic well-being must contend with their acute social backwardness, and their lack of skills necessary for participation in economic spheres dominated by multinational corporations within a hostile post 9/11 environment, it is also a fact that many of the dreams, desires, as well as plans for a future that Muslim youth entertain today were not a quotidian reality before. Hence, given the new possibilities for social and economic mobility, but also considering the Muslim community's acute backwardness in socio-economic and educational spheres, I propose the concept of 'convoluted modernities' to theorize what I refer to as their one step forward and two-step backward processes of transformation in the face of overwhelming challenges. I examine their emerging modernities with reference to their dreams, aspirations, ambitions, self-projections, and articulations of gendered and communal identities. I argue that though Muslim youth's implication within dominant discourse of materialism as well as resurgent global Islam can be conceived as an intersection between oppositional tendencies of tradition and modernity, which have been historically associated with construction of modern ethos within contexts of colonization (Chatterjee, 1999) but for a fundamental difference. Chatterjee argues that in India the momentum and purpose of charting a way forward have been entangled with tendencies for reviving of tradition, because the creation of modern institutions of state and bureaucracy and the formation of a national identity (from an eclectic mix of regional, linguistic, caste-based, and religious affiliations and situated consciousness ultimately leading to the realization of a nation state of independent people), was within a deeply contested terrain of unequal power relations between the colonizer and the colonized. The former often arbitrarily imposed modernizing structures and ideologies on the latter for its own benefit. Therefore, the creative adjustments required of a colonized people, in order to attain modernity while continuing a struggle against the colonizer responsible for implementing the modernizing trends, called for the formation of the dialectic of inner and outer domains of subjectivity. The inner sovereign and zealously guarded domain would be the repository of traditions, cultures, and values and 'far removed from the arena of political contest with the colonial state' in order to shape the very politics of a modern sovereign state (p. 117). One can be inclined to read the Muslim youth's emergent consciousness as paralleling these dynamics and as a unique restructuring of inner and outer domains of consciousness in response to iniquitous conditions, which have hitherto kept a minority population confined to margins of society, but which are now being unsettled by new opportunities for self actualization created by neoliberal discursive and material regimes. But, the Muslim youth's consciousness signifies much more than hesitant negotiations with modernity and/or reworking of the past, tradition, and habitus to enter modernity.

Firstly, this is because the Muslims youth's engagement with religion is not a matter of resurrecting an inherited but undermined past, because, as indicated earlier, the youth are accessing Islamic values through new circuits of communication, travel, and exposure which have been made recently available in the wake of liberalization and globalization of the Indian economy and society. The Islamic ideologies and ways of life are being communicated from global arenas through satellite television channels and the Internet, introducing Muslim youth to versions of global Islam from varied Islamic countries of the world. The youth's investment in Islam is not a matter of working through memories, which would entail foregrounding of their unique Indian Islamic heritage, perhaps creating a demand the reinstitution of the dying Urdu language. However, I discovered that these issues did not preoccupy most middle class and lower middle class Muslim youth. The other factor that marks a difference from the negotiations between tradition and modernity as highlighted in the construction of postcolonial modernity by scholars such as Chatterjee (1999), is that not only are the platforms and mediums for representing and apprehending Islam novelty, but the inherent dynamics of these platforms shape the posturing of religious ideology in a novel way.

I present the example of the highly popular Peace TV, an Islamic televangelist channel uplinked from Dubai, and juxtaposed on satellite television menu with multiple other secular channels representing and constructing the rhetoric of modern life. I argue that this Islamic televangelist channel is similarly involved in creation of modernity, because even if it evokes tradition by way of religious ideology, it does not position it in opposition to progress. It extols the role of religion as a way of coping with uncertainties and dilemmas of modern life, and as a guiding force in everyday struggles, providing confidence and strength to cope, rather than offering an escape from relentless modernity. Therefore, the channel presents a complex truck with modernity, which is also replicated in the persona of its much admired and emulated anchor/presenter, Dr Zakir Naik. In the early days of the channel, Dr Naik spoke and lectured only in English and was usually dressed in a formal pinstriped suit paired with an Islamic skullcap. He was also wont to invite votaries of other religions and to stridently argue with them in fluent English, presenting Islam as a superior moral force, and countering the negative rhetoric demoting and demonizing Islam. Dr Zakir Naik's engagements with the symbols of Western power, both in his use of the English language for his argumentation as well his sartorial style, with the explicit intention of reasserting Islamic ideology, reflect a layered mutuality between seemingly antithetical ideas, and it communicates what I refer to as 'convoluted modernity.'

I use the term 'convoluted modernity' not only to give credence to modernity's ubiquitous presence, but also to highlight how its core concepts, such as freedom and reflexivity, as well as the tendencies to question one's position within evolving contexts, as proposed by Gaonkar (1999), have been internalized in varying degrees in different geographies. Dr Zakir Naik's public persona, announced with the Western title of 'Dr', exemplifies his situatedness within discourses of modernity rather than outside of it. This is precisely the reason why the youth are so effortlessly able to switch between MTV and Peace TV, because despite overt divergence between these texts they share similar grounds—enunciating modernity's endless possibilities for self-creation. The common theme of these seemingly antithetical media outlets is to unequivocally announce the experience of modernity as the conscious-ness of an ever vanishing present, wherein all certainties have been made redundant, and the imperiled self has to announce itself as a project in constant construction—but within protean possibilities created by an increased movement of both ideas and people (see Appadurai, 1996; Gaonkar, 1999; Giddens, 1991; Hall, 1996c; Taylor, 2000 & 2002). However, what the concept of 'convoluted modernity' specifically high-lights is that freedom realized in an attitude of consistent questioning of the present can even put the discourses of Western modernity under attack even while passionately embracing it as Dr Zakir Naik's persona and his popularity among the Muslim youth both exemplify. I propose that the Muslim youth's 'convoluted modernities' are realized through the acceptance and internalization of modernity's core ideas of freedom and reflexivity, and it is the extent of their imbrications within these discourses, which helps construct their new life choices, ambitions, and dreams. And even though many of the new styles of self-presentation and articulations may appear to reject or oppose Western modernity, (such as in the instance of adoption of the veil by increasing number of young Muslim women), however, these oppositional postures have been made possible only by accepting modernity's impulse for relentless self creation and for questioning the extant status quo.

Consumer Citizenship

Moreover, there is something to be said about Enlightenment's opti-mism for ideas of individuality and citizenship when they appear enhanced, if not potentially expanded, as they circulate and reverber-ate within digital and discursive pathways in this era of unprecedented connectivity to become ingrained in life choices and personal politics. Moreover these high ideals of freedom of choice and faith in individual agency, endemic to the breakdown of old stabilities, become even more insidious when packaged within purely consumerist realms. I argue that in today's mediated worlds, modernity exerts its overwhelming salience through its derivative discourses of consumerist, hedonistic individualism, and through instances of effortless-apolitical resistance peddled 'twenty-four seven' by media outlets such as MTV or its myriad clones, and endlessly reiterated through advertising of products, commodities, and lifestyle. Upholding the validity and power of these new circuits, Nestor Garcia Canclini (2001) argues that for the youth, 'the questions specific to citizenship, such as how we inform ourselves and who represents our interests are answered more often than not through private consumption of commodities and media offerings than through the abstract rules of democracy or through participation in discredited political organizations' because 'the relation between citizens and consumers has been altered throughout the world due to economic, technological, and cultural changes that have impeded the constitution of identities through national symbols' and replaced them 'by programming of, say, Hollywood, Televisa, and MTV' (p. 5). And as my research indicates, the Muslim youth's subjectivities are also evolving within contexts wherein they can exercise their agency, as workers and as consumers, given the opportunities for employment and upward mobility, which have become available in the wake of economic liberalization, and which provide unique opportunities for participation to a hitherto sidelined community. I refer to this situation whence a minority population is able to announce its presence as citizens through its efforts towards material well-being and through its act of consumptions as exemplifying an instance of 'convoluted modernity' because as Nestor Garcia Canclini (2001) proposes that though the acts of consumption may be conceived as 'depoliticization' from liberal and enlightened democratic perspective, 'the political notion of citizenship is expanded by including rights to housing, health, education, and the access to other goods through consumption' (p. 5) . Hence, choices such as adoption of the veil, which in liberal-humanist perspectives represent a capitulation to patriarchal authority, are actually arrived at through the internalization and regurgitation of contemporary neoliberal societies' dominating discourses of consumerist expression of choice through unlimited personal reconstructive projects ranging from the diary, to exercise regimes, to drastic surgical reconstructions (see McRobbie, 2009).

I investigate the Muslim youth's emerging subjectivities as their stable worlds of inherited traditions, religious ideologies, and consciously marked and constructed religious and social spheres become intertwined with unstable and interconnected visual, social, economic, and technological landscapes with the notion of 'convoluted modernities' at its core. The concept helps to capture the Muslim youth's engagements with globalizing forces from their historically disadvantaged position, but within contexts of increased connectivity and reciprocity offered by new communication technologies, which not only help counter biases of traditional media, but also make new connections—such as with diasporic Muslim populations. The concept addresses an emergent consciousness and materiality beyond simplifications and obfuscations of questions of power. It highlights not only acts of appropriation, as has been the case with postcolonial notion of hybridity, but also the acts of resistance, confrontations, and negations that equally constitute experience of cultural contacts, which have been hitherto thought of mainly in terms of exchanges between the East and the West. I explore the articulations of 'convoluted modernities' constructed through internalization of myriad possibilities of self-actualization, including those offered by the pursuit of material well being, at cross-cutting vectors of gender, class, and other socio-economic contexts, and within new spaces of sociability enabled by mobile telephones and digital spheres such as that of Facebook. I argue that I find the notion of "convoluted modernity to be most sharply etched in the subjectivities of the doubly marginalized Muslim women, as they challenge their historical disadvantages to seek gainful employment in the highly competitive economic mainstream, and as they express their agency by engaging in extended negotiations rather than in active resistance with the patriarchal order, defying Western feminist discourses of agency. Many of my informants have led me to believe that their professional, educational, and career aspirations could have been realized only through active support of their families, and especially the encouragement received from their fathers, even though in enlisting this support, the young women often acceded to limits on their social and sexual freedom (for example, by wearing a *hijab* or by carefully monitoring their interactions with the opposite sex). However, even if the young women concede to the patriarchal norms and eschewed all overt expressions of feminist agency, their new found financial wherewithal has the potential to subvert gender equations within a traditional patriarchal society even while the young women pose no obvious challenge to it.

I also elaborate on the 'convoluted modernities' of Muslim youth's as they emerge in their mediated interactions, propelling them to think of and construct a community well beyond the physical precincts of the segregated enclave. I focus on communicative initiatives of individuals and organizations which have been instrumental in establishing connections between Jamia enclave's residents, civil society activists, non-resident, and diaspora Muslim populations as well as human rights activists and forums. The interactive exchanges enabled through these forums between residents, diaspora Muslims, and activists, are noteworthy for interjecting in the Indian civil and political public spheres, using not only new media technologies, but also a very different style and language as compared to both the Urdu press and the Muslim leadership. They evoke neither implausible conspiracy theories nor exaggerated language of hurt, as the Urdu press and Muslim leadership are wont to, but systematically expose the denial of justice and challenge the official versions of truth. Moreover, their identity politics is unique, because rather than fragmenting the struggle for universal human rights by arguing for the cause of a few (see Duggan, 2003), they build momentum for justice for beleaguered Muslim youth, arrested and incarcerated under draconian anti-terrorism laws, by mobilizing other civil society organizations working to protect tribal and other subaltern populations, and finding a common cause with them. Hence, their assertion of communal rights within discourses of universal human rights poses a creative challenge to force shrinking the spaces for Muslim existence in Indian society.

Clifford Geertz (1973) has argued that anthropologists do not study sites—villages, tribes, towns, or neighborhoods, but rather they study in these sites, and different sites are suitable locations to observe different phenomena (p. 22). The segregated Muslim colony Jamia Nagar is among the most suitable sites to understand the complex process of neoliberal globalization from the perspective of those at the margins of society, taking into account complex workings power on aspirations, desires, and self imaginations. It is also a site to apprehend alternative modernities, which are constructs of conflating antithetical ideologies such as ideals of consumerist modernity with the precepts of religious identities that are beyond binary frameworks of progressive and regressive identities, neatly divided between those ascribing to religion and traditions and others devoted to flux and opportunities. I undertake this ethnographic exploration as a participative, particular and contextually circumscribed field-study to make, as Geertz has urged, the 'mega-concepts,' which engage social science, not only actual but real and creative tools to think about social reality (p. 23). The following chapters are devoted to extending the debate about emerging identities by exploring questions such as how do contradictions, diversities, and dissensions inform Muslim identities? How are narratives of materialism, consumerism, nationalism (marked with mainly Hindu symbolism), and globalized Islam imprinted on their consciousness? What are the fall-outs of these experiences, which are unique to the current generation, on the matrix of relationships within the community? How is a divergence in attitudes, beliefs, and politics being engendered between the older and the younger generation of Muslims? What are the new dynamics in the construction of gendered identities and in the enunciation of gendered relationships? Is the internalization of these complexities by young Muslim men and women rewriting gendered equations? And finally, what may be the ramifications of these newly emergent subjectivities in the construction of a communal identity and on the ways a marginalized minority population negotiates its place in the Indian democratic public sphere?

Notes

1. *Burkha* is the veil, as worn in the Indian tradition.
2. *Fatwas* or decrees with religious significance are routinely pronounced with regularity by religious scholars, Imams, or leaders of mosques, at will and without consultation with the larger Muslim community.
3. Nehru (1951) also used the term 'palimpsest' a construct of fluid interconnected layers of different epochs of differing cultural significance to describe India.
4. See Bhabha (1994).
5. The tendencies for suppression and negation of the Muslim identity have become so routine given the rising belligerence of militant Hinduism fundamentalism that they fail to raise the ire of even left-wing, progressive, and liberal sections of Indian society. In fact, as Brita Ohms (2010) notes in her analysis of the traditionally liberal English language media's coverage of the proceedings of the Gujarat riots' trials, these sections of Indian

society have become almost acquiescent to the idea. According to Ohms, Barkha Dutt, a leading journalist and commentator, had no qualms about advising Muslims to forget the brutal massacre of children and women by the Hindu mobs in Gujarat in 2002 and to give up their search for justice because their efforts were only accentuating their 'otherness,' and evoking the anger of the dominant community. According to Dutt (as quoted in Ohm 2010), Muslims were only making life more difficult for themselves (p. 124). Ohm argues that Dutt's view marks a critical turn in the "'lefitist- liberal secular" journalist practice in India' (p. 124) and it indicates the break-down of resistance to right-wing Hindu nationalist agenda. For example, BJP even opposed the setting up of a fact finding committee investigating the state of affairs of Indian Muslims headed by Justice Sachar in March 2005. According to the BJP, the government's decision would fan separatist tendencies and set the nation on the path of destruction (see 'BJP Expresses,' 2006; 'Opposition Stalls,' 2006; 'VHP to oppose,' 2006). They instructed state governments of the BJP ruled states not to cooperate with the Committee because they argued no government in the past ever had the audacity to identify Muslims as a separate religious community (see 'BJP to launch stir,' 2006, 'Victims of bias,' 2006). The prospect of a distinctive Indian Muslim identity is patently unwelcome in many quarters, notwithstanding the fact that Muslims have a sizeable presence in India with a population of nearly 150 million (2010 census).

6. Multiple disciplinary fields have documented and analyzed social and economic transformations that follow liberalization of Indian economy since 1991. I focus on the scholarship interested in the intertwining of neoliberal globalization with the opening up of the Indian skies to global media and the rise of indigenous media independent of state funding. To begin, scholarship interested in the intersections of media and society in the Indian context has focused on an event occurring just prior to economic liberalization. There has been a great deal of attention devoted to the role of media technologies/content in the rise of Hindu nationalism and the political party BJP. The focus has specifically on the cultural symbology provided by Hindu epics, Mahabharata and Ramayana, telecast on Doordarshan the Indian state supported broadcaster (see Mankekar, 1999; McGuire & Reeves, 2003; Miller, 1991; Pollock, 1993; Rajagopal, 2001), which lost most of its urban viewers once global satellite television became a reality. The advent of satellite television introduced a rich repertoire of consumerist imagery and a fairly large body of scholarship is devoted to how this imagery is aiding protean visions of selfhood, endorsing middle class's hegemony and creating major shifts in representation and articulations of gendered identity (see Das, 2001; Fernandes, 2000, 2006, Grewal, 1999;

Mankekar, 2004; Mazzarella, 2003; see Munshi, 1998; Parameswaran, 2004a, 2004b).

7. See Khair (2003) for his critique of the hybrid as only being a construct of the mingling between the East and the West. He argues why are other instances of hybridity such as inter-regional mingling as between a Keralite and a Bengali in India not evoked with the same degree of enthusiasm.

8. According to Abu-Lughod (1991), 'culture is the essential tool for making the other', and anthropologists in their attempt to understand cultural difference have helped to 'construct, produce, and maintain it (p. 143). Hence, she argues that is important for anthropologists to undo culture's capacity to freeze and institutionalize difference, as has also been pointed by Said (1978) in his arguments against Orientalism. According to Said, the term culture naturalizes difference in a way that they seem innate, as achieved in Orientalist scholarship establishing an ontological and epistemological distinction between the East and the West.

9. The tendencies inherent in cultural theories 'to overemphasize coherence' and 'to contribute to perception of communities as bounded and discrete' (Abu-Lughod, 1991, p. 146) have been thoroughly exploited in Huntington's essentialis view of cultures which are responsible for the apparent current lack of rapprochement between Islam and ideologies of Western cultures, which has proved so detrimental to world peace.

10. However, according to Abu-Lughod (1991), the fact that interpretative ethnographers marking the cultural turn still evoke the concept of difference, and hence unwittingly continue to feed into hierarchies and power inequations, that feed according to Kalb and Tak (2005) to the cultural xenophobia of our times.

11. Hence, Kalb and Tak (2005) are wont to argue Geertz (1973) focus as an anthropologist aught not to have been on the cock fight, endlessly excavating various meanings of the social conditions as evident from its staging. The matter of import Kalb and Tak (2005) contend is on how the cock fight came to be staged; and what are the social, economic, and other power dynamics that lead to its production.

12. This research would be seen as being sympathetic to the movement to revive the institutionally based 'global ethnography' as articles in Kalb and Tak's (2005) edited volume also do.

13. Discriminatory practices still prevent Muslims from renting homes in other middle class localities of Delhi, and the Muslim character of these enclaves could be seen as becoming further entrenched by increasing number of migrants (mainly from Uttar Pradesh and Bihar) who too must also be accommodated here as they are unable to find housing in other residential areas. According to the Sachar Committee report (2006) and other studies

such as by Hasan & Menon (2004), the migration from rural to urban areas, and the percentage of Muslim living in urban areas is higher for Muslim as compared to non-Muslim populations.

14. According to Kalb and Tak (2005), the cultural and interpretive ethnography highlighted the autonomy of culture, and demarcated it as a network of semiotic relationship cast over society. However, they argue that it is not the internal grammar or semiotic relationships but praxis, networks, and relationship of power and dependency which create cultures.

15. Postcolonial feminist scholar like Purnima Mankekar's (1999b) warn that personal experiences, though useful for launching of feminist critiques, are not valuable in themselves per se (p. 30) and these accounts could be narcissistic. But according to Clifford (1986), if our knowledge about other cultures is 'the problematic outcome of intersubjective dialogue, translation, and projection' (p. 109), then a degree of transparency about the presence of the scientist, the scholar, and the contexts in which they were investigating, exploring, and disseminating their knowledge is required.

16. The experiences of the marginalized population have not been foregrounded despite the fact that exposing workings of power and the constructions of inequalities constitute the core of critical cultural analysis (see During, 1993; Grossberg, 1996).

17. According to Amin, the writing of the 'new Hindu history,' which dissociates Muslims from India's past, overlooking their historical contributions to Indian society, and silences their active presence isin an 'enactment of historical vendetta against Muslim conquest of pre-colonial India'(p. 93).

18. Scholars like Rajagopal (2001) note the role of Hindu epics *Ramayana* and *Mahabharata*,which were telecast on the state broadcaster in the late 1980s and attracted unprecedented viewership, for providing leverage to right-wing Hindu nationalist party, the BJP, by circulatingextensive repertoire of Hindu iconography, symbols and narratives

19. The scholarship explores the structural, political, economic and social contexts, as well the lacuna in the meaning and institution of secularist politics in Indian democracy that open up the grounds for conflict (eg. Asad, 2006; Basu, 1997; Chatterjee, 2006; Engineer, 1988 & 1995; Hasan, 2004; Kakar, 1996; Mehta, 1992; Pandey 1990, 1997, 2001 & 2006; Shiva, 2005; Saberwal, 1986 & 1996; Tambiah, 1990; Varshney, 2002).

20. Ahmed (1983) is scathing in his criticism as to why false perceptions about Indian Muslims persist. He argues that it is because sociologists and anthropologists investigating modernization and social change in India 'have all accepted commonly held stereotypes and clichés about Muslims in India and tried to simply validate them through empirical research' (p. xxi).

21. Said's arguments have been foundational to Mamdani's (2004) criticisms of the categories of 'good Muslim' (who are 'modern, secular and Westernized') and 'bad Muslim' (who are 'doctrinal, antimodern, and virulent') which he argues have simplified and converted the complex category of Islamic cultural identities (an amalgam and interplay between history, traditions, religion, and customs) into one-dimensional political identities, wherein it is possible to identify political ideologies from the manners of dressing, eating, speaking, and praying (p. 20 & p. 34), but which are nonetheless important for condoning the unequal state of affairs between Western powers and Islamic nations and even maintaining it.

22. The two most prominent scholars who have sought to address criticisms that Said's arguments worked within oppositional poles of total domination and complete lack of agency (of the colonized body) have been Gayatri Spivak (1995 & 1999a) and Homi Bhabha (1994)—given their active engagement with theories of deconstruction, post-modernismism, and post-structuralism.

23. Mongia (1996) dismisses the privileging of 'migrancy and exile' in discussions of hybridity for unduly 'confer[ring] a greater critical edge to the migrant intellectual' (p. 7). And according to Aijaz Ahmed, whose 'ideological location,' is that of the 'male, bourgeois onlooker…not only the lord of all he surveys but also enraptured by his own lordliness' (p. 287).

24. And following Bhabha's focus on diaspora and migrant populations, and on analyzing global cultural processes, postcolonial scholars have been overwhelming preoccupied with analyzing tendencies of vagrancy, fluidity, and uncertainties of diasporic lives (see Alexander, 1996; Appadurai, 1996; Bhaba, 1994; Chopra, 2006; Durham, 2004; Faizal, 2006; Hall, 1996b; Khurana, 2004; Mankekar, 2002a, 2002b & 2004; Rajagopal, 2003).

25. Dirlik (1999) argues that the free floating cosmopolitanism of the hybrid hides questions of 'structure and totality' including 'the legacies of colonial spaces which…continue to shape not only configurations of power and political economy, but also diasporic motion and cultural formations' (p. 154).

26. Lisa Duggan (2003) drives home this point when she examines the struggle for equality of IGF,a conservative gay movement,and argues that progressive, egalitarian, and universalist spirit of the earlier gay and lesbian movement are negated to secure a very limited vision of equality for a select few, while ratifying hierarchies of state and capitalist ideologies.

27. Angela McRobbie (2009) gives the example of the aggressive individualism and competitive effectiveness in the figures of 'TV Blondes'—the young female achievers who are mostly white and blonde and are

seen clutching at their A-level examination certificates and headed to Cambridge and Oxford in various media texts. According to her, while these representations uphold these gendered bodies 'as subjects *par excellence* (sic)' they displace feminism as a collective struggle and political movement (p. 15).

1

MTV AND PEACE TV
Global Cool and *Apna Mahol* in Jamia Enclave

It was an extremely cold winter night when my cousin was driving my parents and me home through the narrow lanes of Zakir Nagar after a family dinner. As he drove his small Maruti Zen contorting, cutting, and careening like an expert gymnast through traffic obstacles of cycle rickshaws, motor cycles, scooters, cars, and handcarts, I was riveted less by his impediment driving than by the congregation of young men who were out on the streets at an hour close to midnight and were significantly contributing to the traffic blockage. The young men were attired in rather trendy Western styles—wearing jeans and jackets rather than *topis* (caps) or *payjama kurta*, the dress which is normally associated with Muslims. However, at the hour when we had arrived for dinner as calls for *Isha* prayers were resounding from different mosques, there were quite a few men both young and old dressed in the customary *topi* as they flocked to the mosques in motley attires of pants or pajamas, *kurtas* or shirts paired with loose coats and woolen scarves to guard against the cold. But at this hour the crowd was distinct. In their dress and demeanour, these young men appeared to be no different from the crowd of aspiring middle-class youth who would be congregating on a Saturday night in the various malls and multiplexes—which have reorganized urban public domain in the rapidly globalizing economy to accommodate the encroachment of consumer culture in all realms of public life. And while the glitzy malls were offering a space for the youth of Delhi to gather and to gape at branded attires and products within air-conditioned environs, these young men were congregated here in the narrow lanes of Zakir Nagar. Standing in groups around *pan* shops or sitting check by jowl with the cook in tiny and nondescript restaurants which were still doing business selling *kabab* and *rotis* with steaming cups of tea, they were enacting the sensibility of the spaces from which they were markedly absent. My cousin on noticing our perplexed expressions at the milling crowds at this late hour, remarked, '*yeh saab laadka bahar se aaya hai.*' According to him, the throngs of young men were migrants from smaller towns and rural areas of Uttar Pradesh and Bihar, who had come to Delhi for higher education and/or employment. And he was right, because in the course of my fieldwork, since 2006, I have met many such migrants from these states who were either students at different educational and vocational training institutes or employees of a range of organizations from multinational banks to call centers, advertising agencies, media organizations, travel agencies, and even courier services. And yet, this congregation of young Muslims riveted my attention, not for the sheer force of their numbers, but as a representative microcosm of how the Muslim youth's aspirations and their investment in the materialities and narratives of the globalizing Indian economy were introducing new dynamics in the segregated Muslim community. The faces of these young men, gathered at every street corner and back alleys of Zakir Nagar, mirrored the floodgates of desires, which have been unleashed in a formerly austere socialist country, sweeping away one and all in their torrential force. And in the sheer intensity of the youth's aspirations, diverging from the tendencies of retrenchment that mark their environments and their representation, is a question about its transformative potential—not only for individual subjectivities but also for Muslim communal identity and politics.

There has been a great deal written about how economic reforms, liberalization, and globalization have transformed India's social and economic landscape by releasing pent up energies of an impatient nation, encouraging entrepreneurship, new ventures, new professions as well as extraordinary endeavours to allow a third world country with a bogged down economy to break new grounds and to imagine itself as an emerging super power.[1] But in all of these accounts, Muslim experiences are scarcely mentioned. This is not only because the focus has been mainly on the experiences of the dominant Hindu identity, but also because scholarship has limited itself to those educated sections of Indian society employed in sectors integrated into the global economy, such as information technology, pharmaceuticals, medicine, and finance. These sectors have also been projected as being at the heart of the revolutionary developments in society and as representing the best of Indian talent and entrepreneurial skills, freed from the shackles of bureaucratic control and debilitating red tape (see Das, 2001; Nilekani, 2008). However, notwithstanding the contributions of these sectors, the focus on achievements of a small and indeed privileged section of Indian society in popular culture and discourses has imbued the narratives of middle-class ascendency with a certain coherence, as well as imposed upon middle-class identity a homogeneity, obfuscating its more fractured, diverse, and complex reality (see Fernandes, 2006). These young Muslim men, crowding the bylanes of the Muslim enclave vouched for the power of the sweeping changes in the economic spheres, concomitant with developments in media technologies and mediated narratives to impact even those on the margins, in forgotten corners of the country, and those given up as inert and calcified, such as the Muslims. Their presence also validates the profound force inherent in the desire for upward mobility and its role in shaping new modernities outside the limited though much investigated domain of the dominant Hindu middle class.

The Muslim youth are a part of the exodus from small towns and semi-rural communities propelled by unlocking desires that emerge from globalized media's incessant circulation of images and ideas of westernized standards of prosperity. Hailing mostly from the northern Indian states of Uttar Pradesh and Bihar where infrastructural and material growth have been unable to keep up with the growing ambitions of their populations (see Ciotti, 2010); the Muslim youth are among many that are drawn to the substantively overhauled urban economic spheres, seeking employment in the growing sunrise sectors and industries that have emerged after liberalization and globalization. But, they constitute a population perceived to be particularly backward and lacking in ability to participate in the transformative changes of the Indian society. Indian Muslims have a much higher school drop-out rate and a lower school attendance rate than any other socio-religious community in India, and almost 25 per cent of Muslim children in the age group of 6 to 14 are not part of the educational system because their condition of abject poverty is further compounded by the discriminatory treatment of Muslims in educational institutions (Sachar committee, 2006, p. 58). But, notwithstanding the structural inequities, entrenched powers have imposed upon Muslims, in the way of 'marking difference and exclusion' (Stuart Hall, 1996c, p. 4), the definition of an exceptional national subject within the 'postcolonial condition.' Akhil Gupta (1998) describes the 'postcolonial condition' as being marked with anxieties of keeping up with Westernized standards of development and modernity. However, the Muslim populations have been presumed to be entirely untouched by such concerns, and according to Hasan (2002), they are 'genetically and culturally cast in the role of a religious crusader,' while their lives are imagined and evoked within narrow contexts of the segregated enclaves which define their 'otherness' and qualify their detachment from the warp and weft of the mainstream Indian society (p. 10). Therefore, not surprisingly, the Muslim populations have been mostly overlooked in the extensive debates and analyses of aspirations for upward mobility and the middle-classes phenomenon in India.

But, in observing the young men in the slowly moving traffic as they ambled in the streets with shuttered down shops (many of them selling communication services ranging from cell phones to complete communication packages for independent households comprised of Internet service, satellite television, and telephone), their pulsating ambitions, which had driven them to this urban ghetto, were almost palpable. And even if most of them may aspire only for entry-level positions in many of the new employment sectors, they still represent a significant thrust from below, and an attempt by another marginalized community to make a bid for itself in the expanding economic pie. I wondered as I gazed at the crowd, if the young men, whom I had seen serving customers and loading supplies earlier in the new supermarket in Friends Colony's community market, creating an international grocery shopping experience for its upscale clientele, were included in the crowd present here? Or was Shakeel who had assisted me while I was trying to get a mobile phone connection earlier that day in the same market part of this midnight congregation?

Over the course of my research, my attention has been drawn to the fact that I was meeting and interacting with an increasing number of young Muslim men and women employed in the various commercial establishments that are operating out of Friends Colony's community

market, located less than half a mile away from the Muslim enclave
of Jamia. The complex of shops, business, restaurants, beauty salons,
and cinema halls serves residents of one of the most expensive residential locales of South Delhi, which exist cheek by jowl with Jamia
enclave. The other operations in the complex represent new avenues in
neoliberal, urbanized India, in the field of sales, marketing, customer-
care, hospitality, as well as education, finance, research, and media
that have created new opportunities for employment. The presence
of the diverse sectors and the options of employment in an expanding
economy create a very different situation today as compared to when
I was seeking employment in the early 1990s. I remember that my
option for employment as a broadcast journalist was limited to the
state broadcaster *Doordarshan*, where it was not easy to find a foothold
because within its high-walled bureaucratic bastion, prejudices against
Muslims could be effectively explained as the outcome of static rules
and regulations.[2] However, the introduction of cultures of meritocracy
in Indian economic spheres following liberalization (see Varma, 1998,
& Nilekani, 2008) have opened up the arena; and the Muslim youth's
quiet presence in various employment sectors today is to be taken note
of, especially considering their very conspicuous absence earlier in a
state-controlled economy where opportunities were hard to come by,
even for those with higher education and skills.

But what is even more significant is the new attitude, which accom-
panies newfound ambitions among the youth belonging to a supposedly inert community. I found the young men and women serving as
customer service personnel, technicians, facilitators, trainers, journalist,
among other professions to be quietly confident rather than evasive, as
I remember being, about their Muslim identity. They also expressed a
sense of optimism, which cannot be ascribed entirely to their youthful-
ness. For example, I have often heard my father lament that employment
prospects for the Indian Muslim community were extremely poor; and
he holds this view despite the fact that he himself had been employed
with the Indian government's enterprises (or public sectors as they
are called). However, when I asked my young cousin, who had just
graduated from the Engineering college at Jamia University and was on
the job market, if he feared discrimination on account of his religious
identity, he did not seem to share my father's gloomy assessment of the
employment scenario. He answered my query with a laugh, and added

completely unfazed 'oh but I don't expect to work for the government,' expressing this faith in the new working environment of the globalized economy, where focus on individual merit undermines cronyism and stigmatization to create a more levelled playing field for members of a discriminated religious minority population. I heard the optimism for the new economic order reiterated, even in the voices of some among the older generations; and as a retired teacher at Jamia School shared with me:

> Look at the private sector. Our children are going places in the private sector. Why are they successful in the private sector? In the private sector, when you see our children there, they are intelligent, they have the power... this tells us that there is some feeling of discrimination. Why are [our] children succeeding in private sector and not in the government sector? (personal communication, December, 4, 2007)

I highlight these exchanges to reflect on a certain degree of confidence among Muslims generated by evolving contexts of the globalizing economy, to the extent that the desire to work for a 'big company,' as multinationals were generally referred to, was expressed by almost every graduate student, men or women that I interacted with during the course of my research. In fact, a sense of hope was the enduring narrative that sustained through the extended period of my research from 2006 to 2013, bridging generational, gender, and class divides. But most importantly, their faith even survived negativity and brutality created by critical events, such as the arrest of Dr Hanif in July 2007, the conflagration in Jamia enclave during Ramazan of 2007, and the Batla House encounter in September 2008 that framed Muslims as terrorists and dismissed them as misfits. The atmosphere of fear and suspicion following in their wake overwhelmed me and endangered the bonds that I formed with my informants (Khan, 2009). However, they never did quite manage to completely smother the resolve of the youth, men and women, to entertain new dreams and aspirations.

More importantly, many of my informants even exhibited the audacity to hope in spite of and despite their very Muslim identity. I encountered examples of their determination across gender, class, and educational divides. But I would like to first make a mention of the aspirations of Nabila, a young woman from Bihar, enrolled in the Diploma of civil engineering at Jamia Polytechnic, whose family enjoins her to wear the full-veil. However, even she believed, undeterred by the fact that her full black *naqab* (veil), and *burqa* (the black long coat) conspicuously announced her Muslim identity, that if she got to work for a 'big company' she would rise steadily. She had full confidence because according her, 'I know…I know [I would succeed] because I am very concentrated' referring to her ability to focus and to concentrate on her goal. One of her professors shared with me that Nabila had even interviewed for a position with one of the well-established developers in Delhi, dressed in her full *naqab* and *burqa*. And according to the professor, although everyone around her was very apprehensive about how she would be received by the prospective employers, given the antipathy towards Islam and Nabila's very strident announcement of her Islamic identity, Nabila was actually offered the job to everyone's pleasant surprise (personal communication, August 6, 2007).

And it was only later in a conversation with Nabila that I understood what the dynamics of new economic regimes mean at the ground level. According to Nabila, much to her discomfort, her employers did first ask her if she were a strict Muslim, to which she had nodded her head in agreement. However, after that, according to Nabila, her prospective employers posed only technical questions. And she narrated rather gleefully that one of their questions was regarding reinforcement of concrete, which according to Nabila, was a very basic question, to which she presented a number of alternatives depending on cost and design, and impressed them enough to be offered a job. The next year when I met Nabila, she was still working with the Dutch multi-national design firm during the day but had enrolled for the Engineering degree at Jamia Millia Islamia and was attending classes later in the evening.

Nabila's story can perhaps be referenced as one of the most optimistic scenarios of how the expanding economy is opening up opportunities for both upward mobility and inclusion, overriding discriminatory politics of religion and community by making individual merit to be the only criterion. This optimism is also reinforced in another informant's story. Zain also graduated with an Engineering degree from Jamia University, and then he successfully competed against the best brains in the country to secure admission at the Faculty of Management Studies, Delhi University, one of the most prestigious MBA programs in the country. His admission to one of the best business schools in the country also helped him to later find a position as a portfolio manager at a major financial consultancy firm in London. However, even as Zain and Nabila are the poster children promoting education as the way to middle-class ascendancy in a growing economy for those from modest backgrounds of a marginalized community (considering the fact that Nabila's father was a school teacher in a small town in Bihar, and Zain's father was only a mid-level government employee), the congregation of young men at the street corners of Jamia enclave represented a different and more complex perspective on how the expanding neoliberal economy is drawing even those existing on the extreme margins of the Indian society into the vortex of global flows.

The path of the young men gathered that night in the bylanes of Zakir Nagar is perhaps not assured by white-collar professionalism but probably carved by vagaries of blue-collared nature of work, because education is not everyone's prerogative. And juxtaposed with the success stories of a Nabila or a Zain, there are hundred other cases of young men and women who are denied privileged access to elite professional courses, because universities, including Jamia University, have significantly raised their parameters for granting admission. However, undeterred, many of these migrants refuse to return and instead try to find their way through new opportunities and impediments. I found their presence to be an extremely instructive representation of how transformative changes in economic, social, and especially mediated spheres establishing the dominance of materialist and consumerist discourses were bearing down upon historically contingent realities defined by lack of education, money power, and a general wherewithal to deal with modernity.

According to Gyanendra Pandey (2006), the problems of the underprivileged as they grapple with modernizing forces have not even been widely discussed, let alone theorized in postcolonial contexts. The focus as pointed out earlier has been mainly on the upper echelons of the middle class, who have the ability to consume. But to explain how fantasies woven around new spaces of modernity created by celebrity cultures, products, and brands enthrall all sections of society; I recount my encounter with Faisal, an assistant at a travel agency and a student of the diploma program in tourism, who could very well have been one of the lower-middle-class young men that were out on the streets that night. I was questioning Faisal about his life ambitions and in response he shared with me some newspaper clippings (probably from Page 3 of Delhi Times) that he carried in his wallet and which I believe summed up his life's philosophy. The newspaper clippings included a picture of the world's most expensive watch—a Choppard costing over a million dollars. Then, there were photographs of Sania Mirza, the Indian Muslim tennis player, of Narain Kartikeyan, the only Indian on the Formula One racing track, and of Brett Lee, the world's fastest bowler. According to Faisal, he carried these pictures because these celebrities inspired him, especially Sania Mirza and Kartikeyan who have done India proud by entering fields where few Indians have ventured. And as for the watch, an epitome of luxury, Faisal hoped that one day he too would own something like that ultimate status symbol (personal communication, July 17, 2007). But until then an image of that watch, a status symbol of the global elites, was a folded and worn out newspaper clipping placed in his plastic wallet as safely as in a safe-deposit box. The collage of images in Faisal's wallet is significant as a complex coming together of the symbols of global lifestyle and affluence (as the watch and Brett Lee) with the icons of 'Team India' (like Sania and Kartikeyan). They are indicative of how the Muslim youth's aspirations and dreams are both implicated in and buoyed by larger changes in the Indian economy. But the question that the youth's driving ambitions raise, is not only with regard to how they may inform individual subjectivities, but if they have the potential to influence the way a minority community imagines its position within the changing Indian economic and social landscape, and if herein lies a potential to create new social and political dynamics.

It is important to explore this question, considering that there has been an extensive exploration of how *Dalit* or the Hindu lower-castes' desire for upward mobility have transformed the political landscape in one of the most important and populace state of Uttar Pradesh (see, Z. Hasan, 2000; Omvedt, 1994; Pai, 2002 & 2001). In the light of the fact that Muslims share with Dalits a complex condition of subjugation that Gyanendra Pandey (2006) refers to as 'internal colonization, 'wherein they are not only perceived as second class citizens, but are also unable to assert any independent claims to history or to seek an identity outside of and without assimilating into the dominant culture (p. 1781), the question is: how may Muslim youth's efforts toward economic well-being give new visibility to Muslim citizens in a way that may contradict existing power equations and reconstruct a minority population's politics within the Indian democratic sphere?

The discussions on the *Dalit* community's push for upward mobility have dwelt on the *Dalit* agency and the way it has played a significant role in reshaping the politics of the lower-castes, leading to a realignment of power equations, especially in the Indian states of Uttar Pradesh and Bihar. Nita Kumar (2006) refers to the question of the *Dalit* agency as a 'provincial modernity,' that is a teeming and pulsating alternative to the more organized and hegemonic modernity of urban elites. And according to Ciotti (2010), it not only presents a challenge to the hegemonic upper-caste prescriptions of modernity, but also confounds popular beliefs about caste identity politics and modernity as being mutually exclusive. In a similar vein, Muslim youth's urging for improved social and economic status interjects into existing contestations for resources, and they also require some form of re-enactment of the minority Muslim population's ideological position and practices in order to strategically confront power factions that perpetuate their marginalized status. However, without elaborating on the fallouts of the youth's rising aspirations on the political spheres, which is the matter for my future research project, I seek to present an insight into the way the imbrication of a hitherto in-ward looking religious community in the turmoil of global flows and in the promises of materialist and consumerist discourses is informing the youth's imaginations of selfhood, while also shifting the patterns of sociability within the community. I begin with examining how the significance of community itself has been transformed by exploring its meaning from the point of view of those born before the liberalizing/globalizing narratives realigned the ideological and social structures of the Indian society to compare it with those who have come of age during revolutionary changes in economic and socio-cultural spheres. The sites of this exploration are spaces, such as the segregated Muslim enclave of Jamia Nagar, that are imagined to reflect the quintessential essence of Muslim populations.

Jamia Nagar, *Apna Mahol* and the Churnings

The exclusive and segregated Muslim enclave of Jamia, which lies on the south-eastern end of the city of Delhi, adjoining the sluggish Yamuna river, is imagined along with all other Muslim enclaves dotted across Indian urban landscapes, as a deteriorating moribund space, whose residents abide by an archaic and unchanging social code. These impressions of inertness could perhaps enjoy some credibility when intrusive presence of mediated technologies was not the norm; and when residents of the enclave could expect to find their traditions and values reflected around them, and seek comfort in their continuity. But today, when to hear the sound of the *azan* from the mosque, the volume of MTV has to be first reduced, life within the distinct Muslim enclave cannot be assumed as stagnating. There is a churning in the Muslim cultural life as new media technologies breach the community's isolation and globalizing narratives challenge the singularity of cultural expression. The younger generations are deeply cognizant of the existence of a new rhythm introduced by the reconstruction of the larger economic, social, and mediated spheres. And the Muslim youth's imaginations of the community as well as their conceptualization of its continuity and coherence are constructed as they grapple with forces from far beyond their comfort limits and as they negotiate with dissonances between the real and the virtual.

The older generations on the other hand are deeply invested in the cultural cohesiveness of the segregated enclave. Explaining their preference to live with their co-religionist, they would often pronounce in languorous conversations in fluent Urdu, '*Aur phir yeh apna mahol hai,*' or 'This is after all our environment.' The word *mahol* is hard to translate, but what this proprietary terminology expresses is their sense of comfort and belonging to a community rooted in Islamic cultural and religious moorings. Jamia enclave in many ways exhibits the Indian Muslim social and cultural heritage—especially through its numerous mosques, the small eateries serving authentic Indian Muslim cuisine of *biryani*, *kabab*, *nihari* and *korma*, the presence of women wearing some form of the veil (either the *burkha* or the *hijab*) indicating the decorum and distance maintained between the members of the opposite sex, and the rhythm of life punctuated by obligations of faith that resonate in the residents' lives. On numerous occasions, I have observed that during *namaz*, a sudden hush would fall over the hustle-bustle of the narrow streets where men, women, animals, and vehicles were all jostling a moment ago. For a few minutes the streets would empty, there would be a veritable pause and then life would resume its pace until the next *namaz*. The enactments of such gestures pronounce the enclave's distinctness. And according to many among the older genera-tions such articulations of Islamic traditions in everyday life are very important, because the inability to express core characteristics of their culture would make Muslims 'psychologically depressed'. They would insist that it was imperative to hear the sound of *azan* resound five times a day and to freely celebrate Islamic festivals without the fear of offending Hindu neighbors. Their concern was especially with regard to the celebration of *Eid Ul Adha*—the festival marking the end of *Hajj*, wherein sacrifice of a lamb is essential and which could be deeply offensive to the largely vegetarian Hindu population.[3] As one older gentleman expressed:

> Take the case of the celebration of *Eid* when we have to sacrifice a goat, we can freely do that here. But suppose I was living in some colony like Mayapuri or Punjabi Bagh, can I do that there? And suppose I am thick skinned enough to perform the ritual sacrifice? Then won't all the blood flow out of the house? My neighbors will come and ask why is there blood flowing out of your home. They will say, where will all this mess go? They don't understand the importance of this sacrifice in our culture. (author's translation, original in Urdu, personal communication, December 4, 2007)

However, the primacy accorded to Muslim culture among the older generations is not to be conceived as inflexibility or obduracy, instead it is to be perceived as a reflection of their living connections with the Indian Islamic cultural and literary heritage, because of their ability to read and write in the Urdu language, which situates them within the Indian Islamic ethos. Their fluency in Urdu gives them access to narra-tives elucidating Indian Islamic sensibilities and to the issues surround-ing their historical construction. More importantly, it places within their grasp the rich and incisive debate on how to approach the question of cultural and material domination of the West which has been engaging the community for over a century (Hasan, 2005). Therefore, the older generations are repositories of the Indian Islamic *adab*, *akhlaq*, and *tehzeeb*, which according to Hasan, are questions of proper etiquette and 'didactic morality,' guiding personal deportment and execution of social obligations of the *Sharif* (or high born Muslim) culture. I speak from personal experience of immediate and extended family as well as from the perspectives of close friends and acquaintants that those who could read and write in Urdu (and I refer not only to Muslims but also to older generations among my Hindu Punjabi friends) were not unfamiliar with the large body of Islamic literature that specifically addressed these matters. According to Mushirul Hasan (2005), the literary guides to 'noble character' and 'lofty conduct' written by north Indian Muslim intelligentia in Urdu in the nineteenth century, drew on Persian and Arabic texts often going as far back as the eight and the ninth century (p. 2–29). The facility in Urdu language created an organic link with both, the Indian Islamic culture as well as, with the Muslim *Ummah* or global community. However, younger generations' disconnect with the Urdu language breaks the flow and renders them unable to comprehend, inhere, or articulate the Indian Islamic cultural ethos. Even the concept of *mahol* was difficult for them to comprehend and many of the young on being prodded to articulate the essence of Islamic life would turn around and ask me, often in English, 'what is *apna mahol?*' Once I was even rebuked for my persistent probing of the matter whether Muslim culture was under erasure by a young 19 year old female student of Jamia Polytechnic, who curtly informed me that people who wanted to get ahead in life did not think of such matters.

I find the resonance of this nonchalance in a recent case within my own extended family, when a distant relative and a famous professor of linguistics willed his entire library containing many hard to come by manuscripts in Persian, Arabic, and Urdu to be gifted to the State archives. His bequeathal is a poignant commentary on the younger generation's frayed relations with their own cultural identity, because there was no one among his children or grandchildren who could apprehend the collection's import or even appreciate his contributions to Persian and Urdu languages. We are, in the professor's own words, a deaf and dumb generation, and in comparison to us the earlier generations of Muslims were better able to maintain a level of integrity in the face of what Pandey (2006) refers to as 'internal colonialism' by deflecting unfettered cultural dominance through their own keen understanding and appreciation of their cultural identity. Nevertheless, this is not to say that there exists a straightforward equation with views of the older and younger generation strung at opposing ends of the spectrum, because as I will elaborate in my later chapters, class is also a very important vector in defining the relationship with Indian Islamic culture and in constructing an ability to claim, reassert, and resurrect the Islamic identity in the public spheres. Yet, I argue that because of the living link with the Urdu language the earlier generations were better able to structure a more cohesive response to pressures for unquestioned assimilation into the dominant culture, even if this entailed a withdrawal from the mainstream—an action for which the community has been severely berated and chastised.

However, their insistence on the maintenance of an Islamic way of life within distinct living spaces made them complicit with discriminatory regimes that keep Muslims confined to their closed and segregated enclaves, and it cast upon the enclave an air of 'provincialism' or 'what is seen on the national level as a brake-effect' or 'an obstacle, political, economic, and most of all cultural' in what could be a 'promising march forward' (N. Kumar, 2006, p. 397). According to Nita Kumar, the term provincialism demarcates inferior spaces from normative or superior ones, and it is a 'key trope for interpreting modern Indian history' (p. 397). The idea of provinciality, which marks an absence of discipline and is a hindrance in 'the smooth march forward of unfettered forces of rationality and order' (p. 398), is also seen as the defining condition of the Indian Muslim population. In the larger discourse, the entire Jamia area is marked as a provincial space, because while one side of the Ashoka Park Road lies the posh Friend's colony—a well-planned living space of organized housing with separation between business and residential areas, along with proper footpaths, parks, and motorable roads, the other side represents indiscipline and chaos. In the Jamia area, unplanned spaces replace the carefully laid out of grid of Friend's Colony and hundreds of narrow lanes and barely navigable main streets crisscross and intersect, while there are no parks, no greens, and no open spaces to break the monotony of concrete constructions. Instead, there is an aggressive and highly risky occupation of the river's shifting sands, and nothing remains to remind that this was once a grassy marshland adjoining the lazily flowing Yamuna. Moreover, many pockets of the locality lack civic facilities like potable drinking water and electricity, but this has not checked the relentless pace of construction to accommodate wave upon wave of migrants, who are drawn to the urban centers lured by economic opportunities.

And yet the role of Muslim insecurities, and especially their fear of violence during communal riots, cannot be disregarded in the settlement of this area. According to Baig Saab, one of the earliest settlers, Muslims tend to feel safer living among their coreligionists, and the Jamia enclave was particularly attractive because of its proximity to water. Its location allayed Muslim settlers' fears that in the event of a communal riot the possibility of the community being cornered and tortured through the shutting down of the water supply was infinitely less as the river water would serve as their lifeline. In fact, the latest wave of migrations to the area, which swelled the area's population substantially, was fueled by violence perpetuated against Muslims in the aftermath of Babri Masjid's destruction in 1992. A number of my informants moved to the Jamia area, many as children, from other mixed localities in Delhi and small towns in Uttar Pradesh following this event. Today, the population of the area, as extrapolating from the census figures that give a compounded figure for the larger south-eastern zone, is estimated to be close to 500,000 people. However, some residents argue that given the steady influx of migrants, even this could be a conservative estimate.

However, notwithstanding the press of populations and the impressions of provinciality, the living together of Muslims with other Muslims does not validate dominant perceptions about the segregated enclave as a homogeneous and undifferentiated community. In fact, there was a note of the explicit 'othering' in my cousin's identification of the young men or the new immigrants as 'outsiders' when he himself could trace his place in this segregated enclave to one such wave of migration created by historical forces. My cousin's remark also unsettles the assumptions that communities can be a construct of religious affinities, while overlooking dissensions created by differences in class, education, and economic wherewithal. The majority of young men that night may have been from the lower middle classes, but the Jamia enclave is largely a middle class residential area. However, it is a pointer to Muslim conditions shaped by intractable and discriminatory politics and attitudes that even if different residential areas of Delhi are organized according to economic status and social class of its residents, all classes of Muslims reside in close proximity in Jamia area together. And as the overtones of provinciality that mark this space, become attached to a Muslim identity denoting all Muslims as inferior and backward subjects, they not only jeopardize Muslim subjects' access to globalized modernized spheres, but the marking of Muslim as the 'other' becomes the uniting factor across all different classes and disparate experiences shaping Muslim identity.

Muslim Middle-Class Modernities

However, despite the intractability of dominant impressions about Muslims as backward and anti-modern, and notwithstanding the general tendency of the older generations of Muslims to withdraw in the face of charges of provinciality, it is not as if Muslims have been acquiescent to their own provinciality. In fact, the urge to join the mainstream has been abiding, and the genesis of this entire area of Jamia is deeply implicated within the distinct world vision and imaginations of modernity, nationhood and citizenship entertained by the middle class and the educated among Muslims at the turn of the 20th century. At the heart of what was formerly known as *Okhla Gaon* (village) is the campus of Jamia Millia Islamia, an educational society established by Muslim intellectuals and scholars in response to Gandhi's call for rejection of colonial control and educational institutes by the way of developing and promoting indigenous education. Set up in the 1920s, as part of the larger design to secure independence from the British rule, the educational society's goal, in common with other indigenous educational movements, was to secure a coherent inner core of indigenous knowledge and values from where to launch an intellectual and moral critique of the British colonial regime (see Chatterjee, 1999). Hence, the mission of Jamia Milia Islamia, which relocated to *Okhla Gaon* from its original location in north Delhi in 1935 (www.jmi.nic.in), was distinct from the other Muslim university at Aligarh. The university at Aligarh, popularly referred to as 'The Muslim Oxford,' was established to closely imitate traditions of the hallowed British universities of Oxford and Cambridge. Jamia Milia Islamia's mission, on the other hand, was opposed to such imitative logic and its founding principle was to give precedence to local experiences and systems of knowledge. But both these universities and the communities constructed around them were involved in seeking an appropriate response to the pressures of modernity introduced by the colonial experience. Mushirul Hasan (2002) quotes Lelyveld to describe the Muslim university at Aligarh as a 'formally organized, self-consciously created social establishment' whose purpose was to enable 'transitions of identity and loyalty suitable to the special circumstances of British India' (p. 6). Aligarh University and Jamia Millia Islamia were both involved in shaping the secular life of Muslims. But, as Hasan has argued, dominant tendencies in India, given scholarship's inability to challenge binary frameworks and 'colonial categories of knowledge' regarding Muslim communities, have colored even secular, progressive, and reformist ideas and movements among Muslims as communal, reactionary, and revivalist imperatives, hindering the Muslim community's endeavors to express and realize its independent vision of modernity.

However, the persistence of power equations enforcing the Muslim community's 'internal colonization' have ensured that any effort on their part to search for distinction would be viewed with deep suspicion, and almost always perceived as a threat to the nation state. Hence, despite the initial coalescence of nationalist and anti-colonial objectives and the support that Jamia Millia Islamia received from leaders such as Nehru, it was not easy for the Muslim educational society to establish itself as a place of higher education in India. It was as late as 1962 when Jamia Millia Islamia was finally declared to be a 'deemed university' by the University Grants Commission of India; but it still did not have the right to confer degrees which were considered to be at par with those granted by other Indian institutes. Hence, owing to its demoted position, the university became a place of refuge for those Muslims who felt that they would not be able to secure admission in any other institute in India. However, efforts to improve the educational standing of the institute continued—often in piece-meal and haphazard manner, woefully dependent on the mood, generosity, and political expediencies of the ruling governments. Nonetheless, it has been a march forward and in 1988 Jamia Millia Islamia was declared by the Parliament to be a central university. This development greatly enhanced the university's access to funding and support from the federal government, leading to the establishment of many new departments of excellence within Jamia Millia Islamia, thereby attenuating the notion of provinciality that have so defined its existence.

However, even as Jamia Millia Islamia's academic standing has substantially improved, its efforts to be considered at par with other Indian universities has entailed that the university has become increasingly inaccessible to the majority of Muslims. It can no longer be the last refuge for under-performing Muslims. I believe that many among the young men gathered that night, were most likely to be aspirants, who had come to Delhi hoping to secure admission in the university, but had failed to do so because of their inability to succeed in highly competitive educational fields. According to Zain, an alumni of the university, the majority of students in key departments like Engineering and Computer Sciences of Jamia Millia Islamia University are non-Muslims. The Muslims, unlike the Dalits and other lower caste communities, have not been covered under ameliorative and affirmative action policies addressing their backwardness. So much so that even as other marginalized and historically underprivileged Indian citizens are assured of reserved seats in educational institutes and in government employment sectors, no such palliative measure is offered to the Indian Muslims. In fact during the course of my research, a struggle was going on to secure a minority status for the university, which would ensure that a certain percentage of seats could be set aside for Muslims in the university.

Therefore, given the lack of constitutional protection which the *Dalits* have enjoyed, the path of Muslim modernity has been very different. While the path of the Dalit modernity has been in tandem with narratives of state, nationhood, and development, and according to Manuela Ciotti (2010), 'state mythologies around development through education, employment and democratization practices [have] flourished amongst its most disadvantaged citizens' (p. 6), Muslims have been ignored by the state. Hence, the state's endeavours have held meaning for the *Dalits* because the state has actively interceded on their behalf to secure favourable conditions for their self-actualization through statutes firmly negating centuries of neglect, disenfranchisement, and cultural politics of the deeply hierarchical Hindu society. Therefore, the *Dalit* modernity, despite posing an explicit challenge to forces resisting the backward citizens' efforts for self-improvement, has not involved an explicit rejection of the Hindu high-caste traditions or even polity. Indeed, according to Ciotti (2010), the *Dalit* search for recognition and distinction has proceeded by invoking the logic of high-caste Hindu social reforms movements of the past century, and the *Dalit's* 'retro-modernity' has deflected inherent conflict in the hierarchical Hindu community by ensuring that upward mobility of Hindu lower castes did not offset dominant ideologies and structures. The contradictory situation is similar to the one posed by the opposing demands of 'universal citizenship on one hand, and protection of particularist rights on the other' that lie at the heart of Dalit subjectivity (Chatterjee, 2006, p. 8), and which has been obfuscated by making ameliorations of *Dalit* conditions a constitutional guarantee.

However, the Muslim subjects on the other hand, have faced a very different reality in independent India, when for the first time in their collective history, they were not only identified as a minority population but also as untrustworthy and recalcitrant citizens, responsible for the partition of the territory into two nation states. Moreover, the historical and cultural force of Indian Muslim experiences has been either outright discarded or frozen within archeological sites and historical monuments. But such is the impulse for negating the Muslim identity that even in these stupefied forms they have not been allowed to represent the distinct Muslim identity, rather they exist only as emblems of India's diversity, attracting global appreciation. In addition, any attempt by Muslims to call upon their cultural resources or seek answers within their unique collective history for the situations facing them have been either staunchly resisted or berated and condemned as anti-nationalist (see Hasan, 2002). The dominant response in the face of debilitating negativity among the older generations of Muslims has been to just withdraw from the mainstream. However, this does not mean that they have been passive or moribund.

Regional Modernity

Rather, extrapolating from the lived environment of the exclusive Muslim enclave and analyzing the reasons for its settlement, I argue that it is a site of a minority community's particular articulation of modernity, or what Sivaramakrishnan and Agrawal (2003) define as 'regional modernity,' which while making an argument for ubiquity, multiplicity, and multi-local expressions of modernity, emphasizes the 'social networks and flows that give it [modernity] particular form and content' (p. 13). Drawing attention to particularity of context, structures, practices, and imaginaries underlying the settlement of the Muslim enclave, I see the efforts of older generations of Muslim to address modernizing forces as well as inequities of hegemonic nationalism, as being akin to politics of 'quiet encroachment' or 'redress' (see Bayat, 2004). Asef Bayat describes 'politics of quiet encroachment' as a 'noncollective, but prolonged, direct action by individuals and families to acquire the basic necessities of life (land for shelter, urban collective consumption, informal work, business opportunities, and public space) in a quiet and unassuming, yet illegal, fashion' (p. 81). He refers to the 'politics of redress' as the defining condition of 'urban informalities' or extra legal measures that mark the everyday practices of ordinary people (and not just of the poor and rural migrants as has been noted earlier) in urban settlements of developing countries under difficult conditions of neoliberal globalization. It is the means of survival for scores of people who are increasingly left to fend for themselves after withdrawal of state support in the wake of neoliberal restructuring of global economies (see AlSayyad & Roy 2004; AlSayyad, 2004). The response of Indian Muslims evokes this politics, because they too, unlike the *Dalits*, have always had to fall back on their own resources and have often had to work in opposition to the state's express dictates and regulations to situate themselves in conditions created by modernizing forces. The extra legality, which is clearly evinced in the settling of the Muslim colony of the Jamia area, has also required certain invisibility in order to proceed with the everyday lives away from the state's surveillance and policing forces. However, this seclusion has also meant that the Muslims have been marked out as actively rejecting modernity and embracing their traditional past. Therefore, while the *Dalit* modernities have been perceived as positive and progressive (given the fact that they are endorsed by the state), the Muslim community's struggles to survive and to grow have been positioned in opposition to modernity and in the current stressful environment even as a deeply detrimental force capable of destabilizing the state.

Such impressions about Muslims persist, I argue, because few have attempted to understand from the perspective of a deeply compromised, disregarded and disavowed religious minority their negotiations with modernity and their desire for progress. The Indian Muslim community's everyday experiences are neither in negation of modernity nor in opposition to narratives of progress peddled by the state. In fact, the settlement of the entire area is an expression of their active interjections to secure a space within urban modernities, notwithstanding the state's indifference or its punitive authority. However, I refrain from referring to their actions and politics of 'redress,' as evinced in the residents' defiance of municipal authorities' sanctions and plans, in terms of resistance or protest. It would be, as Asef Bayat (2004) argues, at the risk of identifying both 'both intended and unintended practices as manifestations of resistance,' while failing to 'search for intent and meaning,' and overlooking the way everyday practices' are enacted within prevailing systems of power (p. 89). Instead, I see them as 'protracted' and 'pervasive' and but not openly confrontational struggle for advancement in face of powerful discriminatory forces arrayed against them. These efforts are deeply implicated in desires for progress, growth, and modernity, especially because it is the Jamia Millia Islamia University, which has been the primary reason why Muslims have been attracted to this region in the first place. Many of my informants shared with me that their families moved out from small towns in Uttar Pradesh and Bihar having sold their ancestral lands and homes to exchange for a small house in the area (given the sky-rocketing real estate prices) just because living close to the university would ensure that they would be able to study at least 'something.' And given the fact that Jamia Millia Islamia now teaches all modern subjects, while being a center of excellence for teaching of Islamic history as well as Urdu, Arabic, Persian, it facilitates Muslim community's truck with modernity.

Generational Differences

However, in analyzing Jamia enclave as a unique site and expression of the Muslim community's modernity, a fundamental shift becomes apparent in the relationships and networks, which situated the university in the lives and consciousness of different generations of the enclave's residents. I gather from my varied conversations with Muslims across generational, class, and cultural divides that for the older generations, the Jamia Millia Islamia University was not only a gateway to a modern world, but it symbolized the entire world within which they were content to remain. Many of them confessed that they had not only hoped to study at Jamia Millia Islamia, but also to eventually find employment here. I also came across many cases of generational connections to the university and to the area as fathers and grandfathers had not only studied, but also worked and settled here. Nadeem, an engineer in his mid forties as well as an alumni and employee of the university, shared with me that the grounds of the university where he returns to work every day were once his playground as his father was also employed and housed in the university premises. His confession was almost a poetic articulation of his contentment on having achieved his life's dream; it represented how for many members of the older generations, the university was not only their pivot but an all-encompassing experience. However, its role has been relatively marginalized in the younger generation's lives and plans for the future. And just as the idea of *apna mahol*, stressing the quintessential Indian Islamic ethos had failed to resonate among my informants, I also found that a search for continuity did not necessarily preoccupy even those Muslim youths whose fathers and grandfathers had been employees of the university.

The different generational reactions are clearly entwined with the university's changing positionality within 'networks and flows' shaping life options and opportunities. In India's largely state controlled economy prior to 1991, the university's importance in the lives of the Jamia area residents was immense, because given the limited employment opportunities, it offered an important option for realization of middle-class aspirations for employment, financial stability, and upward mobility. However, in India's globalized, neoliberal, highly interconnected, and mediated society, the university is but one among the many options. The Muslim youth no longer seek their dreams within narrow and limited spaces but are opening up to the promise of an 'imagined India.' This is an idea, transmitted and incessantly reiterated by the media, which has come to dominate the Indian middle classes' utopian and dystopian visions of reality (Mazzarella, 2005), and it has even captured political platforms as exemplified in BJP's electoral campaign of 'India Shinning' (Fernandes, 2006). The Muslim youth's visions of self actualization are not only embedded within narratives of an 'imagined India,' thereby escaping erstwhile spheres of Muslim middle class modernity, but are also informed by dreams of 'escaping India,' which Fuller and Narasimhan (2007) argue is the overwhelming conditions of those with real time connections to global flows created by technology and finance, such as the technocrats of silicon valley in Bangalore. This desire to look outside and beyond is the youth's overpowering reality, and for the Muslim youth, the university of Jamia Millia Islamia is but a preparatory space and a stepping-stone to other more lucrative and exciting professional options, while the Muslim enclave is only an address, as one young female engineering student shared with me, 'till better accommodation was affordable.' The meaning of community for the Muslim youth has become imbedded in circumstances, wherein it is impossible not to be simultaneously present in worlds far beyond the immediate spheres. The omnipresence of communication technologies perforce extended the youth's vision to encompass larger and multiple worlds, and it is not possible for them to be confined to any one singular context, like the older generations.

Moreover, not only is the Muslim youth's world implicitly plural, it is touched by what Appadurai (1996) argues is the distinguishing facet of contemporary globalized modernity—an enhanced imagination. According to Appadurai, in contemporary globalized worlds imagination has become a quotidian reality, capable of deeply transforming everyday practices and cultural ideologies. The congregation of young men gathered at the street corners of Zakir Nagar so enraptured me precisely because they were embodying a concentrated expression of the new dynamics shaped by an enhanced imagination that is propelling Muslims toward new desires for upward mobility and a new way of being. This enhanced imagination as well as the Muslim youth's expressive intensity for their newfound ambitions distinguish their consciousness from that of the older generations of Muslims. And even if both generations continue to be physically entrenched in their enclosed communities, the Muslim youth's subjectivities are expressive of the new mobilities enjoined by media, communication technologies, and a globalizing economy which seamlessly transport them and allow them to participate in vastly different ideological and physical landscapes in ways not possible for the earlier generations.

Emerging Globalities and Modernities

The Muslim youth's experiences, which are in marked contrast to the community's former seclusion, can be perceived as being imbued with the same exhilarating thrill of discovery that so evocatively underlines Appadurai's (1996) encounters when he 'saw and smelled modernity' in blue jeans, in American college catalogues and in Hollywood cinema. However, to conceive their new interactions in amorphous contexts, without taking into account the Muslim youth's limitations or their social and economic constrains, would be to detract from the transformative powers of the new contexts. The Muslim youth's subjectivities arising within deeply transformative contexts of neoliberal globalization bring a new focus to bear on marginalized populations or 'have-nots' beyond the prevalent focus on issues of disempowerment, criminalization, and/or rise of disaffection and religious fundamentalism as highlighted in Castells' (1997) study of networked societies. Their experiences also complicate the defiant optimism underlying narratives of border-crossing, hybridization, and arguments of modernity at large (see Appadurai, 1996 & Bhabha, 1994). Moreover, not only are their modernities shaped by increased intensity of exchanges and coming-togetherness in globalized, deterritorialized, and highly mediated cultures, but they are also indicative of the multi-directional nature of these exchanges. The interactions are not limited to just being between the East and the West or the colonizer and the colonized, as primarily investigated in postcolonial scholarship (see Khair, 2001). The Muslim youth's fecund imagination is fed by influential narratives emanating both from the globalized spaces of the East as well as the West, and it defies their physical position, which is fixed within limited territorial circuits and iniquitous social economic circumstances of a postcolonial nation. The complex criss-crossings of myriad and multi-directional economic as well as cultural forces, which define contemporary inter-actions of people and cultures, have not been adequately addressed in postcolonial scholarship analyzing processes of globalization mainly in terms of migrations and contact with the dominant West (see Brah & Coombes, 2000). In addition, postcolonial scholarship's highly influ-ential ideas have been primarily concerned with analyzing the interac-tions and the interminglings, not in contexts of everyday life, but in the cultural realms of literature (see Bhabha, 1994), art (see Cancilni, 2005; Papastergiadis, 2005), or language (Bakhtin, 1986). Therefore, the ideas of hybridity, translation, or mimicry (see Bhabha, 1994) are not neces-sarily relevant to the contradictions, constrains, and oppositions that may define experiences of increased interconnectedness; and they also do not address the unjust operations of power that structure and modu-late globalization process at the level of everyday lived experiences(see Araeen, 2000).[4] The Muslim youth's lives, while offering an opportu-nity to examine how globalization is experienced at the margins, enjoin a rethinking of dominant perspectives of movements and flows in an interconnected world beyond ideas of unproblematic and/or creative coming togetherness, which also posture as critiques of the status quo, but without excavating the extant structural and material dynamics and conditions.

Global Cool and Politics of Rip-offs among Muslim Youth

The young men at the street corners that evening not only embodied the force of migratory trends in constructing the community of Jamia Nagar, but they also represented a new politics of belonging within new desires created by global cultural flows as articulated from their marginalized social, economic, political contexts. At first glance the young men's globalized imagination and their appropriation of 'global cool' (an indefinable condition pursued by celebrities and brands by expending billions of dollars) was evident in the references as they extended from advertisements of international men's clothing strung on tattered banners outside shuttered stores to their imitative sartorial styles of rip-off jean jackets; while their hairstyles created by local barbers were examples of both imitative art as well as practices of new imaginaries in the mundane and the everyday. I speak here of how an elusive quality integral to branding and marketing endeavours was approached by the economically weak, and the manner in which mark-down versions of out-of-bounds international men's clothing bolstered the youth's self-esteem. Capitalizing on the resonant powers of the 'global cool,' they inverted the defining ideology of consumerist individualism to disguise a situation of lack rather than to pronounce a state of surfeit. Therefore the youth's acquisition of imitation brands is not only expressive of their agency, it is also reminiscent of politics of 'noise' and 'transgressions' as practiced by British punk subcultures, whose sartorial practices, according to Hebdige (1979), intended to provoke and to outrage society in order to expose its inherent inconsistencies and hypocrisies . Similarly, the Muslim youth's donning of fake branded attires, while disturbing the closed ranks of new forms of belonging, structured around consumer-citizenship in neoliberal India, gave them a sense of élan notwithstanding the implacability of the stakes aligned against them. Their rip-offs fashion almost functioned as battle fatigue, deflecting slurs of impoverishment, and hiding scars acquired in the contest for recognition.

The young men were playing with the hedonistic ethos of branding slogans, and resurrecting the qualities of inventiveness, initiative, and individuality as evoked in exhortatory phrases such as 'Just do it' (from a global sports shoe company) to expand the notion of belonging beyond globalized, homogenized, consumerist, and affluent circles to include the stigmatized other. Therefore, instead of practicing a politics of resistance like the punk subcultures in Britain, who according to Hebdige (1979), employed the signs and objects of the late industrial culture to turn these very signs against the dominant culture, the Muslim youth were using the symbols of consumerist modernity to interject in spaces closed to them. These signs of the 'global cool' were being worked upon to overcome their 'otherness.' I found that a similar strategy for belonging, constructed through engagement with glamour and gloss surrounding brands and celebrity cultures, equally involved young Muslim women. They too were approaching celebrity cultures and instances of high-end consumerism with something other than a star-struck gaze. Indeed the young women's involvement in programming showcasing the rich and the famous with anchors flaunting fake foreign accents, (such as in *Page 3* on *Zoom TV*,[5] a favourite of Zakia, a 19 year old enterprising and enthusiastic student of electronics),and their engagement with the world of 'citizens of the sky,[6]' was not an uncritical approbation of what Debord (2007/1977) refers to as the 'spectacle,' an immense accumulations of images and false premises buttressing the logic of late capitalism. Rather, they were strategically working with the 'spectacle's' magical transformative powers to overcome limitations of their own existence as doubly marginalized Muslim women. In the words of Zakia, she and her cohorts were drawn to such programming because:

> Mam, I told you, I want change. I get to learn all those things from the programme, like later on, the kind of people that I will have to meet...I have a strong ambition to become somebody in my life. That program tells me how those celebrities reached that stage in their life, the kind of living standards they have achieved, how they deal with people and their way of doing things. (Original in Urdu, author's translation, personal communication, December 9, 2007)

According to Zakia, these programmes were not only their window into worlds far removed from their own, but also their means to reach those worlds. However, their appropriation and imitation of Westernized worlds of consumerist modernity cannot ascribe to the idealism of agency underlying Bhabha's (1994) accounts of hybridity. And their mimicry of the dominant cultural logic, though containing multiple slippages or gaps, cannot qualify as mimesis. This is because a conscious intention to critique or undo the dominant logic is not part of their project. What is important for them is to find their space within the social and economic scheme from which they have been hitherto excluded. This contradictory positionality is evocative of Raka Shome's (2006) analysis of Indian call centers as sites for both, the operation of 'transnational governmentality' (as in the Indian youth's training to imitate western accents and to take on a westernized persona) as well as a third world nation's highly efficient and successful strategy for interjecting into the global markets (p. 120). Moving our understanding of hybridity in a new direction, she perceives the call centers as a site of expressive agency even while it is being simultaneously compromised. Similarly, the young Muslim women's efforts to learn the manners and other attributes of successful westernized elites featured in celebrity shows are not examples of the 'creative third space' of the hybrid where the power of the colonizer is artfully deflected by the colonized 'other,' because the young women are still imbibing the logic of the dominant order. And yet, these new skills give them the confidence to effectively deal with the changing worlds and think of a life outside of their shuttered enclave thereby endorsing a new visibility, which challenges power equations invested in their silence. Moreover, the Muslims youth's politics of rewriting their isolation rises from their faith in the cultures of meritocracy ushered into neoliberal India by global (mainly Western) corporations.

However, the model of consumer citizenship, which offers the Muslim 'other' such hopes for assimilation and for middle-class respectability, can be restrictive and unjust. The new regimes are yet to create a level playing for a stigmatized religious minority population. This is firstly because Muslims citizens' quest for upward mobility must contend with existing middle- class politics and interests, which as Arvind Rajapgopal (2001) argues, are a construct of seamless ideological flows, despite ostensible discrepancies, between right-wing Hindu nationalism and advocates of economic liberalization.[7] Secondly, as Fernandes (2006) contends, the ideals of consumer citizenship are essentially exclusionary, notwithstanding the high sounding critique of corrupt political classes, because they draw on 'a continual struggle to reclaim the terms of democratic politics from subordinated social groups' and 'the slothful poor classes,' and to redefine it as being more in tandem with the rights and privileges of the consuming middle-classes (p. 182).

The limitations in current economic and social conditions for true mobility lead Corbridge and Harris (2000) to conclude that ambitions to reinvent India are merely 'elite revolts,' which while serving middle class and high caste Indians' interests, obfuscate the middle classes' sense of entitlement and their inherent distaste for a critical agenda for change. Hence, the regimes of consumer citizenship exhibit a proclivity to combine with historical prejudices and create conditions even more fraught and exclusionary than anticipated by the Muslim youth. Therefore, even as I could read in the milling crowds, the Muslim youth's deep desire of participating in what they perceive are new spheres of influence symbolized in new geographies of neoliberal India where cultures of consumption and cultural consumption inextricably intermix as in the new humongous gaudy shopping malls with multiplex cinema screens, I also understand that they are cordoned off from these spaces. And it is not only because of their inability to consume, but as the hostilities, which Indian Muslims have historically faced, become critically exacerbated in the post 9/11 contexts, young men no longer feel safe in the city when extra-judicial arrests and unwarranted incarcerations have become an aspect of their everyday reality, clouding their dreams with lurking fears. Hence, while the Muslim youth from aspiring lower middle-classes may desire to step out, they are not always able to do so. And even my informants who are more middle-class and successful mid-level employees of multinational corporations must return home to the crowded Muslim ghetto—a place to which their identity is both deeply associated and complexly disassociated.

I see the youth contending with tensions and dynamics of their shifting allegiances between two very different worlds of their physical realities and their virtual lives and imaginaries because while being imbedded in new imaginaries of self-actualization, they must also maintain a truck with the norms and set patterns of the segregated Muslim enclave to ensure their continued presence within its precincts. And it was this daily battle to find coherence in dissonance, which was being enacted in the gatherings of young men at that unearthly hour of a cold winter night. I finally understood why they were out so late. It was because only in those few late night hours the young Muslim men could reclaim a space for themselves and perform their different imaginations of being, but without disrupting the essential mores and ways of being of the Muslim community. At this hour, not only had all other residents retreated to the warmth of their homes, but also the activities which are the central focus of the Muslim community such as the mosque were suspended till *fazar* or pre-dawn prayers, when the *azan* would be heard again calling the faithful for prayers. During these limited hours music could play in the *pan* shops and young men could just hang around, smoking, enjoying languid conversations, and just being men about town, engaging in a very male privileged activity of 'time-pass' which women cannot generally indulge in (see Jeffrey, 2010). But their present activity did not mean that these men had not gathered at the mosque earlier for the *Isha* prayers, and it could very well be that many of them would even attend the morning *Fajar* prayers. However, in these few intervening hours they were living a different sensibility, while being mindful of the marked differences between the quintessential Indian Muslim culture and that of the globalized materialistic individualism celebrated in mediated spheres.

The Muslim youth were approaching spaces of globalized subjectivities and ideologies from within their own localities, especially as it was in the Muslim enclave that they found refuge, hence it was not possible to reject its practices. The young men's attempts to avoid openly disturbing the extant state of affairs and their preference to work around, rather than oppose entrenched religious and cultural norms complicates either/or narratives of the opposition between tradition and modernity. However, the dichotomy has also been made redundant by the multiple and conflicting ideas and ideologies amidst which everyday life in the Muslim enclave is being constructed. The complex currents created by rising tides of ambitions, the push of populations (as compounded by unprecedented rural to urban migrations impelled by India's urban centered economic growth), and the new possibilities of engagement with multitudes of competing mediated discourses of differing degrees of endurance and popularity, demand new creative adjustments, whose true imports is yet to be discerned. But just to illustrate the multifaceted and intricate manner of their articulation, I draw attention to the one last image that caught my eye as we were driving out of the colony. I saw amidst the multiple billboards, hoardings and faces of Bollywood stars and other global and local celebrities peddling a range of products and services, an advertisement printed out on a white A4 sheet offering 'A Room for Rent' within a home in the locality. This innocuous image is portentous of the profound import of the compulsions of neoliberal economy and of the Muslim youth's ambitions on the way of life in the Muslim enclave. The relatively less expensive option of sharing a space within a home is an essential requirement for many migrants coming to the big city in search of employment. It is also the only way out in the face of an inverse relationship between living spaces and growing population in the Muslim enclave. And, it is probably the last option for many Muslim youth, given the hostilities toward Islam, and their inability to find accommodation in other areas of the city. However, even if no one is debating this point as yet, but the potential impact of renting a room in one's home to a relative stranger is not going to be negligible on the maintenance of a strict level of privacy, propriety, and segregation between members of the opposite sex, which are so essential to Islamic way of life. It remains to be asked how Islamic cultural norms can command a commitment and investment when changes ushered in by neoliberal globalization can potentially undermine them within intimate and immediate spaces of the home? However, even as this advertisement is but one instance of the complex set of demands that desires for new modernity are making on the ideological and material realities of the traditional way of life in the segregated Muslim community, I seek answers to the 'cultural wars' within other more public contexts. This is because intimate spheres of the Muslim home are to a large extent still out of bounds even for a native ethnographer for the same reasons of strict privacy and proper deportment that are under threat today.

Peace TV and Muslim Youth

One of the spaces to map the Muslim community's internalization of the multiple and conflicting force fields, which are greatly exaggerated by possibilities of pervasive connectivity within networked societies, is the highly popular satellite channel Peace TV and the even more popular presenter, Dr Zakir Naik. The two sites as well as the Muslim youth's engagement with them are illustrative of the profound transitions that defy clarity imposed by binaries of creative hybridity and regressive fundamentalism. Confounding ideas of frictionless coming-togetherness, notions of agency (see Bhabha, 1994), as well as narratives of resistance in arguments explaining the rise of fundamentalism in Islamic societies (see Castells, 1997), Dr Zakir Naik's persona presents a conundrum for his critics. According to Dhume (2010), unlike the foaming mullah of caricature, Dr Naik eschews traditional clothing for a suit and tie. His background as a doctor and his often gentle demeanour set him apart, as does his preaching in English. Unlike traditional clerics Dr Naik quotes freely from non-Muslim scripture, including the Bible and the Vedas. (You have to pay attention to realize that invariably this is either to disparage other faiths, or to interpret them in line with his version of Islam.) The depth of Dr Naik's learning is easily apparent.

However, even as Dhume acknowledges the difference and takes note of Dr Naik's attempts to situate himself within an evolving context, he dismisses the Muslim televangelist for still advancing the traditionalist agenda. But, perhaps it is precisely the apparent contradictions of seeking Islam within modern contexts that draw Muslim youths to him.

My first encounter with Dr. Zakir Naik's resonance in the Muslim youth's lives was over a rather meandering conversation with a group of Jamia Millia Islamia's students and alumni about their ambitions, dreams, desires, and their favorite celebrities and television programmes (in July 2007). And it was when we were discussing Sania Mirza (the Indian Muslim tennis star much admired by many young Muslim men) in the context of the disquiet created by her rather short tennis skirt and her aggressive volleying style among orthodox Muslim clerics, that Faizan, a history, Spanish, and travel and tourism diploma student suddenly asked me, 'Aap ne Zakir Naik ko suna hai?' (Have you heard Zakir Naik speak?). And when I replied that I had not really watched his programme on television, he added, as if to persuade me to do so, 'Bahut sahi bolta hai,' or, 'He speaks very correctly.' However, in the context of our earlier conversations about what young people liked, what they wanted to do with their lives, who were their role models, and how the politics of fatwas were inflecting our position in Indian society, what Faizan really meant to say was that Dr Naik's ideas, or he, or both effectively addressed their experiences and problems. At first I was baffled as to why would the Muslim youth, who profess to be avid viewers of MTV and who admire competitive and assertive Muslims like Sania Mirza, so value his counsel? Samuel & Rozario (2010), in their research among Bangladeshi Muslims admit to be confounded by the same issue as to how young men and women who are desirous of becoming active participants of the globalized modern world, can be drawn to someone like Dr Naik, who seems to oppose and undermine the world, which young people wish to belong to (p. 429). And when I probed my informants further regarding what aspect of Dr Zakir Naik's programme and/or his personality appealed to them, they could not fully articulate their thoughts. But, I only heard over and over again in my various conversations with both young men and women that they completely endorsed his views, while failing to elaborate what exactly they agree with.

Therefore to understand the charismatic televangelist, I tuned into Peace TV, which till late 2008, was still available on our cable network before the Indian government banned the channel and came down heavily on the cable operators, threatening to close down their businesses if they did not heed the injunctions. However, despite the Indian government's low tolerance for the channel, I found nothing in the channel's offerings that was particularly threatening or revolutionary. To begin with, Dr Zakir Naik did not address the very inflammatory subject of internal debate within Islam, and nor did he openly critique the dominant powers arrayed against Islam. He is muted in his critique of politics, and I felt he was more concerned with reaffirming dominant ideologies and patriarchal norms of the Islamic society. Considering his defense of orthodoxy, his popularity continued to puzzle me, when one day while 'zapping' through the multitude of cable channel offerings, I grasped upon the essence of his relevance.

The fact that impressed upon me (much more than his sartorial presentation or his argumentation style or even his command of the English language, which most people vouched for) is his situatedness within the same globalized, interconnected, and interlinked milieus that the Muslim youth were grappling with and his ability to speak to them from within the same contradictory conditions. An integral aspect of his appeal is constructed by Peace TV's positioning on global satellite platforms, whence Islamic discourses are juxtaposed with MTV, and exist alongside multiple other modernizing and globalizing ideologies. Reflecting initiative, entrepreneurial as well as organizational skills, Peace TV represents a pertinent effort to position Islamic ethos in the face of the Western media's domination and the rising right-wing nationalism of indigenous media. This endeavour has been enabled and aided by digital revolutions and the substantial lowering in the costs of television production and distribution. I argue that Dr Zakir Naik's most exemplary achievement has been that he has made it possible to speak about Islam at all. Therefore, it has mattered little to most Muslim youth, in the vein of Marshall McLuhan's (2012/1964) seminal argument 'medium is the message,' what it was that he spoke about. I think for many among my informants it was enough that he (and thereby they) are able to find a voice in contexts wherein Islam is denied respectability. Hence, for many, Dr Zakir Naik as a doctor turned Islamic cleric, presents an alternative model, which is quite divorced from the orthodoxy, rigidity, and tele-visual unattractiveness of erstwhile Muslim 'mullahs,' because in addressing the stereotypes about Islam as obscurantist, moribund, and rigid, he allows them to be both Muslim and modern.

Dr Zakir Naik owes his immense popularity to successfully addressing the Muslim youth's most implicit need to reconcile Islam to new values and ways of being, including resurgent consumerism and materialism in a formerly austere socialist society. And it is with reference to the Muslim youth's struggle to locate themselves within liberalizing/ globalizing contexts and narratives, and considering their search for answers to questions of personal deportment, values, and beliefs in the changing world that I understand Faizan's comment 'Bahut sahi bolta hai.' The concern of finding common grounds between Islam and modernity or more accurately to find Islam in modernity, a tendency which Echchaibi (2011) refers to as 'Islamicization of modernity,' has also been actively pursued by the new generation of Islamic preachers in many countries of the Middle East. According to Echchaibi, these preachers have effectively mobilized as well as monopolized platforms of satellite television and Internet and 'revalorized their religion,' seeking new respectability and enhanced status for Islamic mores in globalized contexts (p. 91). And in many ways, Dr Zakir Naik too is involved in resurrecting the beleaguered Indian Muslim identity, however, unlike the new breed of preachers in the Middle East who are also responding to the 'crisis of authority in Islam and a climate of semantic disarray'(p. 91), Dr Zakir Naik's immediate concern is to alleviate the Indian Muslim population's sense of powerlessness. Therefore, an important aspect of his talks, which are distributed through his satellite channel, Internet, and DVDs is to 'offer a modernist, quasi scientific defense of Islamic knowledge against both 'western' scientific criticisms and US fundamentalist Christians' (Samuel & Rozario, 2010, p. 427). In addition, by attempting to engage with modernity and clarifying

Islam's position vis-a-vis the modern world, he facilitates the Muslim youth's engagement with the expansive experiences of the globalized world order. His style is unique because, according to Samuel and Rozario, he does not vehemently pitch Islam against modern science, but attempts to 'demonstrate that Islam includes modern science, and that the Qur'an is a source of knowledge that anticipates and betters anything the West could offer' (p. 429). His credibility also lies in his logical argumentative style, even as his artful deflections and his occasional use of conspiracy theories keep his audience intrigued and appreciative. And even though the 'quasi-scientific defense of Islamic knowledge, in which western science is allowed to confirm the truth of the Qur'an but the authority of the latter remains absolute' (p. 428) fails to impress many of his critics, it is very important for the Muslim youth because it rescues Islam from charges of retrogression and helps to reinstate their stigmatized Islamic identity in globalized spaces.

Dr Zakir Naik's efforts to prove Islam's explicit edge by employing his formidable knowledge to engage votaries and scholars of both Hinduism and Christianity in fluent English, the language of modernity as well as a modern argumentative style resonates deeply with the Muslim youth (see also Samuel & Rozario, 2010). Almost everyone among the youth who felt any iota of admiration for him drew my attention to it. According to Shazia, a student of Electronic Engineering in Jamia, *'unki knowledge itni hai, itni hai, ke jo loog Hindu hai woh bhi nahin jante aape majhab ke bare mein, aur Dr Zakir Naik unhe bate hai ke unki kitabon mein kya likha hai'* (His knowledge is so deep and (or) extensive that even Hindus whose religion it is supposed to be are unaware of many facts regarding their religion, and Dr Zakir Naik has to tell them what is written in their books)[personal communication, August 2007]. Dr Zakir Naik has helped Muslims deal with their identity crisis in a way that orthodox clergy has been unable to, but the manner in which a doctor turn cleric has captured the imagination of the new generation also reflects the new confidence among ordinary Muslims to appropriate their religion, remove it from expert and sanctimonious circuits, and to make it relevant to their own life experience.

But, my argument is that the true import of Dr Naik's televangelism is to highlight the practice and process of negotiation in contexts when Islam and Muslims are ensconced within definitions of immutability, and when it is difficult to imagine the 'angry Muslim on the margins of 'modern' global culture' negotiating, contesting, or debating their faith or its role in their daily lives (Echchaibi, 2011, p. 90). He imparts an important skill of argumentation and discussion to help Muslim youth deal with their diverse interconnected contexts, and juggle with multiple, dissenting, and conflicting views.

However, these efforts are different from the more idealist politics of the creative 'third space' or the liminal spaces, wherein regenerative projects are largely conceived outside of the limitations imposed by contextual histories and realities and which also do not recognize the more humble notion of compromise. But Dr Zakir Naik's sermons, as they are articulated, circulated, and received within specific third world and highly hostile contexts, must contend with obstructive powers while attempting to address the Muslim population's feelings of marginality and lack of self-esteem. These mediated interactions, also lack the sanguinity of narratives of discovery and agency, which have been highlighted in studies of media and Indian society.[8] Moreover, although Dr Zakir Naik immaculate westernized sartorial style along with his fluent use English generously laced with professional terminologies may be representative of a hybrid positionality, the deployment of this persona has been in the fierce defence of Islam and not in the approbation of Western ethos. It, therefore, defies neat binaries, which conceive East and West, tradition and modernity as opposing poles as well as notions that professing an allegiance to Islam represents an antediluvian perspective. In the words of Sudipta Kaviraj (2005), Dr Zakir Naik can be seen as articulating an alternate modernity situated in the 'historically declining imaginative powers of the West,' when people can no longer 'be persuaded to force their future into versions of the Western past' (p. 524–525). However, I argue that Dr Zakir Naik's complex reality is better encapsulated as a 'convoluted modernity.' This is because even as his critics argue that he negates modern ethics, principles, and ways of being by defending Islam (see Dhume, 2010), Dr Naik's dissenting position has been achieved only by internalizing the very principles of modernity—especially freedom of expression and religion which are protected by modern institutions and constitutional authorities and enforced by the rule of law. To reiterate my point of 'convoluted modernities,' Dr Zakir Naik seeks to establish Islam's credibility by arguing for Islam's a priori awareness of and engagement with modern scientific knowledge, and gives credence to western scientific knowledge even as he posits that the West is only just beginning to discover what Islam already knows about modern science.

The other point to note is that if Dr Zakir Naik's interjections in the mediated spheres instill new confidence among Indian Muslims, and give them a presence, invalidating powers seeking to silence them, they must be conceived as a political project, even if he only talks about instituting Islamic piety and propriety. My position is different from scholars analyzing Islamic revivalism in the Middle East who insist that the cultural significance of Islamic revivalism in the Middle East far outweighs its political purpose and that the excessive stresses on personal piety which is the defining element of these movements is not in any way instrumental in promoting politics of radicalism (see Echchaibi, 2011; Gole, 2000; Mahmood, 2005). However, even as current events unfolding in many parts of the Middle East may defy these assertions about the apolitical nature of personal reconstructive projects based in Islamic ideology, my position is that if Dr Zakir Naik's sermons help to assert and articulate a voice, then they cannot be considered to be above politics. Indeed, they are not unimportant to the way a minority population may position itself in India's democratic public sphere, and this is precisely the reason why despite the orthodox and apolitical content of his sermons, the channel is so feared and blocked by Indian authorities.

But my next question which elaborates on the earlier query is, that if the discourses of televangelist religiosity are situated within an awareness of modernity and are expressive of an attitude given to contesting and grappling with its uncertainties rather than withdrawing from them (like the older generations of Muslims), how may this new consciousness inflect the Muslim youth's negotiations to situate themselves within Indian society as equal citizens, notwithstanding the social and political discriminatory regimes? The question is important because while the older generation's response to the conditions of 'internal colonization' marked by demands for erasure of the Muslim identity and a total subjugation to the dominant identity (see Pandey, 2006) was a tactical retreat from mainstream Indian society, the intensity of the younger generation's desires for material well-being foreclose this option for them. I seek to understand how they contend with discordance and injustices to define themselves as both Muslims and Indians.

Being Muslim and Indian: Investments in 'Team India'

The opportunity to explore this issue was provided by a popular allegorical text of the coming of age of new India, which even as it evokes the material, cultural, and ideological realties of a neoliberal and globalized India, addresses the question of the Muslim identity in these emerging contexts. I refer to the Bollywood film *Chak De India* starring Shahrukh Khan, which was one of the top revenue earners for the year 2007 (Kazmi, 2007; Weekly Box Office Review, 2007). In the summer of 2007, the film's release was being eagerly anticipated by my informants. Many of them were of course fans of Shahrukh Khan, but the reason why they so looked forward to seeing him in this particular film was because for the first time in his highly successful two decades-long career, the Muslim superstar was assaying his very Muslim identity. Shahrukh Khan, whose name immediately invokes Afghan and Central Asian origins, has always been the Punjabi 'Raj' or 'Rahul' of romantic melodramas, but in *Chak De India's* central character of Kabir Khan, he was mirroring the travails of ordinary Muslim citizens. The film, given its popularity among the Muslim youth, became an important meta-phorical space to reference matters of import which otherwise were difficult to discuss in the strive-torn contexts of the summer of 2007.

In the summer of 2007, numerous events seriously damaging the image of Islam and Muslims and greatly attenuating the trust that my informants and I had established for each other, unfolded with relent-less regularity (see Khan, 2008). It began with the siege of Lal Masjid in Lahore in the end of June, followed by the failed bombing of Glasgow airport by a Muslim engineering student, leading to the arrest of a Muslim doctor in Australia on suspicions of collusion, and lastly the announcement of Mumbai High Court verdict on the Muslim accused in 1993 serial bomb blasts. In the strained atmosphere when Muslims were besieged by slurs of being terrorists and anti-nationalists, the story of a rag tag women's hockey team that goes on to win the World Cup against all odds through their sheer dedication, equally matched by their coach Kabir Khan's steely determination to win, became an innocuous way to talk about both the state of Indian Muslims as well as my informants own experiences.

The film *Chak De India* revolves around adventures of the Indian women's hockey team, which defies its third world circumstances, facilities, and status to compete and to win against better trained and equipped teams from the more developed worlds. The story parallels the arrival of India, an erstwhile third world country, on the world stage following economic liberalization and unshackling of bureaucratic controls, while catch phrases like 'Team India' invented by the media, evoking India as an emerging super power (Das, 2001; Zakaria, 2006) inadvertently bolster the film's story line. While it can be argued that the invention of India as a power to contend with has been a major contribution of the world press, these assertions are regurgitated in the Indian media without much reflection on their veracity,[9] mirroring the general euphoric mood of post-liberalization and mostly middle-class India. And the film celebrates middle-class India's belief in the individual's will to win, stressing the importance of hard work and dedication as being essential to success. However, notwithstanding the focus on personal ambitions and on cultures of meritocracy, *Chak De India* is a highly nationalist text.

The film resurrects national pride by focusing on India's potentials and by comparing them favourably with the rest of the world. And its message according to Narayan Murty (2007) (head of Infosys, the leading global computer software company and an Indian multinational), who saw the film with a crowd of mostly twenty-something upwardly mobile Indians in Bangalore (India's silicon valley), resonated deeply with the youth, because they cheered with every goal 'as if India had actually won the women's World Cup in hockey.' The film's popularity among the youth is important because the film emphatically communicates the essence of Indian identity. And it proposes an overarching, homogenized, and universalist Indian identity that demands a complete sublimation and erasure of inherent diversities of region, language, dialect, ethnicity underlying the Indian identity. It is a proposal not dissimilar to right-wing Hindu nationalists' arguments. However, in reading the reactions of some of India's leading figures such as Narayan Murty, who is neoliberal middle-class India's icon of success, it appears that they found nothing amiss with these views, but in fact they concurred with them. For example, Narayan Murty exhorts the youth that for India to win real battles, it is imperative for Indians to 'identity as Indians first' and to rise above affiliations of 'states, religions and castes' in order to present a unified front to global competitors. This is also the message that the film *Chak De India* forcefully conveys within the very first few scenes. Kabir Khan, as the coach of the women's hockey team, strongly admonishes the team members, drawn from different parts of India, for prescribing to their regional, state or linguistic identity, and directs them to erase these affiliations, and to identify themselves only as Indians. However, the irony in the scene is that this strong nationalist message is delivered by a Muslim—a person who would only liked to be identified as an Indian, but is not allowed this luxury. Rather, the story line revolves around how he must prove his Indianess and his loyalty to India. His failure to strike the penalty goal during a crucial India–Pakistan match earlier had cost him his career as well as his life, because since he was a Muslim the missed goal was not considered to be a vagary of the game, but an act of deliberate malice and deceit to make the opposing team and his co-religionists win. Defeated, dejected, and banished, Kabir Khan returned only to takes up a job that no other professional coach thought worthwhile, because for him it was a chance to redeem his lost reputation.

Kabir Khan's character represents the contrariness of the Muslim experience in India, because in the general enthusiasm and calls for creation of an overarching Indian identity, which rises above divisions of caste, religion, region, and language, Indian Muslims are precluded from leaving behind their religious affiliations. Kabir Khan, as a professional hockey player, would only like to be recognized for this skill on the field, but the stereotypes that define Islam became a legitimate basis to judge and appraise him. The Indian Muslims in the audience would immediately recognize the unfair scrutiny and pressures to prove one's loyalty. The Muslims are hailed by their religious affiliations, while all that they ask for, like Kabir Khan the protagonist, is to be perceived as just another Indian. Therefore, this cinematic text breaks new grounds in giving space to the Muslim predicament, and in working with a character recognizable as an ordinary Muslim (rather than a caricature of a decadent rentier *nawab* or terrorist that dominate cinematic representations). Moreover, in its rather frank portrayal of the Muslim condition, in the use of the Urdu language, as well as in the depiction of cultural expressions distinct to Indian Muslims, it sought to appeal to the Indian Muslims. I, for one, was thrilled to hear Shahrukh Khan's elegant and unabashed delivery of Urdu resound in the movie theatre and many of my informants shared my pleasure, even as they were more excited by the fact that for once the central character in the film was a Muslim, and a Muslim actor was playing the part with poignant sincerity.

However, despite the fact that the film gave a certain visibility to the shuttered Muslim identity by featuring a Muslim as the main protagonist and by openly discussing the Muslim condition, something which most Bollywood mainstream films studiously avoid, I found the film to be ultra-nationalist and problematic. Its narrative veered towards inscribing Muslims within 'territorialized' and 'territorially circumscribed. . . .national order of things' (Fazila-Yacoobali, 2002, p. 195). It repeated the feat of another popular Bollywood film *Sarfaroosh* (released during the tense period of the brief Kargil war with Pakistan in 1999), which as Fazila-Yacoobli argues, disrupts the silence surrounding the Muslim identity only to forcibly establish the credibility of the overarching Indian identity and to nullify all other affiliations and loyalties by harshly defining them as anti-nationalist (p. 195). As I proceeded to discuss *Chak De India* with my informants, the Muslim youth, I was most interested to understand how would they, as members of a community known for its attachment to its distinct religious and cultural identity, respond to the proposition of total subjugation, bordering almost on erasure, of their unique identity and heritage. I was preoccupied with the issue, especially as stereotypes constricting the Muslim identity abound projecting them as being unduly defensive and protective about their religious and cultural identity and as giving their cultural and religious affiliations precedence over and above their Indian identity. Hence, I was expecting my informants to critique what I thought was the dictatorial authoritativeness of the overarching Indian identity.

However, as an ethnographer situated in American academia and studying my own community, it was indeed a humbling experience to realize that my personal politics of 'writing against culture,' or disrupting power equations and hierarchies essentializing the 'other' (see Abu-Lughod, 1991), cannot overwhelm the voice and experiences of my informants. In self reflexive recognition of class, economic, political, and cultural dynamics that inflect relationships between the native ethnographer and her informants, as well as, inform interpretative practices and texts (see, Foley, 2002), I had to acknowledge that my priorities may not resonate among my informants, despite our shared religious affiliations. The very different contexts—political, economical, and cultural shaping our everyday lives created very different perspectives and power dynamics. They alerted me to a constant awareness of 'the positionality of the anthropological self and its representations of others' (Abu-Lughod, 1991, p. 141). I could proceed only after recognizing that while my positionality may allow me space to critique and deconstruct power politics debasing and dehumanizing the Muslim 'other,' my informants who lived within the thick of these fraught circumstances had a very different reaction, but which was not to be perceived as a lack of critical faculties on their part. Putting my ear to the ground in an endeavour to speak 'from' my informants' realities, which Abu-Lughod argues is a very different proposition as compared to speaking 'for' them (p. 143), I had to deal with my surprise and frustration in order to grapple with their greater truth.

My open-ended preliminary questions to young Muslim men and women about the film *Chak De India* and its narrative appeal, almost always brought forth an appreciation of the way *Chak De India* highlighted a culture of meritocracy. I rarely if ever heard in reaction to my opening question any reference to its Muslim lead or an admiration for the film's agenda to foreground the disregarded and suppressed Muslim identity. Consider the responses of Farhat who was in her early 30s and a teacher at Jamia University:

Ruhi: Did you see the film *Chak de India*? Is there a message in this film?

Farhat: *Haan, unity, determination, hard work* [Yes, unity, determination, hard work]. (personal communication, January 7, 2008)

I juxtapose Farhat's response with Zain's who is in his early twenties, a resident of the Jamia enclave and a student at the prestigious Faculty of Management Studies, Delhi University, because despite differences in gender, age, and professions, his response is almost identical to Farhat's.

Ruhi: You know a lot about *Chak De India*. Do you think *Chak De India* had a message?

Zain: Yes it had a message. It was [that] if we work together everything is possible. (personal communication, January 11, 2008)

And even on probing Farhat further, she still made no reference to the Muslim question at all, but only elaborated further her faith in India's emerging dynamics:

Ruhi: Can you tell me again, what is the message in the film?

Farhat: It does not matter for national pride, religion does not matter for national pride. It is the goal that matters. The message [is that] in India people will respect hard work despite religion. (personal communication, January 7, 2008)

But on the other hand in my conversation with Zain, who as part of my extended family was more aware of my critical stance towards hegemonic discourses and social practices suppressing Muslim identity, I sensed an even greater reluctance to be drawn into my seeking questions.

Ruhi: Did it have a special message for Muslims?

Zain: STAR TV said that Shahrukh Khan was playing a Muslim in the movie.

Ruhi: What did your friends say about the movie?(I meant his Muslim friends)

Zain: They all came out saying what a great actor Shahrukh Khan is. All the guys who went to see the movie are Shahrukh Khan fans. (personal communication, January 11, 2008)

His elliptical responses disrupted the direction that I wanted this conversation to take. I was keen on discussing with him the two very moving moments for me, when verses from the Quran are recited in the film—once when Kabir Khan is supplicating God to help his team win in the face of insurmountable odds, and the other when his team emerges victorious and he turns towards his God in gratitude. For me, these two scenes were acutely transgressive because they bring both, the Islamic religious identity and India's Islamic heritage, to centre stage, issues which provoke the wrath of Hindu right-wing forces and which the Hindutva politics wish to erase completely. The scenes became even more meaningful in retrospect because these two scenes have been deleted in the DVD version and also in its release on Netflix. But Zain did not allow me to dwell on the film's endorsement of the protagonist's faith or his cultural identity, nor did he allow me to critique the film's explicit support of hegemonic nationalism. Zain mentioned Shahrukh Khan's celebrity status, but only incidentally referenced his position as a Muslim superstar and a Muslim protagonist. He also avoided the issue by alluding to it as an observation made by a third party, a television channel, rather than by him. And I knew that Zain was not avoiding the questions because he was irreligious, in fact he had even confided that he regularly offers his *Isha* prayers in his Delhi University dormitory room, which he shares with another non-Muslim student. I had to continue exploring this issue to ascertain if Zain's and also Farhat's response resonated with other Muslim youth. And I found that even those who were willing to talk about the film's significance, in breaking free of stereotypes to present a believable and identifiable Muslim protagonist, were not willing to dwell too much on the issue. There seemed to be a general tendency to avoid dwelling on the issues that were significant on my radar. Consider my conversation with Rehman, a former student of Jamia University's engineering department, and now employed in the information technology sector in the city of Pune, who has achieved a certain stability and success that most of my informants were craving for:

Ruhi: So you think the movie had a message? What was the message?

Rehman: You can see it from several aspects. First and foremost it touched on the stereotype against Indian Muslims. Usually v r [we are] considered as supporters of Pakistan.

Ruhi: Do you think the movie dealt with the issue well?

Rehman: Actually there were other aspects as well [like] women['s] empowerment, team work, etc. Muslim stereotypism was just a part.

Ruhi: So the movie was not focusing on just Muslim stereotyping alone. It was just one of the themes and not the main theme?

Rehman: Yeah, it was one of the aspects. It also showed Hockey vis-a-vis Cricket and the importance of a coach.

Ruhi: Was there any other message?

Rehman: Yes, [the] importance of teamwork. (personal communication, Google Chat, January 20, 2008)

The pragmatic balancing of the different issues and a rather detached appraisal of the Muslim concerns is remarkable especially as Muslims are known to be highly emotional and totally irrational—charges that are not without substance given the irascibility and fondness for conspiracy theories displayed by the Urdu press. However, the obvious obfuscation of the critical discussions on Muslim identity by Muslim youth is extremely instructive in indicating their emerging politics.

My informants' preference to reflect on cultures of meritocracy rather than to indulge in criticism of systems and social structures that stymie their growth is a markedly different stance from that of the Urdu language press as well as from the older generations of Muslims. And if according to Hall (1985), 'language and behavior are the media, so to speak, of the material registration of ideology, the modality of its functioning' (p. 99), then the Muslim youth's inability to read and write in Urdu creates a break with the symbolic referents imbedded in the language, but at the same time they also open up a space for emergence of new ideas, perhaps in consonance with those circulating in mediated spaces that so captivate the Muslim youth. And as my discussion with a young lawyer at Delhi High Court reveals that perhaps an immersion in the cultures of meritocracy demand a new mindset—one that is less concerned with Muslim identity politics.

Ruhi: You have seen the movie *Chak De India*. What is the movie about?

Aasia: *Chak De India* is about the fact that anyone can make it in India. I have no problems with nationalism; that is what the film teaches. I am chilled out. I am very happy as [an] Indian. (personal communication, January 2, 2008)

I read in the responses of younger generations of Muslims not only an investment in middle- class dreams of prosperity, but also an implicit understanding of the power equations shaped by what Hall (1985) refers to as 'articulations' or synergetic correspondence between popular discourses of nationalism, materialism, and middle-class ascendance.[10] They understand that the 'key conjectural moments' (see, Foley, 2002, p. 472) or the conjoining elements between these diverse discourses cementing the hegemonic ideology are not conducive to socio-cultural plurality and even justice. Moreover, it would also be fairly obvious to them that the ideological power of Hindu nationalism, as it combines with middle-class materialism and underlines the narrative of economic growth and progress (see Rajagopal, 2001 & 2006), must not be challenged, if they as members of a minority community wish to be included in the economic mainstream and in the expanding middle class.

But what is also to be noted is that members of a minority community belonging to different class affiliations differently negotiate the hegemonic ideology. For example, for the few upwardly mobile Muslims with elite school education and assured access to well-paid white-collar professions, the internalization of the dominant Hindu nationalism does not mean a complete erasure of their distinct Muslim cultural and religious identity, because there is some room for the elite Muslim culture, especially if it comes packaged in middle-class aesthetics as in the Pakistani television serials, which were highly popular among Indian audiences in the pre-cable days. In fact Aasia shared with me that her Punjabi Hindu friends at the Delhi High Court would always ask her where are the 'normal' Muslims such as those in dramas like *Ankahi, Ana,* and *Dhoop Kinare.* The feudal, superrich, and aristocratic Muslims of Pakistani dramas were admired both as fashion icons and for their upscale lifestyle. And as the response of the well-heeled lawyer Aasia indicates, in such few instances there is an option 'to choose,' quoting Salman Rushdie, not to be overwhelmed by the dominant Hindu identity. But, as most members of the Muslim population are struggling at the very bottom rungs of the economic sectors and represents in the words of Aasia's friends 'people from Delhi 6' (a derogatory reference evoking disparaging images of Muslims, including their tendency to live in segregated, congested, disorderly and filthy neighbourhoods where meat shops abound), they are more likely to confront an absence of choice. And therefore they are more likely to maintain a prudent silence, especially if they are unable to successfully pose a challenge from their current impoverished position.

My conversations with Faisal and Fahim, young Muslim men working in ancillary positions in travel and courier companies, provided an insight into how questions of identity are often effaced and relegated to a secondary position, when people are involved in bigger battles of securing life and livelihood, and in overcoming financial difficulties, as these two young men were. Their parents are working class people who have sacrificed much to secure basic educational qualifications for their wards. Hence, while established wisdom has argued that the clash between identity and modernity are most endemic in the non-Western [read Islamic](see Göle, 2000)[11] societies, I found attempts at reconciliation with often punishing and unjust modernizing forces to be the more characteristic response in the non-Western, Islamic, and relatively impoverished contexts of the segregated Muslim enclave of Jamia Nagar.

I was finally meeting Faisal and Fahim after a long interval during which they kept a certain distance from me as the tumultuous events of summer of 2007 unfolded, testing the bonds I had formed with my informants. And as we sat in the coffee shop, the palpable tension between us was not only because they were not completely at ease in contexts of westernized leisure and affluence even though they had been eager to meet me in this neutral space. Rather we did not know from where to begin sharing the sense of gloom and despondency that was weighing the community down, following Dr Haneef's arrest in Australia in July 2007, in the wake of Glasgow bombing earlier in June. It was an especially stressful time when a sense of persecution bound the community together transcending all economic and social differences among the Muslims that I mention earlier. We were all acutely conscious of our precarious existence and how easily entrenched prejudice can destroy our lives. I could not but think back on my sense of unease and hurt at the careful inspection of my person as I cross international borders, even as I realized (more so in hindsight) the life threatening implications of such scrutiny for young men like Faisal and Fahim. We sat around making polite conversation about inane matters, too worried to talk about what was bothering us for the fear of being overheard and marked as Muslims by other patrons in the café, when at last, after an hour and more of hedging around, I, very obliquely, in very few words, in a very public place, said very quietly, 'Look at what is happening around us'. This was like a cue for a dam to burst and suddenly we were addressing the same thing and coming straight to the point. Faisal responded, equally quietly, 'Karta koi hai bharta koi hai' [Someone else's misdeeds and someone else has to bear the consequences], expecting us to understand without explicitly spelling out how Kafeel's (the Glasgow bomber and Haneef's cousin) actions had compromised the entire community's future. To this Fahim added, 'Agar yahan naukri karni hai to bahut sabar se' [If you want to work here, earn a living, then you must exercise a lot of patience]. Faisal responded by uttering almost under his breath, 'Sabar, sabar' [Patience, patience] (personal communication, July, 2007). In a few words they told me the complete story about what they were feeling and how they chose to react to their circumstances with patience and forbearance.

This was the only strategy they could conceive of to hold on to their jobs in the highly vexed circumstances. Their response can also be read to indicate their belief that the way forward for Muslims is by first addressing and overcoming their socio-economic marginality. Hence, once again, instead of staging a critique of the powers that deny and exclude them, they are focused on creating a niche for themselves by taking advantage of the small window of opportunity provided by cultures of meritocracy. But, this is not to say that they or my other informants are devoid of agency or politics, even though Foucaldian perspectives of diffuse workings of power, which inform theoretical perspectives of agency, would not recognize their politics of silence and withdrawal as being political. But by proposing to delay the challenge to dominating forces, which negates their existential and cultural identity, till such time when they can successfully argue their case, they are strategizing for a better future.

This prompts me to argue that the burning ambition of being rich, which most of my informants unabashedly harbour and also admit to, not only represents their agency but also informs their politics. Paul Willis (2000 & 1990), based on his study of the British working class youth, proposes that commodity consumption is an important way by which stigmatized cultural identities resist being 'othered.' Refuting Marxist-cultural arguments that commodity consumption completes the cycle of domination of labouring classes, he argues that it is instead a font providing innumerable resources for meaning making as well as being a vehicle for self-expression. However, without fetishizing the agency expressed in cultural commodity consumption, I argue that the Muslim youth's dreams and aspirations to achieve economic stability and consumerist prosperity are a way towards a higher social standing and, thus, towards a more inclusive existence as opposed to their current alienation from the Indian mainstream. Therefore, like Canclini (2001), I argue that this struggle for upward mobility is a political strategy for inclusiveness which requires them to chart a careful path forward taking cognizance of the discriminatory regimes and also thinking through their own predilections and lack of skills, which may be abetting their own marginalization. And while Faisal and Fahim may not have all the answers to the problems before them, the one thing they do not advocate is retreat, as Muslims were earlier wont to, and I argue that the persistence to move forward defines new politics among Muslims.

Convoluted Modernities as Existential Politics

The Muslim youth are approaching modernity or notions of progress and material prosperity from their particular socio-economic and political contexts, wherein their Islamic identity is reinforced not only by social and structural iniquities which keep them confined to their segregated and enclosed enclave, but also by negativity about Islam reverberating from the mediated spheres, which incidentally are also their window to the world and a way to participate and experience the modern worlds outside of their limited spheres. In my encounters with my informants, I find that they are struggling to ascribe to consumerist modernity while still being hailed by their religious identity. Their ascriptions of a hybrid positionality, being both Muslim and modern, lack the exultation associated with tendencies of existing 'inbetween' attributed to the hybrid, and neither do I find instances of heroic resistance or a critique of the dominant structures. Instead, there is certain judiciousness and sagacity defining their tendency to negotiate with their difficult situation—given the intensity of their desire to be included and the tenacity of discriminatory regimes. Their responses are difficult to contain within either frameworks of hybridity or modernity, given the fact that discussions of a hybrid consciousness draw mainly on experiences of a small circuit of diasporic populations within advanced westernized countries[12] and are perhaps stretched beyond their intent in explaining the mixing and the coming togetherness in the contemporary phase of mediated-neoliberal globalization within postcolonial nations.[13] However, if as Ahmad (1995) argues that postcoloniality is not a single condition but highly differentiated experiences and situations of dominance encapsulated in a single amorphous definition, then the notion of hybridity too is over-extended in attempting to stand for variegated experiences of coming togetherness in very diverse socio-political contexts.[14] The need is to address the multiple and multifaceted nature of cultural exchanges and the emergence of consciousness within contexts marked by highly accelerated circulation of people, ideas, and commodities and from different directions (see Lee & LiPuma, 2002).[15]

But even as I propose to seek an alternative concept beyond the hybrid in emergent modernities to understand the experiences from the margins, which my informants' present, I am confronted with certain theoretical difficulties. This is because, if modernity means an enlargement and an enhancement of human freedom and of the range of choices available, enabling individuals to exercise better control over their lives and to exert their presence, according to T. N. Madan (1987 as quoted in Eickelman, 2000), then the Muslim youth's existence in abeyance of their right to chose would not qualify as modernity. Therefore, I propose the explanatory framework of 'convoluted modernity', drawing on arguments of multiple modernities and calling attention to particular circumstances and motivations defining emergent modernities of a religious minority population, which is no longer content with being left out of the general scheme of things. And if modernity is to be understood as an attitude or condition of persistent questioning of one's place within evolving contexts, then the Muslim youth inhabit this modernity in their new attitudes, which is equally concerned with defining who they are as Muslims as with how do they make a space for themselves as consumer citizens, to discard their isolation and to rise above their impoverished status.

As I have described in this chapter they address their question of being both Muslim and modern by borrowing forms and practices from consumerist modernity to rewrite their religious identity. For them having a cell phone, speaking in fluent English, dreaming of buying a car, are all ways of entering and experiencing modernity (see Canclini, 2001). They eagerly seek to inhabit new spaces and to find a job in the glittering cities of India or the Middle East is a dream for almost every one of them. In fact, I would argue that I was able to establish a rapport with young Muslim men and women, and that they welcomed my presence, not because of our shared cultural affinities or our common religious identity as most native ethnographers are wont to highlight, but only because I exemplified to my young informants the promise and the possibility of a life outside the community and within new global-scapes. Moreover, as I have argued that though the Muslim youth's reluctance to be drawn into the contentious issue of the erasure and subjugation of Islamic identity in India (unlike the older generations of Muslims and also the Urdu press), may appear to be an absence of voice, and a sign of their inability to be modern subjects, it is in fact an expression of a heightened rationality, which is indeed a defining condition of modernity. It represents the Muslim youth's strategy to enter modernity, notwithstanding socio-economic, political, and structural constrains confronting them. Their efforts challenge theoretical definitions of modernity, which have been constructed keeping in mind only Western experiences and perceptions. And as I shall explain in the next chapter, their sagacity is communicated both in a new language and style taking advantages of the enhanced capabilities of digital communication technologies to communicate with diverse audiences, transforming them from passive viewers/receivers of information to active members, capable of interjecting and inflecting discourses that define them, and position themselves within globalized and neoliberal Indian society.

Notes

1. According to Das (2001), the economic reform process has 'changed the mind-set of Indian people' and the freedom from the 'License *Raj* [Regime]' has unleashed the entrepreneurial energies of Indians on an unprecedented scale almost marking the 'biggest transformation in its history' (p. 346). And according to Zakaria (2006), the Indian middle class now apes consumption patterns of the citizens of the developed West, and Varma (1998) adds that in a country where an overwhelming number of citizens are poor, the Indian State professed bias towards austerity and the containment of material pursuits has been abandoned. Middle-class Indians desire to escape from the self-denying idealism of Gandhi, and liberalization provides them an opportunity to construct 'a break from the attitudes and thinking of the past' and 'to bring out into the open desires long held back' (p. 175). While Timmons (2007) argues that two decade long reform process has raised India's status from a Third World nation to a 'place to see and to be seen in,' as dignitaries, politicians, and executives from across the world make their way here, drawn by the country's economic potential.

2. According to the Sachar Committee (2006), not only are there few Muslims employed at high levels of state governance, police, and judiciary due to low level of education among Muslims, but 'discriminatory practices, especially at the time of the interviews,' make it impossible for Muslims to be employed even at lower levels of employment such as D class in state agencies and provincial services where higher educational qualifications are not the requirement (p. 20).

3. For the Muslim, the sacrifice of the lamb commemorates Abraham's willingness to sacrifice his son Ismail on God's command. However, as he proceeded unflinchingly with his task, Ismail was replaced by a lamb.

4. Rasheed Araeen (2005) argues that expressions of hybridity in artistic critical practices may be completely unrelated to lived experiences of

displacement and migration. And even Brah and Coombes (2000) argue, pointing to the popularity of Australian aboriginal art, that the relative importance of creative art forms may be totally incommensurate with acceptance and relevance on the ground level, as the continued persecution of the aborigines in Australia reveals (p. 9).

5. The program is a replication of *the third page* in the supplement to the national daily *The Times of India*. The *Page 3*, as it is popularly referred to, represents a new phenomenon ushered in by the most successful English daily to reproduce social events, parties, product launches, celebrities as paid news, which while providing free content also creates a new revenue stream.

6. As Arundhati Roy (1999) refers to them.

7. According to Rajagopal, the liberalization of the Indian economy and the rise of Hindu nationalism have been concomitant events, though it may not have been 'out of conscious design, although design was not absent' but they have shared 'technologies of transmission for expanding markets and audiences respectively' (p. 3). The connection or 'opportunistic alliance' between market reforms and Hindutva has been cemented via the language of consumerism which has helped to overcome the contradictions between BJP's core ideologies and the aspirations of its larger constituency.

8. The issue of audience agency was especially highlighted in early ethnographic studies concerned with a single force field (formed by tele-visual narratives of the Indian state broadcaster Doordarshan), wherein the audience's subversive reception of dominant texts could be easily mapped 'in the ways histories were rewritten, personal and collective memories recast, and notions of personhood, family, and sexuality reconfigured through viewers' active negotiations of televisual reconstructions of tradition and culture' (Mankekar, 1999a, p. 11). However, the investigation of production of culture and identity within the historical context of neoliberalized India complicates narratives of both agency and discovery. Firstly, in the presence of hundreds of satellite television broadcasters, there is a marked absence of any defining or hegemonic discourse influencing the narrative of either gender, nation, or selfhood and the construction of individual, gendered, or communal identity, which engaged media reception studies in the age of captive audiences (see, Mankekar, 1999b; Rajagopal, 2001). Secondly, as the audience's media experiences expand to include Internet and mobile telephony, the question of audience agency, as opposed to passive reception, becomes a matter of fact (rather than an occasion of celebration) because the exercises of trawling the Internet or viral messaging via mobile phone and Internet are acts of volition demanded by technological possibilities, transforming youth from being mere viewers to active commentators and creator of media content.

9. The world press has described these changes in exalted terms, as the coming of age of India, a country which on many counts of human development index is still a Third World nation (see Timmons, 2007; Waldan, 2003; Zakaria, 2006; also see 'The great Indian', 2006; 'Virtual champions', 2006). The euphoria about India also reverberates among political analysts, who project India as the strategic partner of the West, especially America (see Carter, 2006; Das, 2006; Raja, 2006). According to critics like Mishra (2006) and Arundhati Roy (2008), this jubilation without being subject to any critical scrutiny circulates with even greater enthusiasm in the Indian press and other media outlets which appear to be blind to certain abject truths of the exclusionary nature of India's economic growth.

10. According to Douglas E. Foley (2002), ' Hall contends that understanding the construction of ideological hegemony requires focusing on key conjunctural moments or 'articulations' within a given social formation, e.g., the articulations between various popular discourses such as nationalism, Catholicism, racism, and classism' (p. 472).

11. In her insightful essay, Gole (2000) presents an extensive account through four situated examples from Turkey of the interaction of Islamic ideology, practices, and beliefs (which she refers to as Islamism) with modernizing forces that transform, as she argues, both Islamism as well as modernity. However, such is the overwhelming predilection of even nuanced scholars such as Gole to see Islam in opposition to modernity, that she asks after herself presenting instances of 'cross-fertilization. . .between Western and Islamic conceptions of self and modernity, modesty and truth, faith and secularism, community and individualism, conservatism and consumerism' in Turkey, if such intersections are a possibility (p. 114).

12. In the contexts of the backlash against hybridity by social theorists (see Ahmad, 1992; Araeen, 2000; Zizek, 1997) as being a limited explanatory construct elaborating on either relationships of cultural elites in a globalized world order or on the thriving of new creative energies within the workings of the free markets (as in the works of Canclini, 2005), there is a renewed effort to address the criticisms of the detractors and to reinvest in the idea of the hybrid to see how it can be reflective of the complexities of cultural transformations (see, Brah & Coombes, 2001; Papastergiadis, 2005). Critics like Nikos Papastergiadis are invested in exploring the creativity of the hybrid in artistic practices to see if the idea of the hybrid can contribute to the process of decolonization of imagination and a better understanding of the workings of cultural differences given the especially tense and hostile environments towards migrants and the cultural and ethnic 'other.'

13. This is especially so if, as Terry Eagleton (1994) argues in his review of Bhabha's (1994) *The Location of Culture*, that the conditions within

developing nations are not the concerns addressed in the enunciations of
the hybrid in the first place. They remain concerned with dilemmas of
diasporic populations (for example, see Ang, 2001).

14. Ania Loomba (1998) is skeptical of the celebratory discourse of the hybrid
subjectivity, which in her opinion masks the complexities and diversities
to present what is a 'curiously universal and homogenous' condition (p.
178). For example, how does the concept differentiate between MTV's
commodification of cultural difference from the artistic practices of street
vendors and visual artists in Canclini's (2005) elaboration of their unique
hybrid practices?

15. Lee and LiPuma (2002) argue that the analysis of culture itself must
undergo an overhaul from being mere excavation and interpretation of
meaning to how dynamics of circulation propelled by a larger material
force of economy drive globalization and challenge 'traditional notions of
language, culture, and nation' (p. 191).

2

CYBER CITIZENS
Rewriting Social and Political Marginalization

'Mediated' is the qualifying definition of lives immiserated in networks and flows arising from revolutions in communication technologies that increasingly engulf global populations. According to Thomas De Zengottia (2005), these are 'lives composed of an unprecedented fusion of the real and the represented' and incessantly addressed 'through every sensory channel,' and presented in multi-dimensional visions through varied media angles, so much so that such lives become more compelling, present and alive in their performance of the mediated person than in their own paired down realities (p. 6–7). As Zengottia elaborates the 'alchemy of mediation, the osmotic process through which reality and representation fuse' as though through 'method acting,' where pre-written scripts evoke the deepest and most sincere emotions, I argue that this fusion between reality and vision is most compelling when articulated in the performance of the competent consumer. Driving every individual regardless of their ability, and constantly reinforced by omnipresent commercial media, consumer citizenship is the ultimate promise of globalized economies to their citizens. And as satellite television penetration grows to saturation point in India and as mobile telephone subscriber base becomes the second largest in the world with a steady increase in Internet connectivity,[1] media's transformative logic gathers immense valence in the Indian context, especially when contrasted with former conditions of almost negligible presence of communication and media technologies

in pre-globalization/liberalization era prior to 1991.[2] It is in the establishment of the logic of capitalism and consumerism through processes
of mediation which, according to Silverstone (2005), alter both social
and cultural environments, as well as individual and institutional relationships to these overarching environments and to each other, that the
transformation of a formerly socialist country, its citizens, including its
neglected minorities, are to be understood.[3]

However, even as new communication technologies have created
a resonance around certain dominant ideologies, the fact is that the
spread of digital media, Internet, and W-2 platforms have also opened
up floodgates to the articulation of individual and personalized stories
that can potentially challenge the prevailing dominant logic. As Nick
Couldry (2008) exultantly writes, 'a whole range of personal stories
[are] now being told in potentially public form using digital media
resources' and by 'people who have never done so before' (p. 374),
or who like the Indian Muslims never thought that they would have
a voice, or a chance to voice their complex realities. Hence, it is in
the context of digital storytelling's 'liberatory potential' given 'the
remediation capacity of digital media' and its 'multiple possibilities
for transmission, retransmission and transformation' (p. 374) that I
explore the Muslim youth's struggle to secure their space in consumerist modernity and in the Indian mainstream society. Given the salience
of new needs in the construction of the Muslim youth's selfhood, I
argue that while globalized mediated discourses have expanded their
imaginations creating new aspirations, the spaces of digital media, W-2
applications have provided spaces for the expression of this enhanced
imagination and for its full realization as a quotidian everyday reality
(see Appadurai, 1996). They have allowed the Muslim youth to both
re-think the larger public sphere and to explore new possibilities of
representing themselves, countering their marginalization, and confronting the tenacity of the stereotypes defining Muslim as 'others.' As I
have argued in the previous chapter, the defining quality of aspiring and
mediated younger generations of Muslims is their propensity to negotiate rather than to withdraw from the complexities and struggles facing
a religious minority population with a contested history in a rapidly
globalizing neoliberal economy. And in this chapter, I draw attention
to how they employ digital media's flexibility, increasing accessibility, and creativity to address and counter discourses, which draw on

discriminatory politics to disenfranchize and mark the Muslims as the aberrant and abhorrent 'other.'

Digital Storytelling: Negotiating for an Inclusive Status

The stories that Muslim youth tell, exploiting the potentialities of digital media, are first and most about themselves, focusing on individual choices, dreams, and aspirations. These stories carry different nuances or inflections, representing differences in age, gender, family background, economic status, as well as opportunities and skills to effectively communicate their point of view, which in turn are intimately connected with their personal and economic conditions. However, across a spectrum of stories that I read, as told on Facebook, there is one clearly discernable common theme, which is to reclaim some respectability and space that the Muslims are denied in their everyday life. There is a steadfast effort directed at reinstating the self by rescuing it from constrictions imposed by stereotypes constraining the Muslim identity and this makes their communication more complex and relevant than being mere expressions of personal foibles. And even if their presentations of 'highly selective version of themselves' qualify as being narcissistic, like most Facebook interactions of the youth are wont to[4] (see Mendelson & Papacharissi, 2011), their self aggrandizing postures not only endorse social networking sites as spaces facilitating negotiations around the question of identity, but they also alert us to the potential political implications when members of a neglected and disregarded minority community interject in larger public spheres, well beyond the physical limits of their segregated enclaves, to present their version of the truth and to expand their experiences and spheres of influence.

The personalities that the Muslim youth create online are often not only far removed from the dominant descriptions of a typical Muslim but I even found them to be completely unrecognizable from their non-virtual identities. For example, I could not apprehend even my own distant cousin— a shy, respectful young person deeply mindful of the *akhlaq* and *tehzeeb* of the North Indian Islamic culture— in his Facebook avatar, where he pledges allegiance to obscure British rock groups, and surprisingly also to Ayn Rand (being completely unaware of the two groups anti and pro establishment oppositional politics). And even if the highlighting of a westernized lifestyle in the

Facebook persona of a Jamia enclave's female resident on scholarship
to an American university, punctuated with photographs posing with
a glass of wine in hand, and sidelining the issue of scholarship that
merited the trip, was amusing, the fact is that even such ego-centric
self presentations are indications of the open ended nature of change
ushered in by new applications. Couldry (2008) argues that media's
true impact is in promoting 'a process of environmental transformation which, in turn, transforms the conditions under which any further
media can be produced and understood' (p. 380). The possibilities for
self-creation as well as the opportunities to ease the stigma of their
'otherness[5] 'are so endemic and deep-rooted in the digital or virtual
spaces that personal communications of the Muslim youth are bound
to overflow the narrow limits of preserving individual self-esteem and
extend to reinstating the community as a whole. And the efforts to
establish the self by rescuing the Muslim community's collective image
in the public sphere, I argue, would not only constitute the Muslims
youth's 'convoluted modernities' but also count as attempts to stake a
claim as rightful citizens, there by constituting a new form of political
participation by members of a minority community.

In pursuing the Muslim youth's use of digital media I take a leaf
out of Clay Shirky's (2012) *Ted Talk*, where he proposes that if we
are trying to understand the potential for change imbedded in new
technologies then we must look at their adoption and appropriation
at the margins. The efforts of disregarded Muslim youth, who chaff
at their second class citizen status, to assert themselves and to stake
a larger claim in the public sphere through avenues of digital media
exemplifies such an instance. My quest is to understand what kind of
stories would they tell about themselves to contend with the discriminatory regimes? And given the technological permeance, opening of
opportunities to speak to different and new audiences, what would be
the new alliance that they would form, and how would they recruit
support from extended quarters to argue their cause forcefully. I ask
these questions at a point of time when, Internet access becomes as
pervasive as a telephone connection in middle-class homes of the Jamia
area, and when in lower-middle- class homes a computer becomes a
prized status symbol to be displayed in drawing rooms.

These questions are also noteworthy especially as the Muslim populations are generally positioned in that state of opposition between

'the Net and the self' or representing the disconnect between actual and virtual worlds that underlines much of Castells' (1997) earlier writings about selfhood and identity in networked societies.[6] The Muslim youth would be perceived by Castell as defensive identities existing on the other side of the digital divide, in the hope that 'God, nation, family, and community will provide unbreakable, eternal codes, around which a counter-offensive will be mounted against the culture of virtuality' (Castell 1997, p. 66). However, the Muslim youth-mediated interactions are interjections comparable to those made by other disempowered communities— like the Zappatistas— using the tools of information technologies, which Castells (1996) argues dissociate them from global power networks. And even as I agree that these interventions are definitely a factor of individual access, resources, and capabilities, it is important to understand why has the deployment of digital media's new faculties become imperative at this moment? Why has it now become important for the Muslim youth to address the misconceptions that exist about them and to redefine their image? What motivates them to intervene in their environment? As I explore the Muslim youth's interjections I find frameworks of both mediatization and mediations to be useful in explaining their experiences.[7] The former concept stresses a certain directionality of change, while the latter is more concerned with mapping its heterogeneous contours without making any determinist claims about direction or form.[8] Keeping the dialectics of these frameworks in mind I argue that though the highly mediated environment have perforce ended Muslim isolation, igniting desires to participate in the larger public spheres, it is also true that proliferation of media has not attenuated discourses bent on perpetuating the Muslim 'otherness' and marginalization from Indian mainstream society. In fact, the discriminatory discourses are constantly being reinforced by omnipresent media, but there are new possibilities to address these discriminatory regimes. And it is in these paradoxical environments that I focus on the multiple and often contradictory stories that Muslim youth tell which are as much dependent on their capacities and predilections as on the circumstances that they are addressing. But one consistent reality about these stories is that they constitute negotiations for a more egalitarian existence. I trace how these stories evolve in spaces and dynamics created by social networking sites, blogs, and web hosting allowing Muslim youth to exert an influence in spheres that once lay beyond their capabilities and imagination, and include possibilities for creating new communities and forging alliances with groups such as with the diasporic Muslim populations.

Reconstructing Muslim 'Otherness'

On September 22, 2007 there was a conflagration in Jamia area that attracted immense media attention. This confirms my earlier argument that contemporary Muslim existence, surrounded by multitude of national and international media outlets, forces them to confront on an everyday basis the negative impressions about Islam and Muslims. And the occurrence on that day resurrected with heightened volubility all the shibboleths identifying Islam and its followers as irascible, violent, and uncivilized, much to the chagrin of both the middle-class, urbane and educated among my informants as well as those aspiring to this status. But I owe it to my informants' access and connectivity to interactive communications technologies and to its relevance in their everyday life that even if I was miles away from the scene, I could be vitally present in the occurrences unfolding in the Jamia area. I came to know of the event through the emails that I exchanged with many of my informants. And this was a point of time before all of them had acquired a Facebook account and before pervasive digital presence had become the norm. However, their emails not only provided me details of the incident, but also gave me an insight into how my informants framed the event and what issues they particularly focused on. Their mails helped me to understand the event from their perspective, and gauge how increasing access to Internet has transformed passive media consumers to conscious media producers, who are able to interject and to reconstruct the general perceptions about Muslims .

It was the month of *Ramazan* when Muslims the world over fast during the day and spend the evening reciting the Quran and remain immersed in prayers. It is also the month when the Jamia area reflects more than even ever its quintessential Islamic religious and cultural ethos—as routines of life are altered to revolve around religious obligation of fasting and prayers. During *Ramazan*, shops are open till late hours, restaurants serve their clients until wee hours, and there is much activity up till dawns when the fasting period begins with the call to *fazar* or early morning prayers. There is almost a festive air in the evening as Muslim men fill the mosques to pray and recite the Quran, and there is much traffic on the roads as people traverse back and forth from their homes to shops and mosques. The traffic situation is further worsened by pavement vendors who encroach upon narrow roads to sell a range of commodities eagerly taking advantage of the increased hours of business. On the evening of September 22 (Saturday) , one such roadside vendor was also selling the copies of the Quran, and the constable, who had instructions to clear the traffic, perhaps pushed the cart a bit too hard to get it out of the way and a copy of the Quran fell on the roadside. And this triggered a pandemonium bringing the Rapid Action Police Force to the doorsteps of Jamia. The profit driven media was quick to feed off the frenzy. The headlines from *The Times of India*, September 23, 2007, read 'Police posts set fire in mob fury' and another from *The Indian Express*, September 23, 2007 repeated 'Jamia Nagar: Mob torches police post, 4 cops serious,'. Both reports focused on how a mob of about 600 to 700 people, incensed by the desecration of the Quran, attacked the police station and set it on fire. The highlighting of the behaviour of Muslims miscreants and mob in these stories contributes to the important task of constructing and maintaining the Muslim 'otherness.'

According to Barbara Metcalf (1995), the Muslim 'otherness' is not so much a matter of Muslim cultural and religious differences from the majority Hindu community. Instead, it is a product of political expediencies aimed at preserving the hegemony and cohesiveness of the dominant Hindu community and of deflecting attention from the inequalities and lack of redistributive justice within the world's largest democracy. Hence, it is a 'foil against which the unity of others—Hindus, the nation—can be constituted, and injustices of class and wealth obscured' (Metcalf , 1995 p. 963).That is why even if British colonial policies and practices of governance[9] are responsible for codifying discrete Muslim and Hindu religious communities, these divisions continue to be upheld because they are imperative to maintaining the entrenched power equations in independent India. They, in fact, form the very foundations of the Indian national identity.[10] Moreover, boundaries between Muslim and Hindu subjects are daily redrawn by projecting them as homogenous and self-contained identities. Shani

(2007) argues that the specter and logic of Partition are frequently resurrected to consecrate the hegemony of upper-caste Hindu ideologies and constituencies. It is not easy for Muslims to constantly contest the Hindu nationalist's arguments for separation and segregation of Muslims, especially when they are proposed in the interest of national integrity, security, and peace.The older generations had chosen to fall back on their own resources and withdraw from contexts reducing them to the status of second-class citizens,[11] but the Muslim youth, exposed to transnational global regimes and eager acolytes of the consumerist ethos cannot do so.

Therefore, in this context, my first concern was to understand how my informants were reacting to the media's construction of the event as being just another instance of the Muslim community's essential incivility and 'otherness.' How they were reacting to the highly prejudiced media coverage that failed to take into account that if the violence of uncontrollable crowds is one part of the story, the other is the larger context of Muslim existence in India that had an equal role to play in the construction of this incident. And once again, in reading through my informants' responses and emails, I was not at all surprised to notice that they made a conscious effort to present a more balanced picture of the incident that day, and their judiciousness problematizes allegations of irrationality and irascibility leveled against the Muslims. For example Faisal's short email said, *'police waalo ne Quran ki be atbi kr di thi is wajah se bahot tension ho gayi thi jamia me. Bahot zada fight ho gayi thi police aur public me'* [the police disrespected the Quran and that is why there was so much tension and a big fight broke out between the people and the police] (personal communication, September 28, 2007). While Prof. Shahid noted that, 'overall there seems to less sensitivity on both sides, the community and the police authorities in this case. And I guess we tend to overreact because of our own insecurity' (personal communication, September 24, 2007). Hence, even as he criticized the police, he also berated the community for its reaction. But it is the reference to a sense of insecurity among Muslims, which is of paramount importance in understanding both the altercation as well as my informants' reactions. According to Professor Shahid, while it is true that in the month of *Ramazan* religious sentiments are bound to be high, but what riled the situation was the lack of respect for those sentiments, especially at a time when Muslims are particularly conscious of their identity. The timing indeed was crucial, because within the sensitive context, the Muslim sense of negation and suppression was further inflamed and it evoked from the community an extremely strong response. The Muslim community's sense of persecution has further deepened with the resurrection of the hegemonic Hindu identity and right-wing nationalist politics in the past two decades—a reality which owes not a little to the incessant and mostly positive representations of the Hindu identity in mainstream media (see, Brosius, 2005; McGuire & Reeves, 2003; Rajagopal, 1992 & 2001), as compared to negative and derogatory coverage of Islam. In the light of the Muslim sensitivity, it was feared that Muslims across the country may become enraged by the occurrence in Jamia and Delhi's administration issued a directive to television news channels not to broadcast any news of the agitation until the situation had been brought under control (Pratyush 2007).

The coverage of the event which highlighted the Muslim community's volatility was a matter of deep embarrassment for many of my informants, but I also found that some were more mortified than others and exhibited a greater concern with regards to saving the community's reputation. I argue that the feelings of discomfiture were more acute among those who in their quest for middle-class respectability not only experience greater pressure for assimilation, but are also highly sensitive to how they are portrayed in the media. These are the people for whom a job at a multi-national corporation has become a reality but finding a home in a mixed locality is not an easy proposition as yet. And though better integrated in the mainstream Indian society, both in their professional and personal lives, they are still tied down by financial constraints and socio-cultural discrimination of Islam to their Muslim enclave. Therefore, these individuals were more eager than others to address other middle-class Indians and to correct the misconceptions circulating about Muslims. I noted in the communications that I received from them, that they felt almost obliged to perform some form of damage control to both rescue their identity and to ensure their continued participation in the mainstream Indian society by disassociating themselves from the clamorous occurrences of that evening. Hence, it was a more limited, mainly middle-class self-concerned negotiation which motivated and underlined their email messages that were sent within a day or two of being bombarded by newspaper and television reports elaborating the excesses of Muslim fundamentalists and hoodlums.

The emails were drafted to address a long list of friends and acquaintances in their mailing lists. And the first issue, which almost all of them addressed, was the unseemly publicity that their residential area had received. Najma, a journalist working for an international news channel expressed her perplexity and asked herself how such a thing could happen in Jamia where, she stressed, mostly educated and cultured Muslims lived. According to her,

> I always used to think that Jamia has no history of riots and the entire area is 'safe' for Muslims (that's why so many of them, perhaps, migrated to this area from different parts of the city, including my own extended family). (personal communication, September 24, 2007)

To this her friend Haroun, a media consultant with an international foundation, added,

> Having lived over 35 years in this area, I think this is the first time I heard this slogan [referring to the slogan of *Naara e Tatbir* or in defense of Islam] being shouted in Jamia Nagar. My father says he hasn't seen this sort of attitude of people in Jamia area in last 50 years that he's been here. (personal communication, September 24, 2007)

Both of them described the event as anomalous and atypical, while Najma also felt 'confused and slightly taken aback by the whole thing' (personal communication, September 24, 2007). Not only did they wish to be completely disassociated from it all, but the only way they could explain it was by referring to the excessive religious zeal of a motley group of young men. According to Najma, she saw a group of young men 'creating complete situation of panic and confusion by unnecessarily running in groups from one lane to another and shouting slogans against the police, etc.' She also believed that they 'were all waiting [for] something untoward to happen and show how religious they are and can 'sacrifice' their lives when there is a threat to their religion' (personal communication, September 24, 2007). Corroborating her view, Haroun added, 'I took a risk by trying to persuade some youngsters to quit their violence and go back home. It was certainly futile. . . . Many of them told me I was being a *buzdil* [coward] and should go back home' (personal communication, September 24, 2007). And in the atmosphere of mayhem Najma urged action, 'all I want to say is that there is an immediate need to do something. I also don't know what [to do]', but the exchange ended with a plan to hold a meeting with all like-minded residents in order to ensure that such a situation would not arise again. The meeting did not take place as far as I am aware, however, I could not but wonder who would be the 'like-minded' residents invited to this event.

These exchanges are viewpoints of those among the Muslim with the cultural and economic capital to seek and find employment with international organizations. They also point to internal dissent, especially as the upper-classes seem to perceive themselves as occupying a markedly different position in comparison to other residents of the community. However, my other informants, the students of Jamia university, who did not have the same class and educational facilities as Najma or Haroun, were also equally critical of the turn of events in the Jamia area on the evening of 22 September . For example, both Simi and Fawzia, young women from modest homes and students of Diploma in Engineering, were also very angry with the young men. They believed that the policeman did not intentionally drop the Quran, and as Fawzia said, 'then he had said sorry too. So, what was the reason for those boys to go and burn the police station' (author's translation, original in Urdu, personal communication, December 9, 2007). While Faisal was so upset, he did not want to talk about it and brushed aside my email queries with a gruff response, 'leave it mam. Tell me howz ur life going' (personal communication, September 28, 2007); and Zain, expressed his dismay that such incidences prevented his non-Muslim friends from visiting him and gave the area a bad reputation. But then who were the young men that everyone seems to hold responsible for the untoward occurrence?

I found it difficult to answer this question. The snowball method of sampling that I used in my fieldwork allowed me to reach out to the larger population from my former base at the Jamia University. Hence, the young people I was introduced to were either students of the university, or children of those employed at the university, or alumni of the university who were now employed in different sectors. But it appeared that the young men everyone was holding responsible for the trouble had probably no connection with the university, because none of my informants mentioned that there was any one among their acquaintances who was part of the protest or part of the mob that had battled with the police. I believe, that the miscreants could have been part of that migrant population whom Professor Shahid had mentioned are relocating to Jamia area from the small towns and villages of north India with the hope of getting admission in Jamia University, but were unable to do so because of the rising educational standards of the university. However, even if they fail in their desired ambition, according to Professor Shahid, they do not return home. Instead, they choose to stay on and enroll in distance education programs or in other private institutes where the criteria for admission are not so stringent. I did not have access to this population. The only ones that I knew from among the migrant population were those who were fortunate and talented enough to secure their admission in Jamia University. Hence, while this incidence points how a presumably cohesive community is hierarchically constructed by differing access to education, professional qualifications, and ensuing monetary status, it also highlights how these aspirations for education and employment underline the Muslim community's dream for inclusion.

Moreover, an analysis of this event also indicates that access to media, or the lack of access to it, may be another dividing factor; because while these young men had no presence except as miscreants in media reports and in the opinion of my most of my informants, those with educational and cultural proficiencies were able to intervene in the environment to influence perceptions about the community. And it is owing to privileges of education, class, and attendant social networks that some are not just able to rescue the beleaguered Islamic identity but also to reinstate its pride as I discuss in my next section.

Muslim High Cultures: Deploying Exotic 'Otherness'

The middle-class among Muslims are better able to appropriate the possibilities for dispersed, flexible, and horizontal channels of communication of digital media technologies to effectively engage in what Castells (2009) calls 'mass-self broadcasting,' where they become an important node, in not just receiving but also transmitting information and reaching out to diverse audiences across geographic distances. I present the case study of a media collective engaged in promoting syncretic Indian culture of which Haroun, my informant is a key convener. Haroun hails from middle class *shurfa* (or high caste) family from Uttar

Pradesh. He has been educated at good English medium schools and university, and is professionally qualified to work as media consultant for international agencies and government organizations. But his class and professional standing also enable him to be a translator of the Muslim culture. And drawing on his family of academics and scholars of Urdu and Persian, Haroun applies his inclinations towards Islamic culture and heritage to break the silence about Islam's contributions to Indian culture and society. He works with a creative artists' group that includes both Hindus and Muslims who are united by their common interest in Hindustani classical music and its highly diverse and mixed heritage. They hold workshops on Indian culture, focusing especially on Sufi music and philosophy, because it epitomizes the syncretism and eclecticism underlining the Indian ethos.

However, what I find most interesting are the people who enroll in the workshops on Indian culture as well as Haroun's communications with his audiences who according to him are 'mostly well-heeled and well-paid employees of the IT industry looking for some cultural activities.' They represent that section of the Indian society who after having being immersed in cultural products of mainly the western world are now looking for something else to define their cultural capital and to augment their social standing. These are people who are ready to pay approximately $100 for a two day workshop where they think they will dabble in culture and learn some useful tricks like mediation to deal with their stressed life-styles. According to Haroun, their perspective often tends to be utilitarian because as he says 'while we want to talk about literature, music, history, they are looking for things like meditation and ask us 'are you not going to talk about Sufi meditation' (personal communication January 2011). However, the workshop also attracts those who are genuinely interested to know the finer nuances of Sufi music. But nonetheless even the uninformed among the audience, who may have no idea at all about India's eclectic culture are important to Haroun's purpose. They constitute the influential middle-classes and potential agenda setters before whom he has a chance to expertly articulate and assert Islam's claim in the construction of Indian society—something which most Muslims are too diffident or unable to raise even in the passing. And if 'there is something cool about Sufism,' as Haroun acknowledges, it definitely helps him point out how integrated Islam is in Indian society.

However, what is interesting to note is that organization, promo-
tion, and advertising of such events has become greatly facilitated since
the emergence of social media and networking sites like Facebook.
According to Haroun, the workshops are advertized 'on mainstream
mediums like Facebook' (personal communication, January 2011). I
was impressed that he refers to the Internet medium and not to print
or television as being 'mainstream'. However, even if the word 'mainstream' may not apply to Facebook in early 2011, it definitely helps
in understanding the way new digital platforms are becoming incor-
porated in everyday life and parlance of the privileged middle-class
including the Muslims among them. These interactions are essentially
instances of reaching out to other upper middle-class Indians, and they
illustrate the horizontal nature of communications enabled by interactive technologies to which scholars like Castells (2009) and Kallinikos,
Aaltonen & Marton (2010) have drawn attentions to. But they do not
highlight the entrenched socio-economic circumstances or the question of class and its attendant facilities, which make communication
between middle-class members, as represented in this online and
offline collective, easier.

In fact, I was extended the invitation via Facebook, even while
I was still in America, and I was also allowed to view and peruse
the pictures and the programs from previous workshops, giving me
ample opportunity to plan and to know what to expect. Moreover,
not only were there clear instructions on how to register and pay for
the registration but I could also see who else might be attending the
workshop, and be acquainted with a few facts about them, and generally feel comfortable about the middle- class milieu that I was about
to step into. The important selling point about these workshops is
that in an ambience saturated with cultural artifacts from the Western
world, they make nostalgia and appropriation of Indian culture as
self-aggrandizing activities and shape new spheres of inclusiveness.
But even while such events emulate the cultural and social snobbery
of the 'for invitation only' Sufi music soirees organized by the Indian
government's cultural agencies at exclusive and out of bounds Delhi's
historical locations and which are graced by Delhi's high society, its
senior bureaucrats, politicians, doyens of business houses, and celebrities, these workshops are more accommodative of the contemporary
nouveau riche milieus—allowing middle-class individuals to improve

their cultural quotient with the hope of climbing up the social hierarchies.

At the workshop, that I attended, I not only met with the 'IT industry type' (in Haroun's words) but also with others who were genuinely interested in knowing more about Indian culture. However, even those who came to the workshop with the hope of changing their perspective on Indian music, culture, and history, events such as the heritage walk in the heart of the city, a space which they probably crossed everyday, were an eye-opener with regard to Indian Islam's rich history and long presence. Walking in Basti, Nizamuddin, and at the Sufi sacred spots at the back of the famous Humayun's tomb meant acknowledging not only Islam's historical relevance but also its contemporary continuance. The residential locale of Nizamudin is dotted with numerous historical buildings from the eleventh to the eighteenth century; and the tombs, inns, enclaves of erstwhile Muslims rulers and courtiers have now been converted into parks for its rich residents' pleasure. However, there is but one historical monument dating back to the eleventh century, the tomb of the Sufi saint Hazrat Nizamuddin, and his disciple and poet Amir Khursau, which is a living site, marking Islam's continuing history since a thousand years in India. Here, people from across the city and country, both rich and poor, Hindus and Muslims, gather to commemorate the memory of the Sufi saint. And every Thursday evening draws large crowds to hear the *qawwalis* sung in his praise and mainly written by his disciple Amir Khusrau whose poetry fluidly moves between Persian, Turkish, and Hindavi languages that were once interchangeably spoken by the educated Indian middle classes. However, despite the participants' general lack of knowledge about Islam, Haroun's pride in pointing out that on almost every street corner of Delhi there is a monument speaking of Indian culture's Central Asian and Islamic roots, was uplifting for a fellow Muslim; because Haroun in his articulate speech, but without being explicit, was subtly making a strong case for Indo-Islamic cultural relevance, and therefore for his own dignity as an Indian citizen and for his community's claim to Indianess.

However, even if this collective represents a comfortable network of like-minded people from the same social class, differences in religions notwithstanding, where talking about Islam or asserting its significance can be couched in terms of high art and music, Islam's existence in India continues to be a deeply contentious issue. And even as I was working with this group, I was grappling with the realities of my other informants whose experiences with tackling the question of their very Muslim 'otherness' were not so very pleasant. Their experiences of being stigmatized demand that forums such as Facebook cannot be reserved for discussions of soft social-cultural concerns, even if its structure is intrinsically more favourable to horizontal networks such as the one exemplified in this middle-class's cultural forum. However, as Couldry (2008) argues, the possibilities for interactions on W-2 platforms are so heterogeneous and so diverse that it is not always possible to predict the directionality or form that these interactions may take. And as my next example shows the facilities in digital communication technolo-gies of Internet, W-2 applications, and mobile telephone are conducive to helping the Muslim youth find both a political presence and a voice. Within cyber-spaces, the Muslim youth are able to construct new inter-ventions that address discourses reinstating their 'otherness,' and they are also able to employ a markedly different language and style to reach out to a much larger mainstream audience. And therefore, they are able to successfully project themselves in a way, which has never been possible for the Urdu press before.

However, before I elaborate on how enabling cyber-spaces support politics which is different from tendencies for 'redressal' or 'quiet encroachment' espoused by the older generations, and helping Muslim youth to directly call attention to their problems, I outline the political and social circumstances which force the definition of less than equal citizens on Muslims.

Muslim 'Otherness': A Political Necessity

The discourses of Muslim 'otherness,' which as mentioned earlier, have sutured the fabric of the Indian nation, have to be demonized further, according to Hansen (1996), to perpetuate Hindu upper-caste right-wing dominance in national politics. Hansen argues that the brutal erasure of Muslim presence from the Indian soil has been woven into cultural nationalism of the Hindu organization like the RSS as politics of 'recuperation of masculinity.' Internalizing Orientalist epistemology describing India in feminine, spiritual, and organic terminology, and according to Hansen, Sarvarkar, RSS's founding ideologue, proposed the avenging of 'effiminization' of the Indian nation by punishing the

Muslims (p. 138). Hansen also argues that in contemporary Indian politics, the theme of a purportedly lost masculinity has been removed from RSS's high-sounding rhetoric of national purification, and has instead been transformed into a language of lumpen violence as seen in the workings of Shiv Sena, which viciously targets Muslims (p. 153). According to Hansen, the stresses and conflicts created by modernizing capitalism have further contributed to the idea of assertion of masculinity by violently emasculating the Muslim 'other.' The demonization of Muslim 'other' has permeated 'popular communal common sense,' because, according to Hansen, it is only through an aggressive reaffirmation of sexual prowess that the endemic insecurities of capitalism, the injustices of unequal growth, and the destruction of cultural and communal ties can be dealt with (p. 153).

In independent India the notion of the Muslim 'otherness' has also been absolutely essential to preserving cohesiveness of the Hindu community, which has the potential to fray along caste lines, and to protect the upper-caste Hindu hegemony in the face of rising upward mobility of the lower-castes ensured by constitutional promises. Hence, according to Ornit Shani (2007), whenever tensions along 'the boundaries of difference among Hindus' have surfaced in the Indian society, the upper-castes propagators of Hindu nationalism have been quick to exploit sectarian differences between Hindus and Muslims and to divert the hostilities towards the Muslim 'other' (Shani 2007, p. 181). However, the rising aspirations among the lower and backward caste Hindus have now become an endemic source of anxiety and the demands for their upliftment through job reservations in state employment sectors and through preferential admission quotas in educational institutes are creating conflicts over scarce resources. These caste tensions have erupted at regular intervals as accommodations and ameliorative policy decisions supporting underprivileged lower caste Hindus have raised the ire of the middle and upper Hindu castes who are deeply threatened by the potential loss of their own entitlements (Williams, 2011, p. 244). And whenever these tensions potentially damage Hindu electoral politics, or dismantle the myth of the unified Hindu community, the Muslim 'other' serves as the expedient foil against which the Hindu right wing group is able to organize and to regroup, preventing the disintegration of the Hindu constituency. Indeed, as Shani (2011) and Williams (2011) argue, the growing uncertainties and tensions in the caste regimes were the backdrop against which the *Ram Janambhoomi* movement was constructed, and Muslim negativity was raised to such a feverish pitch that it lead to the destruction of a protected archeological monument and mosque on 6 December 1992. However, it prevented internal dissent within the Hindu community. Shani (2007) also points out that the shift from caste to communal conflicts also underlies the Gujarat riots of 2002. The BJP government systematically orchestrated the demonization of Muslims in order to divert growing discontent among the lower-castes as well as middle-class Hindus whose life's ambitions were being thwarted due to the Gujarat economy's inability to accommodate their growing aspirations.[12] According to Shani (2007), in the months preceding the violence, the unemployed youth were advised by the leaders of Hindu organizations such as the VHP to look upon the Muslims as the reason for the loss of their livelihood, and these leaders not only openly propagated violence but also distributed small metal *trishuls* (pointed sharp tridents) as weapons to be used against Muslims (Shani, 2007, p. 183).

However, even as the hostilities towards Indian Muslims have only worsened in the age of global war against terror, when atrocities committed against the Muslim 'other' can be justified as a corollary of the global events (see Williams, 2011), the Muslim youth, driven by their ambitions for better education, employment, and membership in the Indian society must find a way to address these negativities. And it is the need to challenge their iniquitous positioning within the Indian society, which drives the Muslim youth to use digital avenues of communication, which offer them an opportunity to express themselves, air their grievances as well as by pass the prejudiced mainstream media in ways not possible before. The Muslim youth's use of digital technologies is being shaped within their particular life struggles as well as aspirations to establish their presences within the new spaces of a globalized economy, and in response to the odds arrayed against them.

Moreover, the Muslim youth's participation in digital public spheres, heralds the presence of middle-class Muslims in political spaces on a scale not known before. Their participation has the potential to usher in new politics driven by more middle-class aspirations as well as by middle-class Muslims who hitherto were ignored in India's vote bank politics due to their relatively small numbers. But what drives this research is not a desire to establish a definite connection or to measure with precision any links between digital media usage and political participation. Instead I seek to understand how the Muslim youth's usage of new means of 'mass-self broadcasting' is a facet of their situatedness within the expanding Indian economy and of their propensity to raise their voice to demand their inclusion. I address these questions through ethnographic explorations of the Muslim youth's experiences at the intersections of off line dynamics with potentialities for free-expressions offered by online spaces to understand who they address and how.

New Positions: Offline and Online

On 19 September, 2008, in Batla House, one of the many localities within the larger Jamia area, the Delhi Police's Special Cell, in an encounter conducted during broad daylight in a heavily populated residential area, killed two Muslim students from Jamia University and arrested two others in what they claimed was an operation against terrorists responsible for the bomb blasts in Delhi earlier in the month. The targeting of Muslim youth in the month of *Ramazan* was bound to deeply hurt the community and also deepen its sense of insecurity. Many of the residents wondered if this was a cruel coincidence, because according to them, this demonstration of the state's explicit might as cordons of armed police descended on the area and conducted an armed operation exposed the Muslim population's extreme vulnerability. They admitted that it felt as if the ground itself had given away under their feet because they were no longer safe even in their cloistered, shuttered, and exclusive enclaves, where they choose to live with their co-religionists, despite the ghetto like conditions, believing that living among other Muslims would guarantee their safety. But what is more important is that this brutal display of power comes as a forceful reminder of the prejudices and threats of violence that Muslim youth must face in their quest for upward mobility.

I examine the happenings on that day through the eyes of one such Muslim youth desirous of material and professional success. Afrin is a television reporter and presenter for a reputable twenty-four hour satellite news channel, and a resident of the Jamia enclave, who moved here from her hometown in Uttar Pradesh. According to Afrin, she came to Delhi with big dreams of making a name for herself as a journalist, and, 'Mashallah within five to six years I was a fairly well-known face on television' (personal communication December, 2011). I focus on her view of the event not only to illustrate the impending conflict between the Muslim youth's desires and the iniquitous regimes, but also to argue that the Muslim youth's increased presence in mainstream arenas (courtesy the small window of opportunity provided by cultures of meritocracy) both exaggerate this tussle as well as reshape it in ways that has implications for the Muslim youth's political voice and participation. I argue that even if Afrin epitomizes the way the burgeoning economy is opening new doors and creating new opportunities for Muslims, and giving even Muslim women a chance to entertain new dreams and hopes, her experiences also illustrate how increased presence of Muslims in new economic spheres and social and cultural domains is testing the limits of cultures of meritocracy. But on that particular day it was not only her credentials as a journalist, or her standing in the community because of being of her profession that were called into question. It was the journalistic ethics that were put under severe strain. But what is also noteworthy in her account is how practices of journalism are being enhanced by the use of digital technologies (such as the use of mobile phones to link to the studio) and creating new kinds of immediacy in reporting. According to Arfa:

> I was the first journalist to reach the place. I lived in the area and I reached there within three minutes. I was the first one to report. I took pictures. I even uploaded pictures taken from my mobile phone. They were very happy with it. However, the way that I covered the story was very different from the way other journalists covered the story. Later on other senior journalists of XXTV reached the scene. And they reported on the death of the inspector in term of 'shaheed' (personal communication January 2012).

According reverence to security forces by referring to them as 'shaheed' or martyrs and by pronouncing the Muslim youth's guilt before being proven is standard practice of media organizations, and even those channels otherwise known for balanced journalism are guilty of it. It is in these ultra-nationalist contexts, which berate and defame Muslims that Afrin's story as a Muslim caught at the crossfires between dominant equations and minority aspirations becomes important. According to her:

I mean this was the first time that something like this was happening in the city. This was not the Valley where encounters are routine. In all my years as a journalist it was the very first event. It was for the first time that such an encounter took place in my area. I was trying to present a picture of what was happening. (personal communication January 2012).

It is obvious that she presented the story from the perspective of the Muslim residents and perhaps she even condemned the operations of the police, but countering official versions of the truth would not win her any friends. Hence, a Muslim journalist may have a chance to put her point forward but only as far as it does not pose a challenge to the dominant narratives. In fact, if Afrin's presentation of the Muslim residents' point of view had cast any doubts on the news channels nationalist fervor, I was informed by another resident of Jamia enclave that on the evening of 19 September 2008, the well-known and respected journalist who heads the channel anchored the main evening news bulletin, something which he rarely does, to reiterate the slain security personnel's distinctive status as 'a shaheed' or martyr. Afrin's position in the event was becoming increasingly uncomfortable. She said:

The other people created an atmosphere in the office that created a sense of otherness in me. Later on, they did not call me for an important meeting that took place with regard to the breaking story and when I was the first one to report on this story. They sent out the signal that I was not to be trusted any more. ...the Batla House encounter hit something below the belt. I got a lot of hate emails. There was a lot of backbiting, it was to an extent that it started to get back to me. The atmosphere was not harmonious. It was not ok. Even if you work in the best of the milieu but there is this...(trails off) (personal communication, January 2012).

Afrin had to finally leave the organization. But it did not mean the end of her career, because she was able to find a placement elsewhere, and I know her today as someone who is a very vocal critique of hegemonic politics (especially on Facebook which is my main way of keeping in touch). She has evolved into a committed commentator who never fails to point out to over a thousand of her friends or acquaintances on Facebook, the matters of unjust treatment or discrimination of Muslims.

However, according to her, when she first started her career, she was not interested in the Muslim question at all. She had only wanted to enjoy her work, learn new things, and travel. And it is only later on as she started to work that the question of the contested Muslim identity became apparent to her. Therefore, supporting my argument for the Muslim youth's 'convoluted modernity' the opportunities to participate as a journalist in the contemporary (modern) spheres, and to reflect on her own contributions to the construction of the topical contexts, which brought her to the realization of how her own identity was factored in this flux created by neoliberal globalization. Afrin had sought to move beyond her North Indian Islamic identity when she had first set out to become a journalist and traveled to Delhi in search of her dream. She had only wanted to blend into the metropolitan milieu as just another successful person (or consumer citizen) but stepping into the new world changed her perceptions about who she was or what it meant to be a minority Muslim citizen in Indian democratic contexts. Hence, it was by moving forward that she was able to understand her identity as a Muslim, and grapple with all the connotations of being retrograde that are associated with it. However, it is to the new cyber spheres that she owes her facility to inhabit her Muslim identity with great élan, circumventing the oppressive rhetoric of mainstream mediums as well as the powers negating and smothering minority voices.

Brauchler (2013) argues that the Internet has brought into the public domain the remote, the marginal, the disregarded, and the dismissed issues, voices, and concerns, which have been outside the purview of mainstream media.[13] And in the context of Muslim presence in cyberspace, I argue, that though the expanded possibilities for expression of individual viewpoints is extremely important, but what is truly transformative is the opportunity to construct a common cause with other marginalized groups and to demand action and change from dominant authorities in a way that overcomes Muslim isolationist position. It entails not only representing or describing in cyberspace their contesting viewpoints, but as Brauchler argues also altering the dynamics of conflict all together by playing it out in very different contexts of cyberspace (Brauchler 2013, p. 6). It is within the intention of exploring this argument further that I describe other developments that followed in the wake of the police encounter and the death of the two students at the Jamia enclave.

Civil Society Activism and Cyberspaces

I explore the activism spearheaded by the Jamia Teachers' Solidarity Association and the news agency Two Circles.net, two different organizations of civil society members situated at two very different ends of the globe, but which have been able to work in tandem with each other and with the residents of Jamia to disrupt routines of either absolute silence or of defamatory uproar that have underlined discussions on the Muslim identity in ways that neither Muslim politicians nor the Urdu press have been able to do so before.

The Jamia Teachers' Solidarity Association is an organization formed in the aftermath of the incident on September 19 2008, and is a coalition of academics teaching at the Jamia University, residents of the area, along with other activists. According to Manisha Sethi, one of the key conveners of the group, the forming of the collective was the spontaneous coming together of individuals offended by the mainstream media's relentless and constant reiterations of the narrative peddled by state agencies and by the media's blatant efforts to corroborate the police's version of the story, while criminalizing the Muslim youths even before all facts were established. Their group's aim was not so much to attack or undermine the veracity of the police's story, but to find out and put forth the residents' version of the events, which had been consistently denied any space in the media. In many ways, this organization represents a situated and place based response to the overwhelming hegemony of discourses defaming and othering the Muslims.

On the other hand, *Two Circles.net* is an Internet based news organization, whose Cambridge, Massachusetts, based editor works part time with a team of enthusiastic, though not always highly trained, reporters as well as volunteers in India to report on issues largely ignored by the mainstream media. It includes not only coverage of events related to Muslims, but the website also extends space to independent opinions on matters, which the for-profit media has no interest in. The news website has created history not only by rapidly building its credibility among Muslims, but through its in-depth coverage of under-reported and ignored issues, it has become a credible news source and option even among other journalists, activists, and even news organizations.

But again the fact is that it is owing to the possibilities of enhanced interconnectivity offered by digital spheres that disperse organizations, though with shared interests, situated often in diametrically opposing geographical contexts, have been able to find common causes and forge effective partnerships not only with each other but also with other organizations focusing on civil liberties and human rights. The processes of creation, circulation, recreation, and redistribution enabled by digital technologies have destabilized the endemic power structures sustained by networks of traditional media. It has become possible today for new actors, such as the educated middle-class factions of Muslim society situated within middle class settings of an educational institution and within diasporic spheres, who have never before been factored into the construction of Muslim politics, to emerge. And as the working partnership between the two organizations that I refer to reflects, they have also been able to create a sustained response to discriminatory practices and policies authorizing the incarceration of Muslims youth. Their critique of powers sanctioning the destruction of Muslim youth's lives and dreams resounds more powerfully in larger public sphere—a feat which Urdu press could not achieve.

Castells (1996) exhorts us that we must take technology seriously and place the process of technological change in the social context with a keen eye on their interrelationship,[14] an observation missing in Marhall McLuhan's technological determinism, because according to Castells 'the search for identity is as powerful as techno-economic change in charting the new history' (Castells, 1996, p. 4). And yet his dominant perception of the interrelations between media and society has also been conceived in terms of opposition. He argues that 'our societies are increasingly structured around a bipolar opposition between the Net and the self' (Castells, 1996, p. 3), and that there is a structural schizophrenia[15] as 'the networked, ahistorical space of flows' impose their logic 'over scattered, segmented places' and that 'unless cultural, political, and *physical* (sic) links are deliberately built between these two forms of spaces, we may be heading toward life in parallel universe whose times cannot meet because they are wrapped in different dimensions of a social hyperspace' (p. 459). And this view of oppositional relationship between networked spaces and self would be particularly relevant to how the Muslim society would be organized, given their alleged predilections, according to Castells (1997) to withdraw from spaces of modernity. However, these new forms of interconnections that have been made possible when Facebook became such an integral element of everyday sociability, providing new space for constructing and expressing identity, deny Castells' (1996) argument that there exists a fundamental split between abstract realms of global networks and the rooted 'particularist identities' (1996, p. 3). And as we see in this case, even a marginalized population like the Muslim residents of Jamia, perceived to be existing outside digital networks and global flows, can successfully construct a dialogue connecting localized spaces to global arenas through deployment of the new digital technologies.

The work of the Jamia Teacher's Solidarity Association (hence forth JTSA), in the words of another of its members Adil Mehndi, started with the simple objective of finding out the truth, which had been obfuscated by the media hysteria. The army of PCR vans parked outside the colony belonging to different media outlets were all telling only one side of the story, and projecting the event only from the perspective of the security personnel. However, many members of the staff, who were residents of the area, were contradicting this version of the story. They viewed the encounter as an act of vicious targeting of Muslims and a deliberate witch-hunt. They had serious doubts about the veracity of the police's narrative and many among them labeled the encounter as 'fake,' meaning that though the police had no real proof about the involvement of the youth in terrorist activists, they chose to proceed with the encounter to fulfill some other political exigency. Moreover, the show of force created such a sense of despair among the members of the Jamia community that even I could troll its dark depths from so far away in California; it compelled many among the academic community to act, especially as the morale of their students had been so deeply damaged. The youth would have most likely perceived the event as damming the tide of Muslim dreams and of their desire for middle- classes' respectability.

However, I argue that notwithstanding the compulsions for the formation of JTSA and its decision to question the dominant narratives and to project the alternate versions of the truth, their intervention could only have been possible if they had a notion of who they would be addressing and how. Hence, even as they set about on their fact-finding mission, the task of building the association's website, however

rudimentary, went hand in hand. Their report which came out within a
few weeks was published on the website. And according to Adil Mehdi,
this report was picked up by every major newspaper in the country; and
an alternate viewpoint on the events of Batla House, one from the perspective of the Muslim residents and one very different from the official narratives, asserted itself in the public sphere. Adil Mehdi contends
that 'the Batla House event would have been completely forgotten as
just another encounter, and there are many, if not for our part. We had
far-reaching impact, brought the problem to the public' (personal communication, December 2012). Perhaps the impact was much greater
than even what they had anticipated, because once the challenge to the
official version of the truth had been made, its reverberations were felt
in many different directions. Of course there were the Muslim politicians and members of the Parliament who sought to play on the fears,
exploit vote-bank politics, and create a stir by staging protests, rallies,
and demonstration (see Congress joins chorus, 17 October 2008). But
it was the systematic documentation, presentation, and argumentation
of the case in the report of the organization that circulated in legal
spheres and even caught the attention of the courts and other social
activists, thereby increasing the pressure on the government to order
a judicial probe to establish the truth—whether the encounter was
staged or if the young men had been guilty of the bomb blasts (see
'Arundhati Roy joins chorus for judicial probe', 20 October 2008).
Moreover, the efforts for an independent review and collation of facts
to challenge official versions of the story also gave impetus to the other
bold move of offering the young men who had been arrested legal aid.
The call was made from within the premises of the university, and the
vice-chancellor of the university was vociferously condemned by many
in the mainstream media for taking this decision (see Sanjay, 2008).
However, he staunchly defended his view and stood by his decision to
provide legal aid to the students, which according to him was not being
granted from the university's coffers, but was being arranged by donations from members of the faculty. And this decision, which was hailed
as courageous, was an important turning point, because it represents a
new confidence among Muslims to use the legal system to seek redress
of their problems.

    JTSA's work has expanded the sphere of influence to beyond the
boundaries of their community to address a much larger constituency

of Indian Muslims as well as other oppressed sections of Indian society, while still continuing to offer residents of Jamia Nagar counsel and support (see 'Scarred Jamia seeks safe house', 19 October 2008). And after publishing their very well-received first report, the JTSA has been involved in the systemic documentation of innumerable other instances of unlawful confinement and custodial deaths of Muslim youth from across the country, which the security forces have held up as major breakthroughs in the fight against terror. On the fourth anniversary of the Batla House encounter on 19 September 2012 they released yet another report entitled *Framed, Damned Acquitted: Dossiers of a Very Special Cell* that documents sixteen cases of alleged terrorist activity that the courts dismissed, accusing the Special cell of Delhi police for falsifying evidence. The excesses of the Special Cell of Delhi Police, responsible for carrying out the Batla House encounter, which had gone largely unreported and unnoticed became a matter of discussion within both national and international press and forums because of the work done by a few dedicated civil society members from the Muslim community (see Punwani, 2012). The Human Rights Watch based in New York (as quoted on Al Jazeera) praised the JTSA for highlighting 'the serious flaws and limitations on justice when police are under pressure to show results in terrorism-related cases' (see Tilak, 2012).

The release of the report in September 2012 was attended by prominent civil rights activist like Arundhati Roy, and I was able to participate through the You Tube videos posted later and by sharing the Facebook status updates of JTSA members. The JTSA, through its meticulously researched reports which are widely circulated via their websites and on social networking platforms like Facebook has been able to voice criticism of institutionalized violence perpetuated by state agencies. The concerted circulation of independent viewpoints challenging official versions of the truth on social media and later on mainstream media (as it picks up the traction generated on social media) has given visibility to the injustices suffered by the Muslim youth. It has been particularly effective in illustrating the precarious state of the Muslim community, something that the traditional Urdu press was unable to do because it was not read by the general public. The argument is that JTSA's activism is clearly shaped by the possibilities inherent in new media technologies for giving space to expressions and opinions of marginalized groups, which are otherwise suppressed or ignored by mainstream media and by circulating them in the larger public spheres. Therefore if JTSA's work resonated in national and international spheres, it was on no small account due the opportunity created by digital spheres to speak and to be heard, a fact which spurred the creation of the reports in the first place. JTSA's activism highlights the dynamism between the report's ability to find receptive audiences (by challenging official or dominant narratives) and the digital channels' capacity for amplifying their significance by extending the ambit of their resonance. The complex synergy, challenges tendencies to see protest movements and their mediation as two independently constituted events, which plague even scholarship invested in creating an interdisciplinary dialogue between disciplines of political science, sociology, and media and communication studies (see Camaerts, Mattoni, and McCurdy, 2013).

In fact it is due to the inherent architecture of the new media technologies, and the way it defines questions of access and effective communication that mainly the middle class Muslims are drawn to explore its potential to create this new form of politics. The educated middle-class, given their access to networks and nodes of power as well as to their much clearer understanding of their functioning, have been able to create a social response, which has been not only in marked contrast to the position presented by Muslim politicians, but also represents an activism of the kind not seen in the Muslim community before. As seen in the case of JTSA, they are able to structure and build their arguments first in cyberspace through release of their fact-finding reports before presenting a cogent political challenge in the public spheres through demonstrations and press conferences that are reported and covered by mainstream media and circulated in realms outside the Muslim community. And it is not as if the mainstream media have stopped being powerful or the powers that condemn and target the minorities have attenuated in any way, because the criticism of the Special Cell of Delhi Police by JTSA was met with vehement opposition from the police, the government agencies, and the Hindu right wing forces (Tilak, 2012). Reading the vituperative intensity of some of the comments from the police and Hindu right wing activists, I even feared for the safety of JTSA's members. However, despite the persistence of the dominant narratives and of the powers that sustain them, what is new is that alternative viewpoints challenging their hegemony can no longer be completely smothered, as it was possible to do so before the popularization of Internet and digital communication technologies. The voices of the 'other' are able to find a way to be heard despite the prevalence of the old communication networks and their power fields.

Moreover, they are also able to seek and to recruit sympathetic alliances supportive of their struggles, to which they also contribute and support, thereby increasing their sphere of influence. For example, the JTSA's website has active links to other like-minded activist and media organizations. Among those featured is the People's Union for Civil Liberties, which has been involved in a long-drawn-out struggle for rights of tribal populations of India, whose homes, lives, and livelihood are being threatened by inexorable demands for development. Mining corporations' relentless destruction of forests has forced them out of spaces which have been their homes for millennia. One of the other organizations is the Human Rights Watch, an international non-profit agency with employees across the globe that observes and reports on human rights violations worldwide. I take special note of the connection to the website of Two Circles, not only because it is among the few websites run by Muslims, but also because it exemplifies how new media technologies have made it feasible to report on matters affecting the Muslims on a daily basis—giving them a voice, and I believe also a new confidence to be. The low cost of production of news and relatively inexpensive options of webhosting make it possible for them to exist in the same space as the mainstream big budget new businesses that were once perceived to be invincible. But according to Saira, a student of Jamia University and a resident of Jamia, today Two Circles is considered as among the most reliable source of information on Muslim affairs. The distinction of being 'most reliable' was once ascribed to the BBC, and it is no small matter that in such a short time, this honour should be claimed by an organization run on almost shoe-string budget with journalists who excel in their dedication but not necessarily in their training. According to Kashif, the editor who lives in Boston and works full time in pharmaceuticals and part-time and pro-bono for Two Circles, he and his team of journalists and photographers are situated in different parts of India. But, the rapid spread of Internet connectivity in India beyond the metropolitan hubs to smaller towns and even semi-rural areas, has ensured that despite vast geographical distances and different time zones all of them can be on the same page and work together to create a credible news organization. Kashif's evening is typically spent in editing and posting on the website stories that he receives from his team in India, where the day has just begun. Their budget is almost negligible, totally drawn from donations and advertisements posted on the site, and yet they are able to manage as they have no overhead costs associated with hiring of office space. The work stations in the age of new communication technologies are flexible, and most people associated with the news website work out of their homes. But despite their constraints, they are able to speak to emerging Muslim middle and even lower middle-classes aspiring for upward mobility. And as the stories are all written in English, and often translated into English to ensure accessibility to a global audience, it enables the Muslim diaspora as well as Indian Muslims in all corners of the country to come together on a common platform. But this is not to say that a cohesive community has emerged, because despite possibilities for greater connectivity it is not as if the local and global have effortlessly merged.

It is a complex situation, wherein as Adil Mehdi laments that even as it has become possible to forge bonds across the world, it is often difficult to involve the entire community of Jamia or generate a consensus within this localized population. For example, some members of JTSA feel that the import of their work is not adequately understood or valued within the Jamia community. Expressing his frustration at the situation, Adil Mehdi vented, '[there is] a lot of rage at the burning of the pages of the Quran, but where is the anger when young boys are dying?'(personal communication, December 2012). He said that often at their events, it is difficult to get even the faculty involved, and pointing to the gathering for the release of the report *The SIMI Trial of Jaipur*, he said, 'there are 600 faculty members in this university, do count how many of them are present here today' (personal communication, January 2012). However, it must also be acknowledged that there is both a generational and an educational gap working here, because while most of the members of JTSA are relatively young, in their 30s and 40s, they also represent the injunction of fresh blood into Jamia University from other educational centres of excellence, such as Jawaharlal Nehru University. Their appointment is reflective of the larger change within the university itself, which was bound to follow surely, though very slowly, once it had been declared a Central University. Hence, in many ways the members of JTSA represents an intellectual crème, which not only understands the risks but also comprehends the greater perils of inaction.

There is no denying the fact that the question of surveillance of Muslim community is an important factor deterring the community from actively participating at events and protest meeting. There is an underlining fear which even the members of JTSA acknowledge, as Arundhati Roy said at the release of the report *Framed Damned and Acquitted* (as quoted in Tilak, 2012), 'this is all about power, and abuse of power.' And if that is the case then these young scholars would have no protection, if even a celebrity like Roy, has been threatened with arrest by the Home Ministry on her speech about Kashmir. In fact, when I asked Adil Mehdi how the announcements about their meetings were received in the university, he smiled and said nothing. And I persisted and asked if I was rubbing shoulders with the secret police at this particular meeting, he smiled again and said, 'well nothing has happened up till now,' perhaps indicating that none of them had been arrested till date, and which told me a lot about the state of affairs for a minority population in the world's largest democracy. But the fear of the state notwithstanding, according to Kashif, the situation is such that there is no choice, 'Muslims have to speak,' and according to him the middle-class Muslims who had presumed that they were safe in their elite circles are coming to realize that this not so. It is the coming to terms with their own vulnerability, which is compelling middle class Muslim to voice their opinion and to tell their stories. The newfound expressiveness of middle class Muslims in digital public spheres cannot remain. My next project is to map the stories that emerge in the digital spheres from various sections of Muslim society in the run up to parliamentary elections in India in 2014. I am interested in understanding if Muslims will articulate their demands and stake their claim as rightful citizens of India. Moreover, how will these demands be projected, that is, what will be the language and the strategy and who will they address? There has been a lot interest in understanding how digital media has impacted political and civic participation (see, Anduiza, Jensen, & Jorba, 2012; Chadwick, 2012 & 2006; Cantijoch, 2012; Hamilton & Tolbert, 2012; Jensen & Anduiza, 2012); and in the wake of recent events in the Islamic worlds from Algeria to Egypt, the use of digital technology in Islamic societies has become a new area of focus. But there is a qualitative difference between these studies and my future project, because instead of being concerned with the trends in online participation, or the relationships between online participation and voting behaviour, I am involved with understanding how emancipating possibilities of the digital spaces are being imagined by those at the other end of the power spectrum. I wish to map how digital spheres enable members of a marginalized community to shift their position from being a victimized subject to that of potential challengers and even haranguers striving to exert their hitherto invisible presence and point of view. I am interested in seeing what are the stories that a marginalized population tells about itself, how will they frame their demand for justice, and what will be the signification of their rhetoric to their position as citizens of India and as Muslims?

Notes

1. According to Federation of Indian Chambers and Commerce report for the year 2011, the media have grown at nearly 13 per cent annually in the past decade, a figure far surpassing growth rates for Indian economy at 6 to 7 per cent.

2. Nick Couldry (2008) has criticized the stress on media technologies alone in constructing transformations of society as articulated in the concept of 'mediatization' proposed by Stig Hjarvard (2007) and Winfried Schulz (2004). He argues that though the 'theory of mediatization insists that wider consequences follow from this regular dependence of zones of social or cultural activity on media exposure,' this 'linear nature' of the singular underlying logic is in capable of explaining the 'complex dynamics of the interrelations between media and other fields' or the 'heterogeneity of the transformations in question' (Couldry, 2008, p. 378). He proposes drawing on Bourdieu's (1993) field theory that social spaces are multi-polar and to understand 'the multi-directionality of how media may be transforming society' it is necessary to work with an open-ended and flexible concept like mediation.

3. The identifications with a state lack, which were once an important plank of Indian nation building and of national identity, and which were con-sciously embodied by Indian political and social elites in their khadi clothes and modest demeanours, have now been entirely dispensed with. Today, the projects of individual, communal, political identities (Rajagopal, 2001) as well as notions of gendered identities and sexuality (Mankekar, 2004) are refracted through the lens of consumerist desires.

4. See Mendelson & Papacharissi (2011) for examination of Facebook self representations.

5. Even as one balks at the undermining of the potential of the cyber spheres when youth define themselves within and through Facebook provided categories and options such as the books they like and music they endorse, they tilt the scales in favour of a Western cultural ethos notwithstanding immense global diversity.

6. According to Castells (1997), the dissonance at the micro and individual level is a reflection of the larger structural disconnections at the levels of 'power-making in the global networks and the logic of association and representation in specific societies and cultures,' which leads to the disintegration of civil society, creating an unpredictable, hostile, unstable but networked world where 'the search for meaning takes place . . . in the reconstruction of defensive identities around communal principles' (1997, p. 11).

7. Nick Couldry (2008) has argued the relative usefulness of the concepts in explaining the role digital story telling in contemporary networked democratic societies.

8. Most studies of political participation and online engagement have been concerned with mapping with a certain exactitude the types and nature of the online alliances, the age, income, educational demographics of the participants as well as their motivation, and to determine whether the online networks encourage and motivate new participants or if they are just new ways for politically engaged people to communicate and network (see Jorba & Bimber, 2012 for a detailed overview of trends and theoretical concerns in Internet research). The studies, which address the concerns of political campaigners and analysts seeking to understand whether online engagement reinforces or motivates political participation, and if it constitutes a qualitatively new kind of engagement have been largely centered on political domains of the United States and UK and there are as yet few from across the world even if the Internet is a global phenomenon.

9. According to Metcalf (1995), it was the British who first presumed the existence of 'self-conscious communities' of 'Hindus' and 'Muslims,' which their colonial practices then 'systematically institutionalized' through indices of measurement, including 'census and ethnographic surveys' which highlighted religion as a defining category in a way not applicable to Britain at all (1995, p. 954).

10. Metcalf (1995) argues that the Orientalist colonial histories of India, which highlighted notions of an authentic and glorious Indian (Hindu) Golden age and attributed its end to the coming of the Muslims in eleventh century, were appropriated by Indian nationalists not only to explain India's

later subjugation under British colonial rule, but also to inspire nationalist struggles in the hope of recapturing and reinstituting the past glories
(1995, p. 954). Therefore, the nationalist discourses were not only heavily
seeped in Hindu iconography, symbolism, and ideologies, overlooking the
Muslim contributions to Indian culture and everyday life, but the striving
for a pure Hindu civilization actively discredited and silenced the long
historical Muslim presence in India (also see Chakravorty, 1994).

11. A fact which is clearly indicated by the highest percentage of self-employ-
ment figures for the Muslim community as compared to any other community in India (Sachar Committee, 2006).

12. According to Shani (2007), the effects of growing discontent were felt
in the electoral defeats of the incumbent BJP government in *panchayat*,
municipal, and assembly elections between 2000 and 2002 in Gujarat. But,
the BJP, heavily invested in the myth of the united Hindu front, and with
the intention of tiding over this crisis, brought in Modi as 'a defender of
Hindu faith,' and within two months communal riots broke out as Modi
instituted BJP's larger strategy of obfuscating dissent within the community by evoking the threat posed by the Muslim 'other' (Shani 2007: 181).

13. Brauchler's argument (2013) is based on his study of the conflict in
Moluccan Islands in Indonesia. The conflict has not received any attention
in mainstream media. However, the people involved in the conflict have
used the Internet to talk about the conflict and to draw attention to their
experiences. They have successfully put out in to the public sphere their
point of view, and their suffering are no longer a negated or obfuscated
reality.

14. Castells' (1996) detailed historical analysis of the interrelations between
technology, economy, and society in different epochs and contexts is
extremely pertinent to understanding how technology, economy, and
polity have intersected and created conditions for either exploitation or
suppression of their potentialities leading to the very trajectories of development.

15. Castells' (1996) argument is that while people do still live in places but
power is organized in the 'space of flows' such that its structural dominance alters the meaning and dynamics of places and that 'experience, by
being related to places, becomes abstracted from power, and meaning is
increasingly separated from knowledge' (p. 459).

3

MUSLIM WOMEN NEGOTIATING MODERNITY AND ISLAM

The narratives of Muslim women's victimhood have been essential to both imperialist as well as chauvinist nationalist projects. The neat icon of a veiled and subjugated Muslim woman not only reifies Islam as a retrograde and rigid religion, but also helps identify Muslims across the globe, notwithstanding their inherent diversity, as intrinsically backward and conservative communities. More importantly, the emblem of the oppressed Muslim woman has been repeatedly deployed in self-righteous imperialist projects, wherein the task of saving passive and pliant Muslim women from their own people has helped conceal real power dynamics and messy politics motivating and guiding the exploitation of these images and discourses (see Abu-Lughod, 2002).[1] Similarly, in the Indian context, the *burqa* clad Muslim woman not only hails the Indian Muslim community into place as an inward-looking and disaffected minority, but her veiled persona also helps explain the community's poor state of affairs, while obfuscating historical injustices and embedded structural and social discriminatory regimes encountered by Muslims in their everyday lives. In addition, the Muslim community's abject state of affairs as reflected in the Muslim women's disregarded and impoverished status also provides the rationale validating the Hindu hegemonic identity, because how can a community incapable of according dignity and justice to almost half of its members ask for equitable treatment in the Indian national public spheres. The assumptions of Muslim women's victimhood are intrinsic to upholding the

Muslim 'otherness' and to instituting their second-class citizen status, relegating them to the margins of Indian society.

And such is the entrenched power of Muslim women's presumed victimhood that even liberal and socially conscious scholarship is unable to effectively negate its suppositions. Rather, their arguments continue to evoke its framework as well as to perpetuate impressions of Muslim women's lack of agency. Concerned with alleviating the Muslim women's doubly marginalized status within Indian democratic public spheres—as neglected members of a dispossessed minority, Shahida Lateef (1983) argues that 'the tensions and strains, which development activity specific to modernization can produce in a minority community, is magnified for the women of the community, making them vulnerable to pressures from within and outside the community'(1983: 182). A substantial body of research largely from the social-scientific perspective has been devoted to identifying and evaluating the debilitating circumstances facing Indian Muslim women and addressing their historical neglect. These studies draw attention to structural, social, legal, political, and economic constraints facing Muslim women, and map the Muslim women's level of education, employment, and health status, while critiquing secular and religious laws which constructed and rule their lives[2] (see Das, 2005; Fazalbhoy, 2005; Haniff, 1983; Hasan, 1994; Hasan & Menon, 2004 & 2005; Lateef, 1983 & 1994; Siddiqui, 2005; Singh, 1994; Vatuk, 2005). Their aim is to effect social change by providing important indicators for policy review and analysis. However, not only is the consciousness of an Indian Muslim woman hard to decipher in these accounts, but the category of the Muslim woman, which emerges from this analysis, is but a residual afterthought or an effect of the larger structural forces.[3] The Muslim woman is always seen as being at the receiving end of elemental factors, but never a as master of her own destiny.

However, even if the sociological and quantitatively inclined scholarship, in its zeal to present an overarching picture of the Indian Muslim community, has failed to delineate the Indian Muslim woman's subjectivity and the manner in which it emerges from within her everyday life and struggles, the literary and humanist approaches have proved to be equally inadequate to the task. And this despite the overwhelming focus in postcolonial and cultural studies on identifying agency and resistance. I argue that this is because they evoke and seek the Muslim

woman and her capacities for opposition in discursive spheres of literary and artistic representations rather than in lived experiences of
real Muslim women (see, Kazmi, 1994; Kesavan, 1994; Mufti, 2000).[4]
Exhibiting a tendency, which Abu-Lughod (1991) describes as speaking 'for' and not speaking 'from' the Indian Muslim women's perspective, the literary-humanist scholarship qualifies more as a case of what
Benita Parry (1987) refers to as 'exorbitation' or exaggeration of the
literary critics role in giving a voice to the subaltern, rather than serving
as a window into the world of the subaltern itself.

In the event of a paucity of ethnographic research exploring the
Indian Muslim women's subjectivities, and considering the scholarship's lack of tactile connection to Muslim women's everyday lives,
practices, and deportment, the stultification of Indian Muslim women
as signifiers of the community's identity and of its distinctiveness
continues to persist. And although Hasan and Menon (2005) hold the
Indian state responsible for making Muslim women's status so central
to Indian Muslim identity—by unduly supporting patriarchal structures and religious ideologues, and by ignoring the more progressive
consensus advocating change within the community, the fact is that
the authoritative discourses reducing Muslim women's lives as mere
emblematic constructs have not been addressed, let alone successfully
challenged. The Muslim women's existence continues to be smothered
under their crushing weight.

And, it is to unearth their lives from within this discursive clutter of
victimhood and 'otherness' that this project seeks the Indian Muslim
women's realities from their own perspective and in their own voices.
But more importantly, I endeavour to understand their experiences in
contemporary volatile contexts to argue that if the churnings in the
Indian Muslim community created by rising ambitions and desires for a
greater stake in mainstream economic and social spheres, as argued earlier, are to be understood, then the Muslim women's gendered realities
are the most illustrative site to represent the ongoing struggles between
rootedness of entrenched traditions and sway of new ideas and ideologies (see, Sunder Rajan,1993). Turning on its head, established arguments that the Muslim women's lives speak of the community's state of
malaise, I contend that it is the Muslim women's emerging subjectivity
which provides a searing insight into the Muslim community' impulse
for change and into their complex emerging modernities. Indeed, it was

the paradoxes and contradictions of the Muslim community's evolving position in neoliberal globalized India as explicitly staged and clearly elicited in the Muslim women's deportments, which often baffled me and in turn impelled me to study the gender equation as being integral to the Muslim youth's shifting ideological position. Hence, while I too view Muslim women's experiences as being central to the Muslim community's emerging consciousness, the difference is that rather than marking Muslim women as passive signifiers, I examine their struggles as being implicit in construction of the new Muslim communal and individual identity and equation within neoliberal globalized India.

Muslim Women's Lives: Contradictions and Paradoxes

In my encounter with Muslim women across the social spectrum, I am faced with recurring occurrences of both situations and instances of emerging subjectivities, which defy neat dichotomy between agency and victimhood, orthodoxy, and modernity ,while creating an uncertainty regarding the Muslim community's direction of change. For example, even as I meet many more young Muslim women than ever before in technical and professional departments of Jamia University, validating the general desire among Muslim youth population to participate in mainstream economic and social spheres, there is no denying the fact that there is a surge in the number of young Muslim women wearing the veil, the *hijab*, or the *abaya* (as worn by the women in the Middle East) on the university campus than ever before (or when I had left in 1996 to return in 2007). I am forced to make sense of a situation wherein young women, even as they purposefully and passionately pursue new academic fields and career ambitions (something that was rare among Muslim middle and especially lower middle classes a decade and a half ago), they also confidently assay symbols associated with tradition and patriarchy, indicating acquiescence and a lack of agency. Moreover, notwithstanding dominant stereotypes about the Muslim community's financial and social backwardness, and about the overwhelming prevalence of patriarchal norms within the Muslim society, which are alleged to have stymied the women's educational and professional dreams of participation in mainstream Indian society,[5] I encountered the Muslim women's significant presence in new spaces of India's neoliberal globalized consumerist modernity.

It has become fairly commonplace today to see veiled Muslim women from Jamia enclave participating in middle class activities of leisure and consumption in the New Friends Colony community market, which is less than half a mile away from the exclusively Muslim enclave. I have often seen them sitting in the McDonalds' outlet, or sipping coffee with a group of friends in an upmarket coffee shop, or watching a movie in the company of both male and female friends in the cineplex, where ticket prices at 250 to 300 Rupees (five or six dollars) seem very steep to me. But, even as I grapple with their presence in spaces where *burkha* clad or veiled women, with all their connotative associations of poverty, illiteracy, and social backwardness, have not ventured before, and even as I work with the contradictions between Muslim women's rising ambitions and common stereotypes about the traditional Muslim community, I am most baffled by Muslim women's self-presentations as exemplary Islamic subjects, while they fervently pursue ideals of outstanding educational qualification, financial independence, and consumerist modernity.

From Passive to Active Signifiers

The growing presence of Muslim women draped in attires signifying idealized Islamic identity in spaces of modernity is most striking, and even the performance of a religious identity with élan in modern contexts is equally baffling. And to elaborate the extent and depth of change that has occurred in Muslim women's expression of Islamic subjectivities over the short period of a decade and a little more, I first recount my experience at my former alma mater, the Anwar Jamal Kidwai Mass Communication Research Centre (hitherto MCRC), an institution well known for its secular credentials and its left-wing political leanings. The cosmopolitan and secular identifications of the institute have been maintained by the presence of a faculty drawn from the world over[6] and by the fact that the institute in its early formative years enjoyed and maintained a certain level of autonomy vis a vis the larger university. In the early 1990s, and at the time of my association with the institute, there were only a few Muslim students, and none of us would ever draw attention to the particularities of our religious identity, despite being situated within the larger campus of a university with Islamic roots and affiliations. Instead, all of us would adhere to the grueling and demanding schedule—spending days and nights in production and editing studios without breaking for *namaz* or making any special concessions for ourselves even when fasting in the month of *Ramazan*. I can argue that we were evasive, if not outright self-conscious about our Islamic identity, notwithstanding the fact that most of the staff members, if not the faculty members, still are and were largely Muslim. However, an event that I recently witnessed within the institute's precincts, where as I remember religion was never allowed to be an identifying equation, and where a bohemian and an almost irreligious subjectivity was celebrated and even upheld among the student population, leads me to argue that there has been a fundamental shift not only in the way Islamic identity is being articulated in public spheres, but in the way Muslim women are fulfilling their symbolic and emblematic role.

It was the month of *Ramazan* of the year 2010 when I had been invited to give a lecture at the AJK MCRC on the evolving political economy of Indian media. But it was not a Friday or any time close to the final days of the holy month. However, after my lecture, which ended at about 1 p.m., I noticed a flurry, as a number of young women hurriedly left the room, even as some students came forward to engage me in a conversation. I noticed that a short while later this group of about 10 women returned with freshly washed faces. It was obvious that they had just done their *wuzu* (the compulsory ablutions before the *namaz*). Among them, there were only two who were veiled, and whose Muslim identity was clearly discernable, while others, dressed as they were in regular *salwar-kameez* and even jeans, were indistinguishable from other girls in the class. I must admit I was quite astounded to see such a large group of Muslim women in one class, when I remember being the only Muslim woman among my cohorts. And even though the class size at 49 students had almost tripled since when I was a student, the percentage of Muslim women with respect to the total class size was still substantially high. Moreover, their presence was quite remarkable, especially as this institute has trained some of the best broadcast-journalists, filmmakers, film directors, and editors in India; and being admitted to the institute implies that these Muslim women must have displayed strong academic as well as personal skills to qualify the highly competitive entrance exam. But, what surprised me even more was how at this moment there they were so concerned with making some space to pray by quickly and quietly pushing aside a few of the tables, even as they dug into their copious bags to fish out prayer mats and head-coverings. There was a spirit of camaraderie and support which was both touching and amusing, especially as they whisked off from each other all kinds of scarves and *duppattas* as well as fabric pieces serving as prayer rugs to offer their prayers in turns. And the two girls who were dressed in jeans even shared a large triangular scarf which they tied around their waist as they offered their four *faraz rakats* (mandatory set of Quranic verses) one after the other. The motley crowd, dressed in large mismatched *duppattas* or scarves got around the difficulties and constrains and most unselfconsciously and ardently offered their *zohar* (mid-day) prayers. They were not the least bit concerned that there were other people still around in the classroom or that this was not really a private space.

This was very different from the caginess and a certain awkwardness, which I recollect experiencing regarding my Islamic identity at the institute till the mid- 1990s. And this was a general and more pervasive feeling shared by other Muslim students as Yousuf, an alumni and who graduated a few years after me, said, corroborating my viewpoint, that he had never seen Muslim students, male or female, offering their prayers on the campus. According to him, in all his years at MCRC it was but once that he had seen young women offer their *namaz* on the campus lawns. And that too on the final Friday of the month of *Ramazan*, an especially important day when even those who may not have fasted the entire month make it a point to commemorate its spirit, abstain from food, and bow down in prayer. It was on that special day, when the few Muslim male students had accompanied the many staff members of the institute to the mosque, that he saw his three classmates retreat to the very edge of the less frequented lawn to say their *namaz* in the shade of a tree, and in complete privacy, away from public glare. But, the young women that I have been meeting at the institute now are completely uninhibited, defying my memories of silence and evasiveness regarding my Islamic identity.

However, my infinite surprise at such display of affinity to Islam within the institute's secular and westernized ambience, as well as at the presence of so many Muslim women within such elitist and haloed educational settings, was also marred by certain simplifications regarding class and religiosity that have been entrenched in my mind. It has been generally assumed within the Muslim community that while the middle and upper-middle class Muslims are not so keen to announce their religious affiliations, and instead try to blend into the secular milieu, the lower-middle-class Muslims are presumed to being more adamant about proclaiming their religious identity. And while it is true that most of the students of MCRC, who are drawn from some of the best undergraduate institutions across India, tend to be more middle and upper middle class as compared to students in other departments of Jamia University who are mostly from lower middle to aspiring middle classes, I witness that the current contexts are obfuscating such neat demarcations between expected behaviour patterns of different social classes. The young women at MCRC were just as conscientious about their religious obligations as young women in other departments of the university, whom I have also often seen offering their prayers in the empty classrooms and staffrooms of the university, but whose behaviour had not astonished me to such an extent.

But the most important reason for my amazement at the young women's behaviour across class divides was—how would such a deep sense of commitment to their religious obligations complicate their ambitions to participate in extremely difficult and competitive economic spheres and especially the media industry? Initially, I was inclined to believe that the young women in Jamia University and at MCRC were comfortable and not the least bit self-conscious about displaying their Islamic identity in a space such as the Jamia University because of its roots in Islamic traditions and prescriptive morality, and perhaps this would not be the case once they joined the professional world. But to my even greater surprise, many young women, graduates and alumni of Jamia University, and now employed in various sectors of the professional world confided to me that they do continue to offer their *zohar* (mid-day prayer) and *asar* (mid-afternoon prayer) *namaz* in their offices. And though I do admit that most of the young women who shared these confessions were from aspiring middle-class families, recently migrated from smaller towns of Uttar Pradesh and Bihar to Jamia enclave, there were still quite a few young women from middle-class families who also professed to be doing the same. Moreover, challenging old shibboleths, I found no difference in the intensity of their ambitions to work for the multinational corporations, notwithstanding, the difference in access to educational facilities as well as to all the other privileges associated with higher social classes. But what I consistently encountered in the current contexts rife with hostilities toward Islam that can potentially jeopardize individual ambitions, was the co-existence of an intense desire for success accompanied by unabashed articulations of the Islamic identity.

Speaking to Shazia, a young woman of about twenty years employed with a multinational mobile phone company while continuing her education in electronic engineering by taking evening classes, I was immensely impressed with the confidence with which she approached her work environment and described it as congenial and supportive. But Shazia is also a person who has an immense capacity for hard work and an infinite faith in the adage that hard work pays. She has set her mind to overcome her innumerable hurdles, be it lack of access to elite education or fluency in the English language.

> Ruhi: Shazia, you are very efficient, how is your English speaking coming along? You had said that hard work can achieve anything, and I still remember that, and I am very proud of you.
>
> Shazia :Thank you, it is coming fine.
>
> Ruhi: Tell me in English about your job, your colleagues....
>
> Shazia: I used to do testing of the mobile phones, to check, if the software is working properly, if it is not malfunctioning.
>
> Ruhi : And your colleagues, how are they? Do you ever feel that because you are a girl and a Muslim...is there is any discrimination?
>
> Shazia: No they are very nice. They are very supportive and they make us learn many things. Like I offer *namaz* in the office and they never say anything.
>
> Ruhi : How long does it take you to say your prayers?
>
> Shazia: It takes 10 minutes.
>
> Ruhi : That is all.
>
> Shazia: Yes. (personal communication, August 2010)

But Shazia's positive experience was not shared by everyone, pointing to the existence of an ambivalent situation in mainstream economic and professional spheres, wherein cultures of meritocracy, valuing and identifying individuals for their work, co-exist with outright distaste for

Islam as well as with secularist intolerance for display of religion in public places. Some of my informants found themselves isolated for publicly practicing their religion. According to Azra who is a Human Resource manager in a major multinational mobile phone provider, 'It is not nice. Some men complained that I use the conference room to pray. But it is empty when I use it and it is my lunchtime. This company is very stingy...lots of people are leaving' (personal communication, November, 2010). But undeterred by the hostile environment she has faced at one work place, she was planning to leave that job and look for another at the time when I met her, exemplifying the general trend among the younger generations to be constantly mobile and always on the lookout for new opportunities instead of faithfully serving in one job for many years. And it is these increasing interconnections between Muslim women's new choices and the extant conditions and opportunities in a neoliberal market economy that I focus on. I am less interested in how Muslims may be perceived in their work place by their colleagues, even though the offering of daily prayers by Muslim women in professional and secular settings is a completely new phenomenon—an event that I have never seen or heard of before in my entire working life in India.

My intent is to understand why Muslim women are choosing to express their religious identity in public spaces now, when such hostilities towards Islam are so palpable? What events or circumstances are making this performance possible? How have the Indian Muslim women transformed from being mere passive signifiers of the community's identity, especially of its backwardness and of its inability, to embrace modernity, to being active articulators of Islamic identity, through their dress, demeanour, and practices? And my larger argument is that if Muslim women are now framing and rearticulating a new politics of presence and affirmation of Islamic identity in a way never attempted before in Indian public spheres, then this assertion of gendered Islamic bodies in spheres of modernity points to the evolution of Muslim minority identity politics in Indian democratic political spheres in a potentially new direction.

Post-colonial Scholarship and Questions of Agency

However, before approaching the issue of communal identity, it is first important to understand whether the Muslim women's current stance can be unequivocally perceived as representing a new position of agency versus their old passiveness? I turn to postcolonial feminist scholarship, which has grappled with the struggles between modernity and tradition and the question of women's agency as it emerges from within these contestations in contexts of postcolonial modernities. However, I find myself at loss as the dominant trend in postcolonial scholarship has been to seek instances of feminist agency, as well as, of victimhood in discursive spheres of literary and cinematic texts and in the lives of 'imagined' women rather than within real world and lived experiences of women within postcolonial nations (see, Sunder Rajan, 1993; John, 1998; Mankekar, 1999a; Mazzarella, 2003; Oza, 2006; Thuru, 1999/2001). Moreover, Muslim women's experiences have scarcely been explored in this large body of scholarship and in rare instances when they have been discussed, it has been mainly in representative literary and cinematic spheres again. For example, Amir Mufti's (2000) poignant evocation of the prostitutes resurgent womanhood in Sadat Hasan Manto's short stories, or even Mukul Kesavan's (1994) recognition and celebration of the Muslim courtesan's spirit and joie d' vivre in Hindi cinema, have very little to say about the ordinary Muslim women's experiences or struggles. Moreover, the postcolonial feminist scholarship's ideologically driven pursuits to seek 'the (re)constitution of female subjectivity in the interest of feminist praxis' (Sunder Rajan, 1993, p. 5) makes the identification of agency less problematic, especially when it is being explored within contained spheres of representation, where limits of credibility can be infinitely stretched.[7] And even more problematic is that the overwhelming focus on agency reduces all other responses to being either a lack of agency or the subjugation of individuality, perpetuating the very dichotomies and simplifications, which the scholarship had set out to address and negate (see Sunder Rajan, 1993). Moreover, the postcolonial feminist scholarship's critiques of the binary framework defining women as either victims or as agents like the celebrations of agency make no reference to the socio-economic conditions in which subjectivities are created or even enforced. In the absence of an organic link between social-cultural realms and political-economic contexts, the imaginations and descriptions of agency and denunciations of victimhood remain an ideological exercise, not given to illuminating extant conditions.

This is especially notable because in the complex spaces of lived experiences, constructed at the crosscutting junctures of myriad influences and motivations, as evidenced in the multifaceted transformations that I am witnessing in various spheres of Muslim women's everyday life, agency is not always the most obvious reading, even if it is equally difficult to unequivocally identify the oppression of patriarchy and the stymieing force of tradition. I argue that it is time now to move beyond discussions of agency and victimhood, which have substantially engaged postcolonial feminist scholarship in the wake of Chandra Talpade Mohanty's (1991[2012]) seminal article critiquing Western feminist scholarship for perceiving third-world women as a coherent group of victims.[8] I intend to examine in the words of Mohanty ' how the category of [Muslim] woman is constructed in a variety of political [and socio-economic] contexts that often exist simultaneously and [are] overlaid on top of one another,' thereby preventing any generalization about emerging subjectivities, or reductionism with regard to the possible explanations regarding their emergence (1991 [2012], pp. 355–6).The point is to see how Muslim women's agency or lack of it emerges as a result of complex negotiations with evolving socio-economic political contexts of neoliberal globalization. And to drive home my point a little more forcefully I present what may seem to be an extreme or an isolated example, but which nonetheless exemplifies the complex flow of currents created by the salience of mediated interactions and an enhanced imagination, as well as, by the increased possibilities of travel, migration, and employment created by neoliberal globalization. Consider my description of an event which occurred one Saturday winter evening of January 2011 in Connaught Place, one of the busiest shopping centres and a hangout place for Delhi' youth, which reinstates my argument that the Muslim women's complex subjectivities are not only reflective of the Muslim community's current circumstances but that they also provide a glimpse into their future.

Aggressive Articulations

Connaught place was packed with weekend crowds drawn to sales and events in the pre-holiday season and my mother and I were also shopping and enjoying the balmy weather, when tired by our forays we drifted towards a fast-food chain of restaurants famous for their ice-creams and pizzas. After digging through the crowd to get our ice-creams, we stood under the awnings outside the restaurant along with many others to enjoy our little treat before venturing back home as the sun was setting. It was then that I noticed a young woman, not far from us, dressed in black, who took some newspapers out of her bag and spread them out on the floor before her. Then quickly she took off her shoes and before I could blink I realized she was saying her *magrib namaz*. This act of a young Muslim women praying in a public space with such a high incidence of footfalls of almost entirely middle class Hindu population is almost like praying in the eye of the storm. And if I was surprised, the people around us were even more so, and many a gaze was raised from the ice-cream cups and cones to look at her in stunned silence. It was only a little later that I noticed that two other young women dressed in salwar kameez, and a young boy and an older gentleman accompanied her. Her companions were completely indiscernible from the rest of the crowd. They had the same middle class presence and none of them were dressed in Islamic attire. But by the way they stood around her and waited for her to finish indicated that even they were feeling deeply uncomfortable. Her three *rakat* prayers did not take too long, perhaps all of five minutes but I felt that these were the longest five minutes ever. And while no one in the mainly middle-class crowd really said anything, the tension in the air was palpable. I could almost hear everyone's thought, 'Just what is this woman doing?' and I was not only acutely embarrassed but also a bit scared, mindful of the hostilities against Islam given the resurgence of Hindu nationalism. However, my mother was absolutely furious, especially when she saw some children point to the young woman and laugh, but her reasons were very different from mine. Expressing her anguish at what she thought was the young woman's immodesty, she said, '*aurtain tau chup kar kisi kone me ja kar namaz padti hai. Yeh kya behudgi hai, namaz kaza bhi tau padi jati hai*' [women hide from plain site and offer their prayers in seclusion and privacy. And this is indecency, you can read your *namaz* late too'] (personal communication, January 2011). Stressing the viewpoint of the older generation of middle class Muslims, her argument was that when women in India do not as a norm even go to the mosque to pray, and perform all their religious observations away from the public gaze, what was the young woman's intention in this public display of religiosity? For my mother the performance almost bordered on the obscene—akin to the vulgar display of affection in public.

However, I was fascinated by what I discerned to be defiance in the young woman's decision to pray in such a congested spot and by the way she stood her ground, even if some people silently ridiculed her and perhaps even hated her. I know it must have taken some courage, but what motivated her to take on upon herself the task of instating the Islamic identity? I could not ask her this question or engage in any conversation with her family because of my mother's annoyance, but could only read into her motives by examining the outward signals emanating from her person. I could see from the imitation Gucci bag kept by her side, from the style of draping her headscarf, and from the gold bangles that peeped out from under the long black sleeves of her black robe, cut and styled like the *abaya* worn by women in the Middle East, that perhaps she was a migrant or a traveler from these parts who was visiting her family in India. But, then even women in the Middle East would not attempt to pray in a crowded mall or shopping center. And although I have seen women in Dubai and Kuwait offer their prayers on the beach, or in the park, but they too would retreat for that purpose to more secluded corners. The sight of an Indian Muslim woman praying so openly in the public eye, was indeed unique, and though it may be easy to dismiss it as an irrational or 'one-off' behaviour, it is important nonetheless for the way it disturbed the hegemonic Hindu nationalist identity, as well as, the sensibilities of the Muslim onlookers as elicited in my mother's sense of shock and outrage.

This bold exhibition of individuality not only confidently refuted the silence and invisibility endorsed for Muslims as second-class citizens, but in the light of the disruptions that it caused, I argue that it is to be read as a statement for belonging and therefore analyzed as a political speech. Her purposeful presentation of a shuttered identity, especially one mired in negative stereotypes as unprogressive and stagnating in broad day light complicates the discussion of Muslim women's subjectivities as victims or agents, as modern-progressive subjects or as subjugated upholders of tradition. It also throws into great uncertainty opinions and views pointing to practices of veiling and *purdah* as hallmark of patriarchal authority, domestic violence, and general subjugation of Muslim woman.[9] But more importantly, if we are not to read the young woman's performance as an expression of Islamic piety alone, then the question is, what is the complex positionality being articulated here? And even more important is the question why has it become possible to articulate such a position today?

Reading into her performance and reminiscing how she calmly slipped back into her high-heeled sandals, picked up the newspaper, and discarding it in the trash can, walked away with her family holding her head with more poise and ease than they could muster to carry their ice-cream cups, I argue that her performance qualifies as experimentation with the range of subject positions now available to women in interconnected, globalized, and mediated worlds. And it is on this account alone that it cannot be disavowed as an absurd or bizarre act, because if she as an individual (aided by her personal predilections of higher social class or wealth) has presented a rather a spectacular example, average Muslim women are also exposed to varying degrees of the same influences. They all potentially represent subjectivities constructed at the cross-roads of westernized discourses of individuality, self-confident personhood, and agency which seem to seamlessly merge with increasing visibility of globalized Islam emanating from the entrepots of the Middle East, associated with wealth and material well-being. There is no doubt that her sense of élan owed not a little to her affluent status. But her behaviour, which disrupted many entrenched notions and expectations both of the Muslim community and about the Muslim community in the dominant Hindu community's minds, reflects the evolving position of Muslim women in the context of their appropriations and internalizations of myriad conflicting, competing, and contradictory discourses whose reverberations are being calibrated by multiple media platforms, as I will elaborate in the next section.

However, the explanatory framework for the Muslim women's emergent subjectivities cannot be predetermined, even if their difference from previous generations is clearly acknowledged. For example, to describe the young woman's performance, I cannot employ the vocabulary of 'the bold hybrid,' as used by postcolonial feminist scholars to speak of instances when women's positionality has shaken the established notions of women's role in Indian society—as when Miss World beauty pageant was first staged in India and images of semi-clad Indian women permeated the public spheres of semi-socialist traditional Indian society (see Parameswaran, 1994a & 1994b). This is because the young Muslim woman did not simply appropriate westernized notions of individuality or agency, but she internalized them from her own unique positionality—so much so that though in her performance of her Islamic identity she may seem to negate these very ideas, but the articulation of this identity was made possible by her active participation in ideas and spheres of modernity. I argue that even her will to assert her special understandings and her negotiations with modernity owed not a little to the values of individuality and agency, which she keenly ascribes to, but which both the onlookers and the academic scholars would argue that she stands in stark defiance of.

Consider the fact that the young woman did not seek the indefinable 'global cool' by either taking on westernized sartorial style of jeans, short skirts, or dresses or by participating in dating or courtship rituals,[10] rather she staged her distinctiveness and therefore her modernity by marking a clear disassociation with these symbols. In fact, she has turned on their head entrenched stereotypes regarding Muslim women as 'less emancipated, less progressive, and open-minded than Hindu women' and as 'representatives of an outdated form of patriarchy,' which forms a similar 'point of contrast' to middle class modernities as the 'low caste-class status' (Gilbertson, 2014, p. 132) by boldly calling them out, and thereby problematizing them. Therefore, what may seem as an unusually brave assertion of a religious identity is actually a statement of citizenship and belonging, and reflects a homegrown understanding of constitutional rights, especially the freedom of religion. And this understanding informs the sensibilities and consciousness of not only one individual person, but of all Muslim women who announce their Islamic identity through their dress or demeanour in the public spheres.

However, to faithfully deconstruct this complex performance and to understand what it entails, it is important to recognize that this play with symbols and ideologies is taking place within specific socioeconomic contexts of neoliberal globalized India offering new opportunities, even to the members of a disregarded minority, for employment, migration, and imaginations of selfhood, as aided by the permeance of mediated communication technologies in everyday life. My argument is that the Muslim youth's subjectivities are evolving within particular circumstances and socio-economic constrains and possibilities and that they cannot be theorized without reference to how people imagine themselves to be as well as what are the possibilities and constrains influencing the realization of their imagination.[11] And one of the most important aspect of the contemporary realities which also supports my argument for theorization from ground-up, is that the level of ambiguity introduced by the multiplicity of discourses, ideologies, and reference points, make the scholarship theorizing realities within binary oppositions such as between East and West, traditional and modern among others, redundant.

Contesting, Conflicting Discourses and Muslim Women's Subjectivities

The open-sky policies, which were instituted in the wake of liberalization of the Indian economy, have not only overhauled the media- scapes of Indian audiences, but they have also been inarguably embroiled in the extensive refurbishing of the Indian social, cultural, and political scapes by transforming what many scholars refer to as the force-field of imagination.[12] The extensive spread of media technologies and mediated content have introduced Indian audiences to rich and abundant commodity imagery, which scholars argue are creating an equally eventful situation—akin to the release of and coming to the surface of deep-rooted libidinal energies that validate rising materialism and consumerism in a formerly socialist and austere society (Mazzarella, 2003). And, one of the main concerns created by the undue prominence of such enticing and sensuous imagery has been how would encounters with such libidinous forces influence not only representation but also construction of gendered subjectivities (see John, 1998/2000; Mankekar, 2004; Mazzarella, 2003).This concern is pre-eminent, especially as scholars argue that there is evidence to show that the Indian culture and values are being redefined by the 'mutual imbrication of erotics and the yearning for commodities' (Mankekar, 2004, p. 410), and that there is a 'globalization of sexuality' or the adoption of more liberal attitudes towards expression of female sexuality (John, 1998/2000, p. 368; Mankekar, 2004). As the global media flows actively extend and reorganize the Indian audience's visual fields, these tendencies are clearly evidenced in the cinematic representations of gender and in the cultural and economic sphere of product advertising. According to John, the female leads of Bollywood cinema are no longer mere passive receptors of the male gaze, but they are prone to display 'a responsive, active and at times disturbing sexuality' of their own (1998/2000, p. 378), while Mazzarella (2003) argues that the marketing of culturally sensitive products tend to forcefully foreground women's needs, in such a way as to seriously challenge gender norms in Indian society[13].

The vortex of new iconography representing and situating Indian women within sexualized consumerist realms also speaks to Muslim women even if dominant discourses marking Muslim 'otherness' persist in framing Indian Muslim woman's lives strictly within religious practices and ideologies.[14] The images suggestive of women's assertiveness and sexuality are also Muslim women's ineluctable truth because there is no escaping them when they explode from multiple media outlets and implode everyday realities, creating bizarre juxtapositions as when hoardings and banners introducing myriad new product categories and beckoning Muslim consumers with images of scantily clad women are placed in shops and stores existing in close proximity to mosques and seminaries. In these sexually charged contexts, the experiences of Muslim women, which have been hitherto buried under the weight of tradition and patriarchy, but which have been so essential to constructing the question of Muslim difference or 'otherness'[15] would indeed be interesting. My question is what does it mean to be a Muslim woman today when sexualized images of Indian women, which had raised the ire of many factions resentful of the growing western influences[16] in the early phases of globalization, have now become routine? How do they think of themselves and in relation to their traditional society when events such as beauty pageants, which were once violently decried, are now packaged and presented with ease as 'modern ritual[s] of feminine achievement,' offering young women from staid middle-class families a chance to participate in Western modernity (see Parameswaran 2004b, p. 347). But, before I examine these questions and the Muslim women's experiences, it is important to consider whether the normalization of audacious and sexually provocative representations of women is indicative of any real transformation in the gendered hierarchies and if these images and ideas transgress, to any meaningful extent, the patriarchal norms of Indian society.

Govindan and Dutta (2008) argue that the suggestive and hybridized femininity, circulating in representational spaces, and registering the global flows in the sartorial styles and choreography of the gendered body, is actually quite restrictive and limiting. This is especially so since the 'sexualisation' of Indian women and the stress on 'feminine agency' in media narratives are driven by the imperative of recruiting women as consumers, and supporting the development of a consuming class in India(see Parameswaran 2004a & John,1998/2000). For example, the daring and sassy imagery, as first deployed in the advertisement for *Kamasutra* brand of condoms, even if it foregrounds women's sexual needs as Mazzarella (2003) argues, is less about women's empowerment and more about aggressive consumer marketing strategies for western products and services relentlessly peddled in India. The new hybridized Indian woman, which emerges in these constructs combining the energy and enterprise of Western femininity with the care giving qualities of the Indian women, exerts her agency only to the extent of being a competent consumer of global lifestyles and products (see Munshi,1998; Parameswaran, 2004a).

Hence, it is not surprising that alongside images of women's modernity (and its connotative ideas of progress and agency), there has been a resurgence of narratives celebrating the idealized (read submissive and self-effacing) Indian femininity in popular soap-operas on mainstream satellite television channels like Zee TV, STAR TV, and others today in 2013.[17] There appears to be a reversal of trend since Zee TV, twenty years ago in the wake of privatization and globalization of media, first introduced strong female lead characters who did not shy away from pursuing their dreams or making choices that pitted them against the patriarchal norms.[18] But today, according to Govindan and Dutta, the modernity promoted in mediated spheres does not challenge gender hierarchies or propose a change in the Indian women's position, rather 'the global flows of media products and the existing media ecology set the stage where a 'traditional' understanding of Indian womanhood, replete with references to archetypes such as Sita and Draupadi, is rehearsed for the contemporary era through global idioms' (2008, p. 181). Hence the consumerist modernity neither supports women's equality nor individualism, and it can at best be described as dubious.

However, even if the feminist posturing in mediated spheres is only in the interest of consumerist discourses, the emerging economic and employment sectors are creating conditions conducive to women's exercise of their will and agency. The expansion of the Indian economy, since liberalization, has created many new employment options for urban Indian women in the organized sector, and especially in the growing service industries, leading to women's increased participation in the work force (see, Chandrasekhar & Ghosh, 2007; Klaveren, Tijdens, Hughie-Williams & Martin, 2010). And, by participating in diverse economic initiatives and professions, the urban Indian women can now command greater financial wherewithal, that can enormously enhance their personal resources. But, it is the irony of the situation that the true import of women's substantially improved purchasing power should only be duly recognized by the manufacturing and advertising sectors. Taking cognizance of women as powerful consumers, the messages from advertising industry make the concession of addressing women differently—no longer assuming them to be passive, retreating, or diffident but capable of taking charge and making decisions (John, 1998/2000). However, the rather superficial deployment of women's agency in the service of consumptive materialism has only entailed the creation of a wider gap between the images dominating the mediated spaces and the realities of women's lives within a society in transition.

Yet, it is possible to assert that even if patriarchal values have not been adequately challenged, they are nonetheless under considerable pressure. There is no denying the fact that there have been significant changes in the lifestyles of urban Indian women, which facilitate their participation in Westernized spaces of modernity, beyond those created by consumer-marketing strategies. The liberalization of the Indian economy has not only created new employment opportunities for educated and trained urban women in the IT sector, export-oriented industries, and the service sectors—including call-centers, airlines, hotels, and back-office operations (Chandrasekhar & Ghosh, 2007), but the very nature of these jobs requires women to adopt Western attire and attitude (including accented speech), as they deal with international clients. Moreover, many of the jobs, such as those at call-centers, airlines, and media, also call for unconventional working hours. For example, women at call centres must work through the night to serve North American clients in a different time zone. These working hours would have been once frowned upon in traditional Indian society, but now they have become a way of life. Hence, despite the ambivalences of mediated discourses, and the ambiguity of the social contexts wherein extant power equations of a traditional patriarchal society are only obliquely addressed, the enhanced employment opportunities provide the more concrete reality underlying as well as enabling the Indian women's desire to participate in 'Western metropolitan modernity' (Parameswaran, 2004b, p. 376).[19] And it is within these potentially empowering emerging economic spheres, despite the continuing dissonance in the dominant representational and social spheres, that the dreams and desires of marginalized Muslim women must also be analyzed.

Competent Consumers

However, despite the dissonance and ambivalence surrounding questions of women's agency and possible challenges to patriarchal hierarchies, there is a general consensus regarding the overwhelming power of images and ideologies of a materialist, consumerist modernity. Scholars have noted the pull of glamorous and enticing product imagery and lifestyles in defining and shaping the hybrid subjectivities of the neoliberal globalized India (see John, 1999/2001; Mankekar, 2004; Parameswaran 2004a & 2004b). And according to Mankekar (2004), gazing upon commodities and products in mediated spaces and in shop-windows is an important way to seek new worlds. The young Muslim women's idea of modernity cannot but be implicated in these realms of materialist prosperity and modernity, given their overwhelming salience.

For example, my informant Farida loves to watch celebrity shows, and she is deeply involved in the stories of self-made millionaires. She is a great admirer of Shahrukh Khan, the Bollywood star, because according to her, '*woh age bad raha hai, aur sirf apni waja se*' [he is moving ahead, and only on the basis of his own capabilities]. Her friend wholeheartedly agreeing with her added, '*woh itna good-looking nahin hai par phir bhi usme bahut sari qualities hain jaise ke intelligence, wisdom*' [though he [Shahrukh] may not be good looking, but still he has so many qualities such as intelligence, wisdom] (personal communication, 9 December, 2007). They expressed their faith in him because according to them he had overcome his humble beginnings and made his fortune on the basis of his own talent and hard work. The power of Shahrukh Khan's rag to riches story helps strengthen their belief in individualism, and much like the myth of the American middle class, it buttresses their faith in rising materialism of the neoliberal Indian society, making them feel more optimistic about their own future.

Expressing their hope in current social and economic conditions, Farida even brought up a reference from her own life and narrated the story of one of her cousins who in her opinion has experienced a similar meteoric rise. Speaking of her uncle she said, *'pehle unke pas kuch nahin tha par ab bilkul society wali life hai'* [he had nothing before, but now he knows how to live well] (personal communication, December 9, 2007). The phrase *'society wali life'* which she uses to describe a life filled with amenities procurable only by the super rich is very interesting. It not only reflects on how Farida has internalized materialist values peddled on celebrity lifestyle shows, but also how these values have become normalized, and almost beyond reproach. The narratives of *'society wali life'* stir their lives to an extent not experienced before and draw an unquestioning and unstinted admiration from my respondents.

For example, when I asked Farida what she wanted to do with her life, she answered in the most matter of fact way, 'I want to be rich' (personal communication, 3 August, 2007). I was completely taken aback by this succinct expression of her life's ambition. It was not only that the honesty and clarity of her vision was refreshing, but this was a novel response as far as I was concerned, because I know no one in my generation, brought up in India's socialist ethos and a good decade and half their senior, who could utter this so straight forwardly and with such candor, even if it was their burning ambition too. Farida's response is reflective of the force that the idea of material well-being has gathered in contemporary Indian society and the manner in which the Muslim youth, who have always been thought of as lying outside the pale of society, ascribe to dominant and mainstream ideologies. Thus, it was hardly surprising that the need for financial well-being would be one of the primary reasons why the young women of Jamia enclave wished to participate in the emerging economic spheres. But the fact of the matter is that an improved financial standing is inevitably linked with economic and social independence, and therefore potentially challenges the patriarchal order.

Although my informants did not verbalize a desire to contradict gender hierarchies within the Islamic society, the fact of the matter is that they are enamoured by stories of personal achievement and self-reliance as Farida's admiration for Shahrukh Khan clearly shows. Their focus on achievement and self-actualization, which also underlines their dreams and plans for participating in the economic workforce, is bound to project their individuality as well as their heightened sense of self worth, and cannot but upset the current conceptions of gender roles and gender equations. Moreover, I also found the young women to be equally captivated by examples of liberated and fearless femininity. For example, Barkha Dutt, a broadcast journalist and a Jamia University alumnus, who achieved her celebrity status after covering the brief but the fiercely fought Kargil War between India and Pakistan in 1999, featured very prominently in their list of most admired women. And when I met with them in the winter of 2007, they were also incessantly talking about the female lead (played by Kareena Kapoor) of the film *Jab We Met* (translated as When We Met), who runs away from home to marry the man of her choice. According to Sameena, 'every girl should be like Kareena, she is so free, not scared of anything. Mam you must watch this movie' (personal communication, 9 December , 2007). And Farida corroborating her added, 'every girl must be so self-independent, [and] she should fear nothing' (personal communication, 9 December , 2007). On several occasions my young informants even mentioned that they also admired me, which took me by surprise. I pointed out to them that I was not the ideal Muslim girl. I had not followed the traditional route, I was not married and many people would say that I was too independent. I asked them if they could approve this self-sufficiency in real life as opposed to reel-life. Nonetheless, they assured me that they wanted to be like me. And I understood why I was so honoured when they admitted that they really admired my ability to converse so fluently in English. In fact, a few of them openly acknowledged that they wanted to meet me and spend time with me, because they wanted to learn how to converse in English with such ease. My access to their private worlds was facilitated by their desire to enter the expanding transnational worlds and to escape 'the stagnant margin of India's vernacular languages' by becoming fluent in the language of global modernity (Parameswaran, 2004a, p. 359).

Hence, even if the power of enticing and glamorous mediated images implicates them in materialist discourses and desires, the inevitable fall-out of pursuing paid employment is that it brings with it a promise of being able of take charge of one's life. And my informants are also interested in being independent and competent, much like the characters they admire. According to Nazneen, a twenty one year old student of architecture, 'everyone has to be self-independent' and her friend Fawzia, also a student at the same institute added echoing her, *'apne pairon par khada hona bahot zaroori hai* [it is *very* important to stand on your own two feet]. 'To be self-independent is very important' (personal communication, December 9, 2007). While another friend of theirs, Sameena, who was aspiring to be a computer engineer, said much more bluntly, 'I want to have a job and be independent so that no one can boss over me' (personal communication, December 9, 2007). Sameena's disavowal of tradition and authority challenges the current gender equations. However, even if such expressions present a more open threat to established power equations, I believe that the silent push for self-actualization will have a more permanent impact. This is because the desire for fulfilling one's potential is deeply ingrained in the concept of individual self-worth, and it can greatly enhance the Muslim women's commitment for change in their own position within their socio-economic religious contexts.

For example take the case of Nabila, a diploma student in civil engineering, who is the only one from the group wearing the full veil. She wears the full black coat and a black head scarf, which makes her look so much more conspicuous in the Delhi heat, as compared to the other girls who sport various versions of the head scarf. Moreover, her family background is not only more strained but it is also more traditional, considering the fact that she hails from a small hamlet in Bihar. She and her brothers have come to the city for better education and all of them are pursuing courses in various engineering fields. And I believe that Nabila's old fashioned and rather shabby veil (as noted and commented upon by one of her teachers) is an enabling condition, facilitating her mobility from the small village to the big city, because it vividly declares her affinity to the traditional order even as she makes a transition to the new world. She wears the veil regardless of the weather or the situation. In fact she is the one who interviewed with a prominent multinational developer in Delhi wearing the full-veil. And her brothers keep a strict watch over her movements; for instance, I had to always call one of her brothers to make an appointment to meet her. Moreover, they often insisted on declaring in public that under no circumstance will Nabila ever discard her veil. Moreover, the force of this pronouncement was in direct proportion to Nabila's increasing participation in the professional field. Hence, it was a bit of a surprise to hear the desire for self-actualization and of the need to fulfill one's potential so clearly articulated by one who seemed to be eschewing this position as evident in her dress, demeanour, and family relations. However, Nabila, shared with me in halting English (which has immensely improved over the years that I have known her),'I want to work, [and] only for [a] multi-national. I know, I know, I will go very up. I know I am very concentrated' (personal communication, 13 August, 2007). She meant to say that she is keen to do her very best and that has set her aims high because she believed in her ability to succeed, given her immense ability to focus and concentrate on her goals.

Hence, when to everyone's surprise Nabila did find employment with a Dutch multinational design firm after graduating with honours from the diploma course in civil engineering, I remembered her words. Her employment offer came as a shock even to her mentors who knew her as an excellent student, but were sceptical about her chances, given her veiled persona and the general hostility towards Islam. However, Nabila succeeded on the basis of her superior merit and her sharp intelligence—skills that would have counted for less in the pre-liberalization India. Today, she still pursues her job at the design firm during the day and in the evening she attends classes for the degree course in engineering. And she has even overcome her inability to speak English fluently, and appears buoyed by her extremely good standing in her new job and in the engineering school.

But, what is important is that Nabila's is not the only inspirational story. There are others among my informants who are living a similar life. For example, Farida is also an undergraduate electronic engineering student, while being a full time employee of a Japanese multinational telecommunication giant. But what is even more significant is the fourteen hour work day, five days a week, and a gruelling routine that she and Nabila share. The young women's ambitions and desires not only call upon their inner most resources and strengths, but they also unsettle the staid routines of Muslims by making new demands on their families. Their daily routine includes setting off from home at about 6:30 a.m. in the morning only to return at about 9:15 p.m. after attending work till 4 p.m. or so, and then classes from about 5:30 p.m. in the evening. And when I pointed out to Farida that she works excruciatingly hard, she replied as a matter of fact: 'No I don't work hard, *main kahan mehnat kar ruhi hoon* [how am I working hard]. Seventy per cent of the people in my class are working and studying and they even do night shifts. I am not doing anything different, I am not doing anything special' (personal communication, August 2010). Her response reflects her sagacity and persistence, which define their dreams of self-realization. And more importantly, it indicates that even if Muslim women are seen as the markers of Muslim 'otherness,' the young Muslim women today are alike and united in their thinking as well as in their dreams with other Indian youth.

However, it would be naïve to assume that the dreams of the young Muslim women are their's alone, or that they can pursue them without support from their families and even the larger community. I know that both, Nabila and Farida, along with others were deeply grateful to their parents and even to their siblings for making the realization of their dreams a possibility. In fact Hina, studying commerce and marketing, related that her father chose to dissociate himself from those members of her large family who criticized her decision to travel to the United States on a scholarship supported by the American Embassy and Youth Education and Study program (YES). However, despite the predominance of these heartening stories, there is no denying the fact that the instances of Muslim women's increasing participation in economic and social spheres challenge entrenched notions about appropriates roles and behaviours for Muslim women. And this is what complicates the narrative of the Muslim women's aspirations for self-realization, calling upon new negotiations and strategies, which are instrumental in constructing what I refer to as their 'convoluted modernities.'

Negotiating Convoluted Modernities

Hence, even as my informants desire to extend their repertoire of experiences, and participate in the economic spheres, overhauling many assumptions about Muslim women and about the Muslim community in general, the fact is that in the North Indian Muslim society, there is still an inordinate amount of stress on circumscribing women's behaviour. The dynamics of living in an environment surrounded by other Muslims, as in the Jamia enclave, entails an overwhelming preponderance of traditions, norms, and ways of life that are supposedly drawn on Islamic ethos. A modest behaviour is strictly emphasized for women, who are also under constant surveillance and everyone is interested in where they are going and what they are doing. The community's watchful gaze is especially focused on those young women who are approaching the 'marriageable age'. And the parents, mindful of this vigilance, also carefully monitor young women's interactions, especially with members of the opposite sex, as a chance negative evaluation by a neighbour might damage the young woman's reputation and hence her prospects for marriage. I heard from parents and even from young women themselves that people should think well of them, and that they should have a good reputation in the community. As a Muslim woman, I understand this very well, and I share the same concerns because it has been drilled into me that we never just represent ourselves, but our entire extended family and clan. And yet, I could not resist teasing one of my informants by asking her why it was so important to be independent when the ultimate goal was just to get married. But, my flippancy was not appreciated, and Fawzia appeared as if I had not only hurt, but also insulted, her. She replied, 'I, too, want to become somebody in life. Just because I am a girl, it does not mean I do not have any dreams. Like men have dreams, I, too, have dreams to do something in life' (author's translation original in Urdu, personal communication, December 9, 2007).

But what is interesting is that even as my informants like Fawzia assert that women have as much right to dream as men, and declare their unabashed desire to pursue financial independence, their outward behaviour is still very guarded and careful rather than being bold or assertive like their declarations. I not only found them to be very cautious in managing their public image as respectable Muslim women, but they also never openly challenge or critique any aspect of their religion or culture. And if ever I opened up the issue regarding veiling or about the position of women in Islam, I was almost always met with a certain silence, which I read as their quiet resistance to the critique of Islam. And if at all they chose to engage with my query, I found their responses to be both confusing and conflicting with their other posturing as self reliant and forward-looking women. For example, consider my conversation with Farida, a fan of Dr Zakir Naik, whom I once asked in a bit annoyed tone why she liked his lectures:

Ruhi–But he says *hijab, hijab,* all the time, how do you, a working girl, deal with that?

Farida–*Cover to rehna chahiye, yeh baat to saach hai, magar aaj kal ke jaamane mein yeh baatein kuch galat ho jati hain. Waisa tau itna busy schedule hota hai keh yeh sab sooachne ka time hi nahin milta. Magar main manti hoon ke cover rehna thik hai, magar Saudi Arabia mein bhi aurtein chehre ko cover nahin karti....aur hum bhi cover hi karte hain...* [Yes I agree that you should be covered, but in today's world we do many things that can be considered wrong. Actually, I have such a busy schedule that I do not have time to think about all these things, what is right or wrong. But I still agree that you should be covered, and I know that women in Saudi Arabia do not cover their faces and we do not cover our faces either.](personal communication, August, 2010).

Her response, as one can read, is rather muddled. She does not critique the stance on veiling even if she does not follow it, while clearly pointing to the rising influence of globalized Islam associated with the affluent Middle Eastern societies on the Indian Muslim women.

And the other aspect which puzzled me was their very calm acceptance of the limits placed on their experiences and dreams by the patriarchal norms of the Indian Muslim society. Nabila, for example, is an exceptional student and the brightest in the diploma programme in civil engineering, who even managed to secure admission to the civil engineering degree programme after clearing the highly competitive entrance exam (conducted at an all India level), which her older brother failed to pass despite two attempts, had no plans or dreams of pursuing higher education abroad. And when I asked her why was that so, she answered that her family will not allow it and that she cannot discard her veil, or get on a plane and go so far away from her family. She said, *'family ke saath relationship zaada important hain. Agar woh achche hain tau aap happy hain aur aapke results zaada achche hain. Akhir yeh saab family ke liye hi tau hai'* [it is more important to have good relations within the family. After all what you achieve is for your family. If your relationships are good, you are more satisfied, you have better results] (personal communication, August 2007). Nabila preferred to contain her dreams rather than upset her family. Moreover, even Soha, the only one among my informants who was actively moved by images of glamour and excitement and wished to be an air-hostess, pushing the limits of Indian Muslim cultural values, had given up on her plans and was training to become a kindergarten teacher.

Hence, should the assertions of independence and the pursuit their dreams be dismissed as mere rhetoric? I believe that though the young women's articulation serve a limited rhetorical function, in that these statements allow them to introduce themselves as modern young women who have not been left out of the changes/developments that are taking place in India, the question of participating in the larger picture of national growth as equals is a matter of great import for them. It definitely goes far beyond a mere rhetoric as one can see that many of these young women were actively pursuing professional studies and many of them over the years have joined the professional worlds. And even those who have chosen to get married did not given up their studies. For example, Fawzia, who had been very hurt by a comment about how important it was for Muslim girls to get married, did get married even as she was still enrolled in the engineering degree program, but she did not give up her studies. In fact, according to her, her mother-in-law was even more insistent than her own mother that she should get good grades.

These lives present a complex scenario wherein Muslim women, seeking independence and personal fulfillment, choose to pose no explicit challenge to establish equations, and instead are deferential to religious and cultural norms as well as to patriarchal authority. However, I argue that this does not point to a static or regressive scenario, instead what appears to be a contradictory situation represents the young Muslim women's negotiating position with several difficult and different social and economic structures within which the Muslim women's lives are situated. Chandra Talpade Mohanty (1991/2012) argues that women emerge as 'sexual-political subjects' by interacting with multiple and often contesting structures within which they are situated, and that 'it is only by understanding the *contradictions* (sic) inherent in women's location within various structures that effective political action and challenges can be devised' (1991/2012, p. 356). Extending this argument, I add that it is only when navigating the inconsistencies and oppositions within various social, cultural, economic, and discursive regimes within which women are located that their agency is exercised and expressed. Hence, the Muslim women's subjectivities must be considered not only against the backdrop of multiple, contradictory, and conflicting circumstances, but also in their encounters and struggles with the inconsistencies within all these different spheres—including the changes that are taking place in the Indian economy, creating new opportunities for an ignored and impoverished minority population; the new influences from media and the way they may have been integrated in the Muslim women's life plans, aspirations, and ideologies as well as the particular predilections of a religious minority including its anxieties and its rules of deportment for young men and women.

Patriarchy and Muslim Women's Modernities

Hence, while on one hand there are the young women's dreams and aspirations, which are given a new dimension and depth by mediated discourses, creating an inexorable pull towards an 'at large' or viral modernity (see Appardurai,1996) as young women seek to explore worlds, which could never be approached by their mothers even in their imagination. But on the other hand there are clearly expressed anxieties in a traditional patriarchal society. There is no denying the pain that transitions are creating, and I encountered one young man among my informants who vocalized these apprehensions with hostility and sarcasm. And even though other young men in the group did not share the intensity of this young man's critique, the fact is that they only scoffed at him, but did not openly challenge or refute him, and this indicates that somewhere his extreme words have varying levels of relevance for them too. According to Yasin, 'girls want to be free, they now want to do everything' (personal communication, 3 July, 2007). The word 'everything' is broad and unclear, but, given his derogatory tone and the smirk, which accompanied it, I read his intention to mean that women now desire sexual freedom. His attempt to ridicule women's dreams for education and professional attainment by equating them to frivolous and even unseemly desires reflects the essential prejudices of a patriarchal order. However, even if his disdain for women's individuality represents an extreme aspect of entrenched prejudices against women in a traditional patriarchal society, the fact is that women's rights are also stymied by the excessive concern of involved fathers worried about the safety of young women as they move about precarious Delhi urban-scapes. The reality is that the young women must grapple with the many slow evolving social and structural forces even as their imaginations soar past them at high speed because support from within the community is extremely essential to the realization of their ambitions.

Their dreams are pitted against the increasing precariousness of the neoliberal globalized world order, which is posing many challenges and demanding an excruciatingly high level of professional competence from the discriminated and disregarded Muslim women. They have a very difficult task ahead of them and the family in these increasingly difficult contexts provides that crucial enabling space.

As mentioned earlier, most young women were deeply grateful for their family's help and support, they cannot afford to isolate themselves from the family's safe and nurturing spaces. Hence, learning to strike a balance between established ways of life and new ways of being by accepting appropriate norms for Muslim women and not critiquing the limits placed on their potentials constitutes their strategy to get ahead. Therefore, it is hardly surprising that the young women did not dwell upon Muslim cultural norms or patriarchal values, or see them as being in any way hampering their path forward. This is because, as Farida clearly indicated, the small injustices of a patriarchal society are very trivial problems in comparison to the larger issues they had to face in order to succeed in the highly competitive economic mainstream. In fact, she dismissed my concerns about discriminatory treatment of women in patriarchal Muslim societies as being irrelevant and referring to my objections to the differences in religious obligations for men and women in Muslim society, she said, '*ladkiyon ke liye har cheez, bahut si cheezen, mushkil hai. Yeh to chooti si baat hai*' [everything, so many things are complicated for women. This is such a small incident] (personal communication, 9 December, 2007). I must accept her argument because abiding within accepted cultural norms and avoiding confrontation saved them energy to prepare for the more difficult task of finding their foothold in Indian society. And if I reflect upon my life, I would agree that despite our difference, this would be true for me too. I too had learned to place certain limits on what was possible for me to maintain a cordial relationship with family and community. For example, when Sameena, who greatly admires Barkha Dutt, once questioned me about my career path, saying, 'why didn't you become like Barkha Dutt?' (personal communication, 31 July, 2007), (meaning why did I not build an equally illustrious career though we had both graduated from the same communication program), I admitted that my upbringing within a conservative Muslim family did not give me many of her social skills. Moreover, as the good Muslim girl (as I thought myself to be), I was also quite consciously reserved and inhibited. Covering a war like Kargil was quite out of the question for me. My family would ostracize me for sharing my personal space with unknown men. And this small bit of information about myself, and the acknowledgement that we Muslim women finely balance our life ambitions with our cultural norms brought me infinitely closer to them.

In many ways the Muslim women's struggles appear to be similar to Gilbertson's (2014) analysis of middle class Indian women's experiences of balancing 'demands of respectability' with their desires for 'cultural capital' as reposited in 'high-status forms of leisure consumption,' including dating, pre-marital romance, and fashion, but there is an essential difference here. This is because even though young Muslim women in their subjective personal spheres may be seeking to strike a balance between oppositional worlds as contained in the mainstream economic and social spheres and the traditional Muslim society, their conscious behaviour is to show a greater preference for the Islamic way of being, rather than seek social status by indulging in rituals of dating or by appropriating Western fashions. For example, as argued earlier, many Muslim women have accepted the veil, because it aids their mobility by assuaging patriarchal anxieties. But to continue wearing it, like Nabila does, even after working at her job for more than four years and despite having achieved financial independence, (her income is more than what her two brothers earn by giving tuition in Maths and Science to High School students) indicates a tendency to not challenge patriarchal norms. She brushes aside the question of her veil but volunteers to speak enthusiastically about how she is learning the Dutch design codes and building regulations and teaching her Dutch boss about building regulations in India. And according to her, no one at work has any problems with her. However, Nabila's optimism notwithstanding, it must be acknowledged that she provides an excellent service for almost manual labour pay to a multinational company (her overall pay-scale is approximately Rs 40000 or about $ 800 a month). And it must also be accepted that considering the state of Muslims in India, this amount seems quietly princely to Nabila. However, she has dreams of earning more and of rising in the corporate hierarchy, and this extremely difficult task calls on her to substantially improve her skills, and as Farida had mentioned while rebuking me, she has little time to fight non-essential battles at the moment. Hence, the veil stays on and patriarchal anxieties continue to be appeased because from their pragmatic and practical perspective, tradition and patriarchy are not always regressive forces, just as spheres of employment and economic participation cannot be identified as the ultimate utopias for a minority population.

Their lives, dreams, and aspirations are being shaped within an increasingly precarious neoliberal globalized order, which promises no security and nothing to fall back upon. It is a complex condition of hope and apprehensions, because if the ascendance of a market economy following liberalization and globalization has created increased employment opportunities and new career options, the dismantling of socialist state structures and increased privatization has also lead to increased job insecurity, and this at a time when the phenomenal expansion of media has been associated with rising consumerism and materialism in a society where millions are still to secure basic necessities of life. These tensions become especially heightened for Muslim women given the vast disparity between their life plans and the social and economic backwardness which they must overcome in contexts of increasing hostility towards Islam. Many of my informants are among the first generation among women in their families, not only to secure a westernized education in a proper school, but also professional education, which allows them to participate in paid employment, outside their homes and community, and in the emerging sectors of the Indian economy. And given their difficult circumstances, the many hurdles in their plans to explore new grounds as well as grow as individuals, many of my informants conceded to the fact that strong ties to their families are imperative.

Patriarchy, Rising Materialism, and Sense of Imminent Lack

However, the problems created by rising materialism are also making it necessary for Muslim women to participate in the economic mainstream. Despite the slow changing nature of the North Indian Muslim society's traditional norms, the predominance of consumerist notions in the Indian society, are validating Muslim women's aspirational pursuits. I argue that this is because pervasive presence of media and mediated discourses in their lives is not only embroiling them within rising consumerist materialism, but is also making them intensely sensitive to their state of relative impoverishment. Muslim women are beginning to question the fall-outs of the Muslim community's state of impoverishment and backwardness on future generations. They are acutely aware of the deep discrepancies between their extant realities and their projected dreams. I found their buoyant assertions about dreams of independence and self-reliance to be sharply underlined by their understanding of hard economic realities. And I say this because once their posturing as modern and progressive women had sobered down in their long drawn out interviews with me, they finally confessed rather obliquely that they were indeed keen to explore new employment opportunities, driven as they were by a sense of an imminent lack, and by a consciousness of what the inability to possess commodities would entail to their sense of self and to their future within such materialist contexts. The consumerist ethos promoted by media and advertising has deeply affected them, and I argue thus even if none of my female informants had actually showed any interest in acquiring or possessing material things. (They were surprisingly uninterested in any cosmetics or other fineries that I would sometime ferry for them, and only accepted with enthusiasm the gift of chocolates). But I still continue to hold on to the position that my informants are being compelled by dominant materialist and consumerist ethos of post globalization and liberalization Indian society to think of different life options than those which have been traditionally ordained for Muslim women. And even when they were not expressing a keen interest in acquiring products and goods, they were working within a mindset apprehensive of a state of lack, which may beset them in the event of their inability to possess materialist possessions, because, as Fawzia and Sameena quietly admitted, almost like an afterthought, 'everything in life is so expensive' (personal communication, 20 August, 2007), and Fawzia further clarified by adding, 'and then children want so many things today,' even as according to her children's education has become so difficult and so costly (personal communication, 20 August, 2007). Both the young women believed that in the contemporary inflationary contexts, both husband and wife, had to chip in together to make ends meet. And they both believed that it was absolutely necessary for a woman to work so that they could provide well for their families and not deprive them of anything that they might need or want.

However, what is interesting to note is that while the stress on commodities as markers of social inclusion have created anxieties among young women, making them fearful of how a possible state of impoverishment might damage their children's self-esteem, similar anxieties regarding adequate provisions for the future generations among their parents and other members from the older generations, have cleared the case for Muslim women's participation in the economic sphere. The community's deep insecurities regarding the Muslim community's rising economic and social marginalization provide a valid argument for the women's active participation in the organized workforce, and for acquisition of educational qualifications and social skills, which were hitherto outside the purview of the Muslim women's life experiences. I argue that the Muslim women are both consciously as well as subconsciously operating in the gaps which exist between the Muslim community's current vulnerable status and the imaginations of a more secure and prosperous future, albeit one arrived at through the women's active participation in new economic spheres. And it is in successfully negotiating these inconsistencies that young women are not only able to deal with tensions that their aspirations produce in a patriarchal society, but they are also able to subtly reinstate the women's enhanced status within the Indian Muslim society.

But to illustrate how these tensions play out in everyday life and how Muslim women are positioned between antithetical trends of expanding possibilities for the women's self-actualization and tenacity of impulses to contain the women's lives, I present the views of the older generation from the perspective of a professor at the university and a father of two daughters. As a father and guardian, he has ensured that both his daughters have access to elite professional education, and at the time of this research one of his daughters was enrolled in Law school, while the other was studying computer programing and electronic engineering. But, even as these investments in women's education reflect the acceptance of the Muslim women's new positionality in Muslim society and a recognition of the essential role they may play in ensuring the community's stability, preventing any further deterioration in its status, his defense of the practice of veiling can be read as resistance to the new conditions of Muslim women's lives. However, it is not simply a reaction against threats to gender equations within a traditional community accentuated by new opportunities for women. This is because according to him 'there is safety in *hijab*,' and it indicates his greater anxiety about his daughters' safety than about possible transgressions of male authority because he clarified himself further by adding, 'but I never forced them [his daughters] into anything. Not what they wanted to study, nor what they want to do, and definitely not for the hijab. They took it up on their own. I only forced them to learn driving. If they have to live in a city like Delhi, they must learn to get around' (personal communication, December, 2010). However, even if one knows that the women's affection and respect can often translates into a different kind of coercion and many of my informants did point out instances of their friends or of other young women in their extended family who adopted the veil to please their fathers, I still do not perceive the situation as a case wherein patriarchal society's excessive control or authority are arrayed against the young women's subjectivity, demanding their abject submission to the dominant logic. On carefully reading the professor's response, it is clearly discernable that he is a concerned father who is keen on ensuring that his daughters are adequately equipped to deal with the changing worlds. And from his perspective, both driving skills and a modest persona (garnered by donning the hijab), are equally essential qualities and skills, which would help young women find their way around the busy city and the precarious pathways of modern life more efficiently. Hence, while he has not denied a woman's right to navigate the city, he has tried to make sure in his own way that it is as painless a process as possible.

Moreover, his response would be more understandable if perceived within the contexts of rapid changes in the Indian society. The fact is that these new roles for women have emerged with such force only in the past two decades or so, and the demand for women to inhabit these roles have accelerated only in the past decade. And these transitions demand an adjustment and realignment of established gendered norms, roles, and behaviour from all quarters. The older generations too must make their own negotiations with the Muslim society's expectations from young women and the demands of the new world, and I argue that the professor's responses, while reflecting these internal contestations, cannot be simply explained as a case of patriarchal society rising against women's self-actualization projects. This is especially so because the problems and challenges facing Muslim women are not simple either, and indeed the women's dreams can be realized with express support of their family and even community. And many of my informants, despite their class and educational differences, vouched for the fact that it was their fathers who have been most actively involved in their educational and professional schemes. Not only had they provided financial support, such by paying for extra tutorials and other fees, but more importantly they were a steady source of emotional support in the face professional difficulties and hazards of finding one's way in the unsafe city of Delhi. In fact, support from male members of the family has been as essential to their mobility as the veil. For example, many of my informants also shared with me that they could attend evening classes or keep late hours at work only because they had their fathers or their brothers volunteering to escort them back home. And according to Hina, she could never have accepted the scholarship to learn English in the United States had her father not staunchly defended her decision in the face of general opposition from her extended family. And according to Mariam, a mother of a toddler, it is owing to her husband's and to her mother-in-law's constant propping up and unflagging support that she has been able to complete her degree in journalism and even hopes to pursue a career in the field.

Hence, rather than it being a case of generational gap or gender divide, it is an instance of coping with changing socio-economic contexts from within the complex physical and sociological spaces of a Muslim ghetto and Muslim socio-economic circumstances. It is an effort to move forward sustaining and validating each other's struggles, while strategically balancing traditional gender expectations with challenges of the contemporary contexts to secure their wards' new modernities. For example, Fawzia's mother confessed, 'It would be better if she [Fawzia] spent the time studying, as her course is quite demanding. But, she must do housework too, because it is important to keep a good house. What is a home where food is not cooked well?' (author's translation, original in Urdu, personal communication, 19 August, 2007).

However, most feminist scholarship is unlikely to perceive agency or modernity within contexts defined by the lack of open conflict between traditional structures and ideologies and women's desires for self-actualization. And as Muslim women continue to work within patriarchal norms, and even uphold religious dictates such as with reference to veiling, my task, like other scholars of Islamic society, has been to understand the complex and contradictory dynamics between religious ideologies and draws of modernity. And I refer to Saba Mahmood's (2005) study of women's mosque movement in Egypt, wherein she tries to analyze the paradox of Egyptian women's participation in the arena of Islamic pedagogy and their active support of a movement inherently inimical to their interests, endorsing their subordination to male authority, at a point of time when 'emancipatory possibilities available to them' and were increasing exponentially (2005, pp. 2–3). According to Mahmood, the Egyptian women's choice indeed presents an enigma for feminists scholars who tend to perceive human agency as discernible only in acts challenging the social order but not in those acts upholding them (2005, pp. 2–3). And Mahmood's main concern has been to speak to 'liberal assumptions about what constitutes human nature and agency,' which have become so integral to 'humanist tradition,' but which from the very core of their intellectual tradition would dismiss the women's mosque movement as a non-liberal and unsuitable site for analyzing questions of moral and political agency, despite its role in mobilizing women. However, Mahmood argues that women's endorsement of the very ethos of religion and patriarchy in the Islamic teaching sessions held at the mosques were also their way of entering modernity, even if the women did not explicitly realize how their actions were implicitly restructuring civil society (deeply and fundamentally as current events now show), and even if the women had no knowledge that while they paid obeisance to both tradition and patriarchy, they were empowering many to take charge of their lives. I argue that the Muslim women's position shares similar dynamics with the Egyptian women's mosque movement, because it is their complex pact with patriarchy as well as active support from established social structures that allow them to approach the new modern worlds and the innumerable attendant trials and travails.

However, even as Mahmood highlights the unintended consequences of women's religious movements and their inadvertent role in constructing civil society, my focus is on Muslim women's active engagement with modernizing impulses (as imbedded in almost revolutionary developments in the fields of media, communication technologies, and audiences engagements in digitized, neoliberal, globalized economy) and the manner in which it shapes their self-consciousness and lives. This is because, as I said earlier there is something to be said about Enlightenment's optimism for ideas of individuality and citizenship, especially when they appear enhanced, if not potentially expanded, as they circulate and reverberate within digital and discursive pathways in this era of unprecedented connectivity, and become ingrained in the everyday, moulding life choices and personal politics. For example, the decision of the young Muslim women of Jamia to wear the veil cannot but resonate within the larger debate about increasing the adoption of the veil as a challenge to state imposed nationalistic ideologies and modernizing missions which deny the voice and the choice of their populations in countries stretching from Algeria to Egypt. Given the salience of mediated discourses, they cannot be totally unaware of the significance of the veil in the construction of political identity in Arab countries, which had experienced colonial rule, and how the veil was adopted to resist and to defy the colonial gaze, even if later discarded in the process of nation building by modernizing elites, who perceived it to be a symbol of social and economic backwardness and a source of all of society's problems (as Leila Ahmed [2011] argues). And even if young Muslim women understand the mere skein of the story of how the veil is being resurrected again in public spheres of many Islamic countries, where it had been rejected, through snippets of images of conflagrations and struggles, symbolizing political reconstructive projects undergoing in these Islamic countries, they are being drawn into new political positions. And even if the same level of political consciousness may not inform the Indian Muslim women's decision to adopt the veil as has been the case with women in other Islamic countries like Egypt, Algeria, or Turkey, where they challenge established powers and assert popular will, I argue that Indian Muslim women draw on Arab women's voices of resistance discarding the hegemonic nationalistic missions, which equated modernity with unveiling, to support their own decisions. Moreover, the struggle around public veiling in France as it utilizes the language of human rights, individual freedom, and equality to counter entrenched perceptions equating veiling with the denial of individuality and negation of women's right cannot but silently reverberate and inform choices; because the young woman who I saw praying in the public space was exhibiting the same aggressiveness about her right to be Muslim that French Muslim women are accused of (see Chrisafis, 2013). A synergetic cross-referencing is enabled by circuits of digital media and vastly extended facilities of travel in the globalized economy engendering awareness, which may fall short of comprehension but which nonetheless permeates the practice of veiling among Indian Muslim women.

Therefore, I argue that it is by being firmly situated within and actively negotiating with modernizing forces that Muslim women's 'convoluted modernities' are shaped. And it is only after having acquired a repertoire of skills along with a knowledge base to contend with the new world order that the defense of religion and even patriarchy can be staged, because as the professor's daughter and a computer engineer confessed to me, 'I wear the veil now, because I am able to explain to others why I wear it and why it is an important part of my being a Muslim' (personal communication, December 2011). Hence, even in their defense of family structures and gender equations, the young women are expressing their agency and creating a place for themselves within highly contentious contexts defined by contesting ideological and physical spaces in which their lives are situated. And as one of the professors at the university observing her students said:

> They are modern girls…and girls today are very focused. They are not like the Muslim women earlier who wore the *burkha*. Today if they wear the *hijab* they know why they are wearing it. They know what they want. They know what kind of a career they want, which kind of boy they want to marry. And this is not only in the towns and cities. It is more in the villages. The girls wear the *hijab* and they drive. I tell my daughter-in-law, you wear the long coat and cover your hair with a scarf and you can wear, jeans and trousers, whatever you want. I also tell her that since she wears the *hijab* she must be very conscious of her appearance. She must look smart. Also you must speak English that is very important. No one should think that you are illiterate or *jahil*. This is very important in society. If you speak English, you will not be looked down upon.

Hence, the defining quality of the Muslim women's subjectivity is a constant negotiation. But even if feminist scholarship is most likely to discard this positionality as being appeasing and lacking of agency, there can be no denying of the fact that Muslim women arrive at their conciliatory posture only after having actively acquired certain core strengths, including and not only formal education, but also heightened awareness of their own standing as a member of a minority community within its larger political-historical-social-economic contexts. It is only on account of this that they are able to valorize their own religion and tradition which is otherwise berated and belittled within dominant social and economic spheres. And the rising display of the veil in the public spheres is akin to the staging of what can be labeled as a form of 'reverse Orientalism' that seeks to address the iniquitous power relationships by accepting essentialist terms of construction of the 'other' only to turn them on its head 'the rigid sense of difference based on culture' (see Abu-Lughod, 1991: 144). And as the young Muslim women asked 'why does being Hindu or the *bindi* not disturb anyone and why does my being Muslim and my veil question my Indianess' (personal communication, December 2012). Hence, Muslim women are deeply political subjects but their politics is beyond frameworks, which see emergence of agency and politics only in contestation of patriarchy (see Mohanty, 1991/2012). However, what the feminist assertions of agency fail to realize is that patriarchy is but one of the many intersecting vectors of powers that shapes the Muslim women's life. And it leads me to my concluding remark that the Muslim women's decision not to challenge patriarchal norms is not to be considered as a sign of their passivity or even as a strategy of deferring a struggle till more propitious times. Rather, the Muslim women's politics and their effective agency are clearly exhibited as they find enabling spaces within their own family, community, and ideology to take on bigger struggles against their poverty, marginality, and general disempowerment.

In many ways the Muslim women's contemporary circumstances expose the inadequacy of constructs, which theorize emerging globalized subjectivities in terms of assimilation, or blending, or churning, as highlighted in postcolonial discussions of the hybrid. Overturning the inherent simplifications embedded in these arguments, which as I have argued earlier have been arrived at without reference to material and lived realities, the Muslim women's complex responses to modernizing forces within particularities of their socio-economic-political contexts demand a more nuanced approach. This is because even as the Muslim women's emergent subjectivities appear to oppose modernity, they could not have arrived at the position without first embracing modernity's discursive and material realities. Moreover, even as they appear subservient to the established order, their rising consciousness which yearns for a position within the new economic and social spheres outside the precincts of home and community, undercuts the permanence of the same order which it purportedly upholds. Hence, in my opinion, their experiences best exemplify a 'convoluted modernity'— a consciousness which while acknowledging modernity's myriad projects, has garnered enough confidence to question the significance and meaning of many of its established wisdoms.

Notes

1. The question of saving brown women from brown men (see Spivak, 1988) has been as fundamental to the justification of colonial rule, as releasing Muslim women from their supposed subjugation to oppressive patriarchal order has been to current imperialist projects, Abu-Lughod (2002) argues.

2. The dominant framework in the investigations of the condition of Indian Muslim women has been the issue of Muslim personal law and its effects on women's agency, especially the curtailment of their rights as equal citizens guaranteed by the secular law of India (Hasan & Menon, 2004 & 2005). Hasan and Menon (2004) also argue that the emphasis in most scholarly analyses, including feminist research, has been on legal equality rather than on socio-economic, historical, and contextual factors which construct their impoverishment, and this shortcoming is equally evident in campaigns and struggles aimed at Muslim women's social and economic upliftment. (2004: 3). However, the authors attempt to illuminate the Indian Muslim women's condition by drawing attention to their key life experiences such as access to education, work, decision-making ability, and marriageable age by conducting an all India survey focusing on districts with notable Muslim population does not do justice to their own key argument that Muslim women's experiences must be seen as a construct of complex 'gendered politics of minority location' and in relation to the rise of sectarian politics in India (2004, p. 3). And even if Hasan and Menon (2004), argue that Muslim women's experiences, subjectivity, and consciousness are effected by their minority status, the overarching approach of the survey methodology is not suitable for illustrating/illuminating the complex negotiations with structural, social, and economic challenges which underline the construction of self perceptions and identities.

3. The production of victimhood as a residual effect of larger structural forces by way of sociological testing has been stringently critiqued by Mohanty (1991/2012). She argues that women are constituted as women through complex interactions between structural and ideological forces and by them being situated at the center of a hegemonic, exploitative world and are not to be thought of as the end result of these forces (1991/2012, p. 355), and therefore totally devoid of agency.

4. This body of scholarship shares an overwhelming concern with discursive and representational spheres of literature, cinema, and other arts. This tendency to highlight secondary experiences filtered through the medium of

art rather than focus on real lives of ordinary women is also exhibited in postcolonial feminist studies.

5. This argument has been made even by the Sachar Committee in its Report (2006)

6. AJK MCRC was set up with support from York University, and Canadian film-makers and engineers were part of the faculty. Moreover, they were also members of staff who were visiting professors from film schools in London.

7. Sunder Rajan(1993) makes an argument for studying the embodied subject, shifting concerns from examination of consciousness to 'a logistics of realism' (1993, p. 19). But her study of *sati* in 1988 in Rajasthan locates the argument for 'sati-as-burning', foregrounding experience from the discourse of 'sati-as-death (murder, suicide, authentic, or inauthentic),' in an event where it cannot be realistically investigated. The woman has perished in the event and the discussions of agency however nuanced can only be conjectures.

8. Mankekar (1999), in her study of construction of gender and nationhood specifically posits that the analysis is being undertaken to validate the notion of third world women's agency by seeking proofs of their active negotiation and the subversion of dominant discourses. This theme also permeates Parameswaran's (2004a & 2004b) analysis of the Indian participants in the beauty queen pageants and underlines Oza (2006) discussions of neoliberal globalized gendered subjects. And even arguments, which critique the binary framework, such as Sunder Rajan's (1993) investigation of *sati*, are unable to look beyond the opposition of agency and victimhood.

9. Chandra Mohanty (1991/2012) severely critiques simplistic association of veiling with 'sexual control' and segregation of women in all Islamic countries in western feminist writings (1991/2012, p. 356). She refers specifically to the arguments of Dearbon (1975) and Hosken (1981), which unproblematically equate *purdah* whatever may be the contexts with severe violations of basic human rights such as in instances of rape, prostitution, pornography, or genital mutilations.

10. See Parameswaran (1994b, p. 376).

11. I take leaf from Mohanty's (1991/2012) arguments for building theory from within contexts under investigation, when referring to Maria Mies (1982) study of lace makers of Narsapur, she contends that 'this mode of local, political analysis which generates theoretical categories from within the situation and context being analyzed, also suggests corresponding effective strategies for organizing against the exploitation faced by the lace makers' (1991/2012: 356).

12. Appadurai (1996) argues that enhanced imagination lies at the heart of new individualities and subjectivities and it constructs the new 'Modernity at Large'. Benedict Anderson (1983) very early on makes a similar argument in his analysis of emergence of nationalism and nation states, while Stuart Hall has long argued for potency imagination as the driving force of human creativity, individuality, and agency.

13. In this regard, mention must also be made of the advertisement for KamaSutra brand of condoms (released in mid 1990s), which according to Mazzarella, was a landmark text for its treatment of sexual intimacy in highly conservative Indian society. The advertisement turned the discussion about sexuality, dominated by the need for population control, on its head. The tagline that declared 'For the pleasure of making love,' and the explicit imagery (of a man and a woman in passionate embrace) came under heavy criticism. According to Mary John (1998/2000), the advertisement was not particularly brazen when compared to suggestive imagery and crude display of women's bodies in Indian film songs (also see Bagchi, 1996). However, the advertisement's stress on sexual intimacy between partners contested patriarchal authority of the traditional Indian joint family.

14. See Ahmed (2008); Ahmed (1983); Lateef (1983); Roy (1979); Vatuk (2008).

15. Zoya Hasan (1994) argues that 'Muslims in general, and women in particular, are treated as separate from the rest of the society' to augment the myth of a 'homogenous community' and one 'unified by the common symbols of Islam' (1994: xi)

16. See Parameswaran (2004a & 2004b) and the analysis of the protests surrounding the staging of the Miss World contests in India.

17. In fact, one of the most popular television dramas with high viewership ratings and advertising revenues revolves around a child bride in Rajasthan. *Balika Vadhu* runs on Colors TV, a joint venture with Viacom, and has one of the highest TRPs.

18. As the long-running soap opera in late 1990s aptly entitled *Hasratein* or Desires (see Oza, 2006).

19. And one of the sites where the combined effect of this phenomenon is being mapped is the impressive growth of beauty industry in the past two decades or so, penetrating markets of even small town and semi-urban India (see, Runkie, 2005) in a way as to ensure the hegemony of a hybrid modernity that serves the interests of marketers and manufacturers.

CONCLUSION

This book explores the everyday life of Muslim youth of the Jamia area in New Delhi to understand how their interactions with media, in a globalized Indian economy and society, were shaping their identity. The youth of Jamia were among the first generation to be born after economic liberalization, and in a society marked by a rapid expansion of the media. And though the younger generation shares with the members of the older generation the experiences of being physically removed and cut off from the cosmopolitan Delhi, their sustained interactions with the media technologies of satellite television, cell phones, and Internet have increased their connections to the world far beyond their discrete neighbourhood. This research has investigated how mediated experiences are woven into the identity of the Muslim youth, and have influenced their self-perceptions as members/residents of a distinct community, as citizens of India, as Muslims and as gendered individuals.

Voices from the Field: Key Observations

My key observation has been that the media's salience in the Muslim youth's lives has been instrumental in shaping a sensibility distinctly different from the one professed by the older generations. The older generations of the Jamia enclave expressed their link to their community in emotive terms of *apna mahol*, and spoke of their decision to live in an area separated from the rest of Delhi, in order to be immersed in their own culture, *mahol*, and traditions, and to freely practice their way of life. However, the younger generations have lost this sentimental attachment to their community, which their parents and the early settlers of the Jamia area so deeply nurtured. Moreover, they also do not harbour any anxieties regarding the Indian Muslim culture's continuity or perpetuation, because their increased repertoire of experiences, given the permeance of mediated discourses, and thereby the increased contact with the world outside their community, have diluted their attachment to their distinct Muslim community.

The Muslim youth's conceptions of what constitutes an Indian Muslim *mahol* have become further problematized because of their rather weak link with the Indian Islamic cultural heritage, given their inability to read and write in Urdu. According to Hasan (2005), an extensive body of Urdu literature is devoted to clarifying the intricacies of *adab* and *akhlaq* (translated as good manners and righteous conduct) that were the core of Muslim *Sharif* (urbane and upper class) culture. Adab and akhlaq were the 'lubricant of social relations,' which sweetened personal exchange and softened conflict (Hasan 2005, p. 2). And the nineteenth century writers like Nazir Ahmed were especially concerned about the Muslim community's espirit de corps as the British colonial rule rapidly established itself and took over reigns of power from the Muslims. Their writings stressed and elaborated on values central to Muslim cultural ethos, and because Muslims were the ruling class, the values of Indian Islamic *adab*, *akhlaq*, and *tehzib* were the defining characteristics of urban north India, so much so that even British colonial officers had to be well-versed in them. But, as the Muslim high urbane culture steadily collapsed in the years following the end of the Mughal rule in 1857, these values and moralities were sidelined. However, they were preserved in myths, poetry, stories, and other forms of literature. But the Muslim youth have no access to literatures which enunciate unique sensibilities of the Indian Muslim *mahol*. In an age of unprecedented media growth in India, the Muslim youth would be unable to recognize even Iqbal, the voice of the resurgent Muslim nationalists of the twentieth century, let alone Mir or Ghalib, the raconteurs of the dying Mughal Empire.

This disconnect is perhaps germane to new sensibilities. Notwithstanding the general stereotypes about Muslims as inward-looking, inert, and unchanging, I found among the Muslim youth a new desire to end their isolation and be part of the larger Indian society.

Meyrowitz (1985) and Appadurai (1996) would argue that this is but an outcome of the media's ability to dislodge the sense of space and to create communities with no sense of place. However, the experiences of Muslim youth do not unequivocally support either of these premises, because if on the one hand the media has increased their connections with the Indian society, then conversely the media has also generated a heightened awareness of the negative perceptions about Muslims, while simultaneously increasing their access to material and discursive realities of globalized Islam. The Muslim youth's subjectivities are emerging within contested and conflicting ideological flows even as materialism and consumerism have emerged as the most vociferous and overwhelming discourse. There exists in India today an aggressive consumerist culture, where wealth is considered to be the most important marker of identity (Das, 2001; Nilekani, 2008; Varma, 1998). However, this deflection of attention from identities based in class, caste, and religion, coupled with regimes of meritocracy as introduced by multinational corporations have created new hopes and aspirations among the Muslim youth to participate in the expanding economy and also benefit from the rising prosperity. The compounded effect of the expanding economy, and of the raising salience of consumerist regimes, created by constant reiteration in ubiquitous media outlets, has been that for the first time in independent India's history, the Muslim population has been so committed to the ideas of participating in the mainstream.

Therefore, this new positionality also calls for very different strategies than the ones adopted by the older generation's to come to terms with their minority status. The youth definitely cannot entertain the option to retreat into their closed society, rather, they have to contend on a daily basis with the power regimes that are arrayed against them. And one of the ways that they approach their new situation is through their heightened sagacity, which does not give credence to the rhetoric of victimization, or indulge in hyperboles and conspiracy theories much favoured by the Urdu press. In fact I found my informants to be rather reluctant to speak about the lack of space accorded to the Indian Muslim culture in the Indian public sphere. Contrary to the commonly held belief that Muslims are defensive about their identity, the youth of Jamia avoided excavating the issue of why the Indian Islamic identity is being marginalized. They did not have a problem with emphasizing their national identity as opposed to their cultural and religious identity. They even endorsed the media's nationalistic rhetoric captured in phrases of 'Team India' and 'India Shining,' while professing to hold a positive outlook towards liberalization and increasing privatization.

But, this is not to say that the Muslim youth have been overwhelmed by Hindu right wing political parties' extreme nationalism, which dictates to Muslims the choice of assimilating into Indian [read Hindu] nationalist ethos by erasing their cultural and religious particularities completely, and which threatens them that in the event of their failure to comply, they would not be allowed to live in peace (see Metcalf 1995). However, despite the right-wing Hindu nationalism's increasing stridency, the acceptance of Muslim subjugation would be a fallacy, because notwithstanding their desire to participate in the economic mainstream, this generation is also the most vocal in staking its claim to a distinct identity. And these claims are being made within complex contexts of 'cultures of circulation' where they reverberate in digital spheres connecting them to new audiences even as they give the Muslim youth a new space to express themselves. The new influences also include the rise of a different version of spirituality, built around televised sermons delivered by religious leaders so well-versed in the English language as to grace not only the homes of middle-class Muslims eager to expand their repertoire of experiences, but also television studios of mainstream Indian channels where they effectively present their point of view. Hence, I argue that often the question of sublimation of their Islamic identity in the larger pan-Indian identity was avoided because of the duplicity surrounding it. It was acceptable to the Muslim youth only as long as it was instrumental in fulfilling their aspirations for inclusion in the economic workforce.

I define the emerging subjectivities as 'convoluted modernities' which leave scholars perplexed because they are so used to framing emerging realities within neat dichotomous frameworks while Muslims problematize such clear-cut divisions by their embrace of modernity only to stage a critique of it.

The key point that I have tried to make through this research project on minority Muslim youth is that the investigation of reality in postcolonial contexts cannot be within frameworks of knowledge developed in vastly different contexts. Based on my critique of postcolonial scholarship, I have concluded that postcolonial theories have been unable to explain the experiences of Muslims because the arguments of hybrid identities have been developed without attention to material conditions and without reference to privileges of class, education, and wealth. The scholar's aim, to quote historian Vinay Bahl (2002), ought to be to forego 'a top-down approach and replace it with the study of the culture of the people' (2002, p. 358). There is a need to analyze actual conditions in postcolonial nations and to explain, ' how do the social order and social institutions articulate in the formation of the subject (individual),' and 'how is the link between social and psychic reality to be spelled out' (Bahl 2002, p. 359). I support Bahl's views that there is a need to invest in social research that accepts the role of both material culture and human agency. He proposes that the emphasis on textual analysis should be replaced by social analysis to show how material culture is shaped by human agency and to show the way material culture influences the creation of values and identities. This is not very different from the anthropologist Geertz's (1973) view that there is a need to build theory from the ground-up. Geertz argued that theoretical concepts must be developed through the study of actual social settings and should not be formulated on the basis of suppositions or without concrete findings of research. This book has attempted to follow these prescriptions through the example of an Indian minority Muslim population.

BIBLIOGRAPHY

Abbas, T. (2001). 'Media Capital and the Representation of South Asian Muslims in British Press: An Ideological Analysis', *Journal of Muslim Minority Affairs*, 21 (2): 245–57.

Abu-Lughod, L. (1990). 'Can there be Feminist Ethnography?', *Women and Performance: Journal of Feminist Theory*, 5 (1): 7–27.

———. (1991). 'Writing Against Culture'. In R.G. Fox (Ed.), *Recapturing Anthropology: Working in the Present* (pp. 137–162). Santa Fe, NM: School of American Research Press.

———. (2002). 'Do Muslim Women Really Need Saving? Anthropological Reflections On Cultural Relativism And Its Other', *American Anthropologist*, 104 (3): 783–90.

———. (2002a). 'Egyptian Melodrama: Technology of the Modern Subject?' In F. D. Ginsburg, L. Abu-Lughod, and B. Larkin (Eds), *Media Worlds: Anthropology on New Terrain* (pp. 115–33). Berkeley: University of California Press.

Agar, M. (1980). *The Professional Stranger: An Informal Introduction to Ethnography*. New York: Academic Press.

———. (1986). *Speaking of Ethnography*. London: Sage Publications.

Ahmed, A. (1983). 'Introduction'. In I. Ahmed (Ed.), *Modernization and Social Change among Muslims in India* (pp. xvii–xlix). Delhi: Manohar.

———. (1992). *In Theory*. London: Verso.

———. (1995). 'Postcolonialism: What's in a Name?' In R. de la Campa, E. A. Kaplan and M. Sprinker (Eds), *Late Imperial Culture* (pp. 11–33). London: Verso.

———. (1996). 'The Politics of Literary Postcoloniality'. In P. Mongia (Ed.), *Contemporary Postcolonial Theory: A Reader* (pp. 276–93). London: Arnold.

Ahmed, Z. (2003, May 23). 'Bollywood's Full Monty'. *BBC News*. Retrieved May 21, 2008 from, http://news.bbc.co.uk/1/hi/world/south_asia/2931870.stm

Ahmed, I. (2008). 'Cracks in the "Mightiest Fortress": Jamaat-e-Islami's Changing Discourse on Women', *Modern Asian Studies*, 42 (2/3): 549–75.

Ahmed, L. (2011). *A Quiet Revolution: The Veil's Resurgence, from the Middle East to America*. New Haven, CT: Yale University Press.

Akbar, I. (2011, March 11). 'The Good Word: Twocircles.net, a website on Indian Muslims is becoming popular for news beyond stereotypes'. *Indian Express*. Retrieved from, http://www.indianexpress.com/news/the-good-word/760752/

Alexander, C. (1996). 'Street Credibility and Identity: Some Observations on the Art of Being Black'. In T. Ranger, Y. Samad, and O. Stuart (Eds), *Culture, Identity, and Politics* (pp. 112–20). Hants, UK: Averbury.

Ali, M. (2003). *Brick Lane*. New York: Scribner.

AlSayyad, N. (2004). 'Urban Informality as a "New" Way of Life'. In A. Roy and N. AlSayyad (Eds), *Urban Informalities: Transnational Perspectives from the Middle East, Latin America, and South Asia* (pp. 7–30). Oxford: Lexington Books.

AlSayyad, N. & Roy, A. (2004). 'Prologue/Dialogue-Urban Informality: Crossing Borders'. In A. Roy and N. AlSayyad (Eds), *Urban Informalities: Transnational Perspectives from the Middle East, Latin America, and South Asia* (pp. 1–6). Oxford: Lexington Books.

Altorki, S. (1988). 'At Home in the Field'. In S. Altorki and C. F. El-Solh (Eds), *Arab Women in the Field* (pp. 49–68). Syracuse, NY: Syracuse University Press.

Altorki, S. & El-Solh, C. F. (1988). 'Introduction'. In S. Altorki and C. F. El-Solh (Eds), *Arab Women in the Field* (pp. 1–23). Syracuse, NY: Syracuse University Press.

Amin, S. (2004). 'On Representing the Musalman' *Sarai reader 04: Crisis/media*. Retrieved January 21, 2006 from, http://www.sarai.net/publications/readers/04-crisis-media

———. (2005). 'Representing the Musalman: Then and now, now and Then'. In S. Mayaram, M. S. S. Pandian and A. Skaria (Eds), *Subaltern Studies XII: Muslims, Dalits, and the Fabrication of History* (pp. 1–35). Delhi: Permanent Black & Ravi Dayal Publisher.

Anand, S. (2006, September 2). 'It's a cell-out! Delhi set to join 10m club' *The Times of India*. Retrieved from http://www.timesofindia.com

Anderson, B. (1983/1991). *Imagined Communities: Reflections on the Origin and Spread of Nationalism*. London: Verso.

Ang, I. (2001). *On not Speaking Chinese: Living between Asia and the West*. London: Routledge.

Ang, I. (2000). 'Identity Blues'. In P. Gilroy, L. Grossberg and A. McRobbie (Eds), *Without Guarantees: In Honour of Stuart Hall* (pp. 1–13). London: Verso

Anngard, E. (2005). 'Barbie Princesses and Dinosaur Dragons: Narration as a Way of Doing Gender', *Gender & Education*, 17 (5): 539–53.

Anzaldua, G. (1987). *Borderlands: La Frontera, The New Mestiza*, San Francisco: Spinsters/ Aunt Lute Book Company.

———. (1982/1985). *Watching Dallas*. London: Methuen.

Appadurai, A. (1996). *Modernity at Large: Cultural Dimensions of Globalization*. Minneapolis: University of Minnesota Press.

Araeen, R. (2000). 'A New Beginning: Beyond Post-colonial Cultural Theory and Identity Politics'. *Third Text*, 50 (3): 3–20.

Ardizzoni, M. (2005). 'Redrawing the Boundaries of Italianess: Televised Identities in the Age of Globalization'. *Social Identities*, 11(5): 509–30.

Asad, T. (2006). 'Responses'. In D. Scott and C. Hirschkind Powers (Eds). *Of the Secular Modern: Talal Asad and his Interlocutors* (pp. 206–43), Stanford, CA: Stanford University Press.

Bagchi, A. (1996). *Women in Indian Cinema*. Retrieved May 21, 2008 from, http://www.cs.jhu.edu/~bagchi/women.html

Bahl, V. (2002). 'Relevance (or irrelevance) of Subaltern Studies'. In. D. Ludden (Ed.), *Reading Subaltern Studies: Critical History, Contested Meaning and the Globalization of South Asia* (pp. 358–99). London: Anthem.

Bajaj, V. (2007, February 11). 'In India, The Golden Age of Television is Now'. *The New York Times*, Retrieved from http://www.nytimes.com

Bakhtin, M. M. (1986). *The Dialogic Imagination: Four Essays by Bakhtin* (C. Emerson & M. Holquist, trans.). Austin: University of Texas Press. (Original work published 1975).

Banaji, S. (2006). 'Loving with Irony: Young Bombay Viewers Discuss Clothing, Sex and their Encounters with Media', *Sex Education*, 6 (4): 377–91.

Banet-Weiser, S. (2004). 'Girls rule!: Gender, Feminism, and Nickelodeon'. *Critical Studies in Media Communication*, 21 (2): 19–139.

Barber, B. (2004). 'Jihad vs. McWorld'. In F. J. Lechner and J. Boli (Eds), *The Globalization Reader* (pp. 29–35), Malden, MA: Blackwell Publishing.

Basu, A. (1997). 'Reflections on Community Conflicts and the State in India'. *The Journal of Asian Studies*, 56 (2): 391–97.

Bauman, Z. (2001). 'Identity in the Globalizing World', *Social Anthropology*, 9(2), 121–129.

Bayat, A. (2004). 'Globalization and the Politics of the Informals in the Global South'. In A. Roy and N. AlSayyad (Eds), *Urban Informalities: Transnational Perspectives from the Middle East, Latin America, and South Asia* (pp. 79–102). Oxford: Lexington Books.

Bhabha H. K. (1994). *The Location of Culture*. London: Routledge.

Bhargava, G. S. (2006). 'Sachar Committee Report: Barking up the Wrong Tree.' *Asian Tribune*. Retrieved January 25, 2007 from, http://www.asiantribune. com/index.php?q=node/3664

Bhaskar, B. (2005). 'Mainstream Indian Media: 1990s and after'. In N. Rajan (Ed.), *Practicing Journalism: Values, Constrains, Implications* (pp. 231–41). New Delhi: Sage.

'BJP expresses concern about Sachar Committee' (2006, July 20), *Hindustan Times*, Retrieved January 25, 2007 from, Lexis-Nexis database.

'BJP to launch stir on Muslim status survey' (2006, February 17), *Indian Express*, Retrieved January 25, 2007 from, Lexis-Nexis database.

Brah, A & Coombes, A. E. (2000). 'Introduction'. In A. Brah and A. E. Coombes (Eds), *Hybridity and its Discontents: Politics, Science, Culture* (pp.1–16). London: Routledge.

Brass, P. R. (2003). *The Production of Hindu-Muslim Violence in Contemporary India*. Seattle: University of Washington Press.

Brauchler, B. (2013). *Cyber Identities at War: The Moluccan Conflict on the Internet* (Jeremy Gaines trans.). New York: Berghahn.

Brosius, C. (2005). *Empowering Visions: The Politics of Representation in Hindu Nationalism*. London: Anthem Press.

Burch, J. (2008, April 17). 'Indian soap operas cause a stir in Afghanistan'. *International Herald Tribune*. Retrieved May 26, 2008 from http://www.iht. com/articles/2008/04/22/asia/22soaps.php

Burke, J. (2013, March 11). *Delhi gang rape victim's tragic death transforms her family's life*. Retrieved March 12, 2013 from, http://www.guardian.co.uk/ world/2013/mar/12/delhi-gang-rape-death-transformed-lives

Butalia, U. (2000). *The Other Side of Silence: Voices from the Partition of India*. Durham: Duke University Press.

Butcher, M. (2003). *Transnational Television, Cultural Identity, and Change: When STAR Came to India*. New Delhi: Sage.

Cammaerts, B., Mattoni, A. & McCurdy, P. (2013). *Mediation and Protest Movements*. Chicago: Intellect.

Canclini, N. G. (2001). 'Consumers and Citizens: Globalization and Multicultural Conflicts.' (George Yúdice trans), Minneapolis: University of Minnesota Press.

———. (2005). *Hybrid Cultures: Strategies for Entering and Leaving Modernity*. Minneapolis: University of Minnesota Press.

Cantijoch, M. (2012). 'Digital Media and Offline Political Participation in Spain'. In E. Anduiza, M. J. Jensen and L. Jorba (Eds), *Digital Media and Political Engagement Worldwide: A Comparative Study* (pp. 118–37). Cambridge: Cambridge University Press.

Carstens, S. (2003). 'Constructing Transnational Identities? Mass Media and the Malaysian Chinese Audience', *Ethnic & Racial Studies*, 26 (2). 321–44.

Carter, A. B. (2006, July/August). 'America's New Strategic Partner?', *Foreign Affairs*, 85(4): 33–44.

Castells, M. (1996). *The Rise of Network Society. Volume I, The Information Age: Economy, Society and Culture*. Oxford: Blackwell.

———. (1997). *The Power of Identity. Volume II, The Information Age: Economy, Society and Culture*. Oxford: Blackwell.

———. (2009). *Communication Power*. New York: Oxford University Press.

Census Data of India. (2001). *India at a Glance: Broad Age Groups*. [Data file]. Available from Census of India Web site: http://www.censusindia.gov.in/Census_Data_2001/India_at_glance/broad.aspx

Certeau, M. de (1984). *The Practice of Everyday Life* (S. Rendall, trans.). Berkeley: University of California Press.

Chadwick, A. (2012). 'Recent shifts in the relationship between the Internet and democratic engagement in Britain and the United States: Granularity, Informational Exuberance, and Political Learning'. In E. Anduiza, M. J. Jensen, and L. Jorba (Eds), *Digital Media and Political Engagement Worldwide: A Comparative Study* (pp. 17–39). Cambridge: Cambridge University Press.

Chakrabarty, D. (2011). 'The Muddle of Modernity', *The American Historical Review*, 116 (3): 663–75.

———. (1999). 'Adda, Calcutta: Dwelling in Modernity', *Public Culture*, 11 (1): 109–45.

Chandrasekhar, C. P. & Ghosh, J. (2007, February 06). 'Women Workers in Urban India', *The Hindu Business Line*. Retrieved May 24, 2008 from, http://www.thehindubusinessline.com/2007/02/06/stories/2007020600770900.htm

Chatterjee, P. (1999). *The Partha Chatterjee Omnibus*. New Delhi: Oxford University Press.

———. (2006). 'Fasting for Bin Laden: The Politics of Secularization in Contemporary India'. In D. Scott & C. Hirschkind Powers (Eds), *Of the Secular Modern: Talal Asad and his Interlocutors* (pp. 57–75). Stanford, CA: Stanford University Press.

Chopra, R. (2006). 'Global Primordialities: Virtual Identity Politics in Online Hindutva and Online Dalit Discourse', *New Media & Society*, 8 (2): 187–206.

Chrisafis, A. (2013, July 22). 'France's Headscarf War: It's an Attack on Freedom', *The Guardian*, Retrieved from, http://www.theguardian.com/world/2013/jul/22/frances-headscarf-war-attack-on-freedom

Ciotti, M. (2010). *Retro-Modern India: Forging the Low-caste Self*. London: Routledge.

Clifford, J. (1986). 'Introduction: Partial Truths'. In J. Clifford and G. Marcus (Eds), *Writing Culture: The Poetics and Politics of Ethnography* (pp. 1–26). Berkeley: University of California Press.

Cooley, C. H. (1902/1964). *Human Nature and the Social Order*. New York: Schocken Books.

Corbridge, S. & Harriss, J. (2000). *Reinventing India: Liberalization, Hindu Nationalism and Popular Democracy*. Cambridge: Polity Press.

Couldry, N. (2008). 'Mediatization or Mediation? Alternative Understanding of the Emergent Space of Digital Storytelling', *New Media and Society*, 10 (3): 373–91.

———. (2002). Ethnography (Multi-sited Ethnography: Made for Television?). In T. Miller (Ed.), *Television Studies* (pp. 14–7). London: BFI Publications.

Craig, J. (2010). *Timepass: Youth, Class, and the Politics of Waiting in India*. Stanford: Stanford University Press.

Das, G. (2001). *India Unbound*. New York: Alfred A. Knoff.

———. (2006, July/August). 'The India Model', *Foreign Affairs*, 85 (4): 2–16.

Das, M. B. (2005). 'Muslim Women's Low Labour Force Participation in India: Some Structural Explanations'. In Z. Hasan & R. Menon (Eds), *In a Minority: Essays on Muslim Women in India* (pp. 189–221). New Delhi: Oxford University Press.

Das, V. (1995). *Critical Events: An Anthropological Perspective on Contemporary India*. New York: Oxford University Press.

Dasgupta, S. (1996). 'Feminist Consciousness in Woman-Centered Hindi Films', *The Journal of Popular Culture*, 30 (1): 173–89.

Datta, S. (2000). 'Globalisation and Representation of Women in Indian Cinema', *Social Scientist*, 28 (3/4): 71–82.

Daura, A. (2005, June 19). 'On the Verge of Extinction', *The Hindu*. Retrieved May 21, 2008, from http://www.hinduonnet.com/mag/2005/06/19/stories/2005061900110500.htm

Dearbon, A. (1975). *Arab Women*. London: Minority Rights Group Report no. 27.

Debord, G. (1983). *Society of the Spectacle*. Detroit: Black & Red.

Defense Minister's statement on Justice Rajinder Sachar Committee report in Rajya Sabha. (2006, February 21). *Hindustan Times*. Retrieved January 25, 2007, from Lexis-Nexis database.

Deshpande, S. (2000). 'Hegemonic Spatial Strategies: The Nation-Space and Hindu Communalism in Twentieth-century India'. In P. Chatterjee and P. Jeganathan (Eds), *Subaltern Studies XI: Community, Gender and Violence* (pp. 167–12). New York: Columbia University Press.

Dhume, S. (2010, June, 20th). 'The Trouble with Dr. Zakir Naik', *The Wall Street Journal*, Retrieved June 22 from http://online.wsj.com/article/SB10001424052748704365204575317833268479268.html

Dilawari, S. R. (1996). 'Communicating the Indian Tradition: A Hermeneutic Study of the Mahabharat Television Serial', *Dissertation Abstracts International*, 59 (12): 4310A.

Dirlik, A. (1999). 'How the Grinch Hijacked Radicalism: Further Thoughts on the Postcolonial', *Postcolonial Studies*, 2 (2): 149–63.

Dubrofsky, R. E. (2006). 'The Bachelor: Whiteness in the Harem', *Critical Studies in Media and Communication*, 23 (1): 39–56.

Duggan, L. (2003). *The Twilight of Equality? Neoliberalism, Cultural Politics, and the Attack on Democracy*, Boston: Beacon Press.

Durham, M. G. (1999). 'Girls, Media, and the Negotiation of Sexuality: A Study on Race, Class, and Gender in Adolescent Peer Groups', *Journalism and Mass Communication Quarterly*, 76 (2): 193–216.

———. (2004). 'Constructing the "New Ethnicities": Media, Sexuality, and Diaspora Identity in the Lives of South Asian Immigrant Girls', *Critical Studies in Media Communication*, 21 (2): 140–61.

Eagleton, T. (1999). 'In the Gaudy Supermarket'. *London Review of Books*, 21 (10). Retrieved October 15, 2006 from, http://www.lrb.co.uk/v21/n10/print/eagl01_.html.

———. (1994, Feb. 8). Goodbye to Enlightenment. *The Guardian*, A12.

Echchaibi, N. (2011). 'Gendered Blueprints: Transnational Masculinities in Muslim Televangelist Cultures'. In R. S. Hegde (Ed.), *Circuits of Visibility: Gender and Transnational Media Cultures* (pp. 89–102). New York: New York University Press.

'Education only way out for Muslims: Sachar's Most Senior Member', (2006, November 10). *Indian Express*. Retrieved January 25, 2007 from, Lexis-Nexis database.

Eickelman, D. F. (2000). 'Islam and the Languages of Modernity', *Daedalus: Multiple Modernities*, 129 (1): 119–35.

Engineer, A. A. (1995). *Lifting the Veil: Communal Violence and Communal Harmony in Contemporary India*. Hyderabad, India: Sangam Books.

———. (1988). *Delhi-Meerut Riots: Analysis, Compilation, and Documentation*. Delhi: Ajanta Publications.

Faisal, M. (2006, August 20). Chak de India! *Indian Muslim blog: A Window into the Indian Muslim life*. Retrieved from, http://indianmuslims.in/chak-de-india-review/

Fazalbhoy, N. (2005). 'Muslim Women and Inheritance'. In Z. Hasan and R. Menon (Eds), *In a Minority: Essays on Muslim Women in India* (pp. 69–107). New Delhi: Oxford University Press.

Fazila-Yacoobali, V. (2002). '*Yeh mulk hamara ghar*: The "national order of thing" and Muslim identity in John Mathew Mattan's *Sarfaroosh*', *Contemporary South Asia*, 11 (2): 183–98.

Fernandes, L. (2000). 'Nationalizing 'the Global': Media Images, Cultural Politics and the Middle Class in India', *Media, Culture & Society*, 22, 611–28.

Fernandes, L. (2006). *India's New Middle Class: Democratic Politics in an Era of Economic Reform*. Minneapolis: University of Minnesota Press.

Foley, D. E. (2002). 'Critical Ethnography: The Reflexive Turn', *International Journal of Qualitative Studies*, 15 (5): 469–90.

Foucault, M. (1977/1995). *Discipline and Punish: The Birth of the Prison* (A. Sheridan, Trans.). New York: Vintage Books.

Fox, R. G. (1991). 'Introduction: Working in the Present'. In R. G. Fox (Ed.), *Recapturing Anthropology: Working in the Present* (pp. 1–16). Santa Fe: School of American Research Press.

Friedman, T. L. (2007, November 11). Democracy's Root: Diversity. *The New York Times*. Retrieved from, http://www.nytimes.com

———. (2006). *The World is Flat: A Brief History of the Twenty-First Century*. New York: Farrar, Straus and Giroux.

Fuller, C.J. & Narasimhan, H. (2007). 'Information Technology Professionals and the New-Rich Middle Class in Chennai (Madras).' *Modern Asian Studies*, 41 (1): 121–50.

Fung, A. (2004). 'Postcolonial Hong Kong Identity: Hybridizing the Local and the National', *Social Identities*, 10 (3): 399–414.

Gaonkar, D. P. (2002). 'Toward New Imaginaries: An Introduction', *Public Culture*, 14 (1): 1–19.

———. (1999). 'On Alternate Modernities', *Public Culture*, 11 (1): 1–18.

Geertz, C. (1973). *The Interpretation of Cultures*. Basic Books: United States of America.

Ghoshal, B. (2010). 'Arabization: The Changing Face of Islam in Asia', *India Quarterly: A Journal of International Affairs*, 66 (1): 69–89.

Giddens, A. (1991). *Modernity and Self-Identity: Self and Society in the Late Modern Age*. Stanford, CA: Stanford University Press.

Gilbertson, A. (2014). 'A Fine Balance: Negotiating Fashion and Respectable Feminity in Middle Class Hyderabad, India', *Modern Asian Studies*, 48 (1): 120–58.

Ginsburg, F. D., Abu-Lughod, L. & Larkin, B. (2002). 'Introduction'. In F. D. Ginsburg, L. Abu-Lughod, and B. Larkin (Eds), *Media Worlds: Anthropology on New Terrain* (pp. 1–36). Berkeley: University of California Press.

Goffman, E. (1959). *The Presentation of Self in Everyday Life*. Garden City, NY: Doubleday.

Gole, N. (2000). 'Snapshots of Islamic Modernities', *Daedalus: Multiple Modernities*, 129 (1): 91–117.

Government of NCT of Delhi. (2006). *Delhi Human Development Report 2006: Partnership for Progress*. New Delhi: Oxford University Press.

Govindan, P. P. & Dutta, B. (2008). '"From Villain to Traditional Housewife!": The Politics of Globalization and Women's Sexuality in the "New" Indian

Media'. In K. P Anandam & A. Punathambekar (Eds), *Global Bollywood* (pp. 180–202). New York: New York University Press.

Gray, John (1998). *False Dawn: The Delusions of Global Capitalism*. The New Press.

Grewal, I. (1999). 'Travelling Barbie: Indian Transnationality and New Consumer Subjects', *Positions*, 7 (3): 799–826.

Grixti, J. (2006). 'Symbiotic Transformations: Youth, Global Media and Indigenous Culture in Malta', *Media, Culture and Society*, 28(1): 105–22.

Grossberg, L. (1996). 'Identity and Cultural Studies: Is that all there is?' In S. Hall and P. Du Gay (Eds), *Questions of Cultural Identity* (pp. 87–108). London: Sage.

Haines, C. (2011). 'Cracks in the Façade: Landscapes of Hope and Desire in Dubai'. In A. Roy & A. Ong (Eds.), *Worlding Cities: Asian Experiments and the Art of being Global*, pp. 160–181. Malden, MA: Wiley-Blackwell.

Hall, S. (1985). 'Signification, Representation, Ideology: Althusser and the Post-structuralist Debates', *Critical Studies in Mass Communication*, 2(2): 91–114.

———. (1990). 'Cultural Identity and Diaspora'. In J. Rutherford (Ed.), *Identity: Community, Culture, Difference*, pp. 222–237. London: Lawrence & Wishart.

———. (1992). 'The Question Of Cultural Identity'. In S. Hall, D. Held and T. McGrew (Eds), *Modernity and its Future* (pp. 274–316). Cambridge: Polity Press.

———. (1996a). 'Cultural Identity and Diaspora'. In P. Mongia (Ed.), *Contemporary Postcolonial Theory* (pp. 276–93). London: Arnold.

———. (1996b). 'Politics of Identity'. In T. Ranger, Y. Samad, and O. Stuart (Eds), *Culture, Identity and Politics* (pp. 129–35). Hants, UK: Averbury.

———. (1996c). 'Who Needs "Identity"?' In S. Hall and P. Du Gay (Eds), *Questions of Cultural Identity* (pp. 1–17). London: Sage.

Hamid, M. (2006). *The Reluctant Fundamentalist*. Orlando: Harcourt.

———. (2000). *Moth Smoke*. New York: Farrar, Straus, and Giroux.

Hamilton, A. & Tolbert, C. J. (2012). 'Political Engagement and the Internet in the 2008 US Presidential Elections: A Panel Survey'. In E. Anduiza, M. J. Jensen and L. Jorba (Eds), *Digital Media and Political Engagement Worldwide: A Comparative Study* (pp. 56–79). Cambridge: Cambridge University Press.

Haniff, N. Z. (1983). 'Muslim Women and the Minority Mentality'. In I. Ahmed (Ed.), *Modernization and Social Change among Muslims in India* (pp. 185–206). Delhi: Manohar.

Hansen, T. B. (1996). 'Recuperating Masculinity: Hindu Nationalism, Violence and the Exorcism of the Muslim "Other"', *Critique of Anthropology*, 16(2), 137–172.

Haq, A. (1993). *Urdu-English Dictionary*. New Delhi: Star Publications.

Harvey, D. (2005). *A Brief History of Neoliberalism*. Oxford: Oxford University Press.

Hasan, M. (1994). *Legacy of a Divided Nation: India's Muslims since Independence.* Boulder, CO: Westview Press.

———. (2002). *Islam in the Subcontinent: Muslims in a Plural Society.* Delhi: Manohar.

———. (Ed.). (2004). *Will Secular India Survive?* Gurgaon, India: ImprintOne.

Hasan, M. (2005). *A Moral Reckoning: Muslim Intellectuals in Nineteenth-Century Delhi.* New Delhi: Oxford University Press.

———. (2007). *Living with Secularism: The Destiny of India's Muslims.* New Delhi: Manohar.

Hasan, Z. (1994). 'Introduction: Contextualizing Gender and Identity in Contemporary India'. In Z. Hasan (Ed.), *Forging Identities: Gender, Communities, and the State in India* (pp. vii–xxiv). Boulder: Westview Press.

———. (2000). 'Representations and Redistribution: The New Lower Caste Politics in Northern India'. In F. Frankel, Z. Hasan, R. Bhargava and B. Arora (Eds), *Transforming India: Social and Political Dynamics of Democracy* (pp. 146–75). Delhi: Oxford University Press.

Hasan, M. & Asaduddin, M. (2000). 'Introduction'. In M. Hasan and M. Asaduddin (Eds), *Images and Representation* (pp. 1–16). New Delhi: Oxford University Press.

Hasan, Z. & Menon, R. (2004). *Unequal Citizens: A Study of Muslim Women in India.* New Delhi: Oxford University Press.

———. (2005). 'Introduction'. In Z. Hasan and R. Menon (Eds), *In a Minority: Essays on Muslim Women in India* (pp. 1–17). New Delhi: Oxford University Press.

Hasan, M. & Roy, A. (Eds). (2005). *Living Together Separately: Cultural India in History and Politics.* New York: Oxford University Press.

Hebdige, D. (1979). *Subculture: The Meaning of Style.* London: Routledge.

Hirji, F. (2006). 'Common Concerns and Constructed Communities: Muslim Canadians, the Internet, and the War in Iraq'. *Journal of Communication Inquiry*, 30(2): 125–41.

Hjavard, S. (2007). 'From Bricks to Bytes: The Mediatization of a Global Toy Industry'. In I. Bondjeberg & P. Golding (Eds.), *European Culture and the Media*, pp. 43–63. Bristol, U.K: Intellect.

Holstein, J., & Gubrium, J. (2000). *The Self We Live By.* New York: Oxford University Press.

Holt, S. (2006, March 27). Delhi Looks to 2010. *BBC News.* Retrieved March 10, 2008 from, http://news.bbc.co.uk/sport1/hi/commonwealth_games/4848528.stm

Hosken, F. (1981). 'Female Genital Mutilation and Human Right', *Feminist Issues* 1 (3).

Hungtington, S. P. (1993). 'The Clash of Civilizations', *Foreign Affairs*, 72(3): 22–50.

India looks forward. (2007, October). *OECD Observer*, 263, 9–11.

Jamia Nagar: Mob torches police post, 4 cops serious. (2007, September 23). *Indian Express*. Retrieved September 24, 2007 from, http://www. expressindia.com/latest-news/Jamia-Nagar-Mob-torches-police-post-4-cops-serious/220056/

Jeffrey, C. (2010). *Timepass: Youth, Class, and the Politics of Waiting in India*. Stanford: Stanford University Press.

Jensen, M. J., Jorba, L. & Anduiza, E. (2012). 'Introduction'. In E. Anduiza, M. J. Jensen and L. Jorba (Eds), *Digital Media and Political Engagement Worldwide: A Comparative Study* (pp. 1–16). Cambridge: Cambridge University Press.

John, M. E. (1998/2000). 'Globalisation, Sexuality and the Visual Field: Issues and Non-issues for Cultural Critique'. In J. Nair and M. E. John (Eds), *A Question of Silence: The Sexual Economies of Modern India* (pp. 368–96). London: Zed Books.

Jorba, L. & Bimber, B. (2012). 'The Impact of Digital Media on Citizenship from a Global Perspective'. In E. Anduiza, M. J. Jensen and L. Jorba (Eds), *Digital Media and Political Engagement Worldwide: A Comparative Study* (pp. 16–38). Cambridge: Cambridge University Press.

Juluri, V. (2003). *Becoming a Global Audience*. New York: Peter Lang Publishing Inc.

Kakar, S. (1996). *The Colors of Violence: Cultural Identities, Religion and Conflict*. Chicago: University of Chicago Press.

Kalb, Don & Herman Tak (2005). 'Introduction: Critical junctions—Recapturing Anthropology and History'. In D. Kalb and H. Tak (Eds), *Critical Junctions: Anthropology and History beyond the Cultural Turn* (pp. 1–27). New York: Berghahn Books.

Kaviraj, S. (2005). 'An Outline of a Revisionist Theory of Modernity', *European Journal of Sociology*, 46(3): 497–526.

Kazmi, F. (1994). 'Muslim Socials and the Female Protagonist: Seeing a Dominant Discourse at Work'. In Z. Hasan (Ed.), *Forging Identities: Gender, Communities, and the State in India* (pp. 226–43). Boulder: Westview Press.

Kazmi, N. (2007, December 11). Comedies Keep Cash Registers Ringing', *The Times of India*, p. A 13.

Kesvan, M. (1994). 'Urdu, Awadh and the Tawaif: Islamic Roots of Hindi Cinema'. In Z. Hasan (Ed.), *Forging Identities: Gender, Communities, and the State in India* (pp. 244–57). Boulder: Westview Press.

Khair, T. (2001). *Babu Fictions: Alienation in Contemporary Indian English Novels*. New Delhi: Oxford University Press.

Khalidi, O. (2006). *Muslims in Indian Economy*. Gurgaon, India: Three Essays Collective.

Khilnani, S. (1997). *The Idea of India*. New York: Farrar, Straus and Giroux.

Klaveren, M. V., Tijdens, K., Hughie-Williams, M. & Martin, N. R. (2010). 'An Overview of Women's Work and Employment in India'. *Decisions for Life MDG3 Project. Country Report No. 13. University of Amsterdam.* Retrieved January 2013 from, http://www.uva-aias.net/uploaded_files/publications/WP90-Klaveren,Tijdens,Hughie-Williams,Ramos-India.pdf

Kohli-Khandekar, V. (2006). *The Indian Media Business* (2nd ed.). London: Sage Publications Ltd.

Kumar, S. (2006). *Gandhi Meets Primetime: Globalization and Nationalism in Indian Television*. Urbana: University of Illinois.

Kumar, N (2006). 'Provincialism in Modern India: The Multiple Narratives of Education and their Plan', *Modern Asian Studies*, 40(2), 397–423.

Lahiri, J. (1999). *Interpreter of Maladies*. Boston: Houghton Mifflin.

———. (2003). *The Namesake*. Boston: Houghton Mifflin.

———. (2008). *Unaccustomed Earth*. New York: Alfred A. Knopf.

Lakdawala, M. H. (2005). 'The Relevance of the Urdu-language Media'. In N. Rajan (Ed.), *Practicing Journalism: Values, Constrains, Implications* (pp. 198–207). New Delhi: Sage Publications.

Lakshmann, N. (2007, February 12). Star India Counts on Star Power. *Business Week Online*. Retrieved from Academic Search Complete database.

Larkin, J. (2006, May 5). Newspaper *nirvana*? 300 dailies court India's avid readers. *The Wall Street Journal Online*. Retrieved from, http://online.wsj.com

Lateef, S. (1994). 'Defining Women through Legislation'. In Z. Hasan (Ed.), *Forging Identities: Gender, Communities, and the State in India* (pp. 38–58). Boulder: Westview Press.

———. (1983). 'Modernization in India and the Status of Muslim Women'. In I. Ahmed (Ed.), *Modernization and Social Change among Muslims in India* (pp. 153–84). Delhi: Manohar.

Lee, B. & LiPuma, E. (2002). 'Cultures of Circulation: The Imaginations of Modernity'. *Public Cultures*, 14(1): 191–213.

Leong, S. (2006). 'Who's the Fairest of Them All? Television ads for Skin-whitening Cosmetics in Hong Kong'. *Asian Ethnicity*, 7(2): 167–81.

Littlefield, M. (2008). 'The Media as a System of Racialization: Exploring Images of African-American and the New Racism'. *American Behavioral Scientist*, 51(5): 675–85.

Lofland, J., & Lofland, L. H. (1995). *Analyzing Social Settings: A Guide to Qualitative Observation and Analysis*. Belmont, CA: Wadsworth.

Loomba, A. (1998). *Colonialism/Postcolonialism*. London: Routledge.

Lull, J. (1988). 'The Family and Television in World Cultures'. In J. Lull (Ed.), *World Families Watch Television* (pp. 9–21). London: Sage Publications.

Malkani, G. (2006). *Londonstani*. New York: Penguin Press.

Mahmood, S. (2005). *Politics of Piety: The Islamic Revival and the Feminist Subject*. Princeton, N.J.: Princeton University Press.

Mamdani, M. (2004). *Good Muslims, Bad Muslims*. New York: Pantheon Books.

Mankekar P. (1999a). 'Brides Who Travel: Gender, Transnationalism, and Nationalism in Hindi Films'. *Positions*, 7(3): 731–761.

———. (1999b). *Screening Culture, Viewing Politics: An Ethnography of Television, Womanhood, and Nation*. Durham, London: Duke University Press.

———. (2004). 'Television and Erotics in late Twentieth-century India'. *The Journal of Asian Studies*, 63 (2): 403–31.

———. (2002a). 'Indian Grocery Stores and Transnational Configurations of Belonging', *Journal of Anthropology*, 67(1): 75–97.

———. (2002b). 'National Texts and Gendered Lives: An Ethnography of Television viewers in a North Indian City'. In K. M. Askew and R. R. Wilk (Eds), *The Anthropology of Media: A Reader* (pp. 299–322). Malden, MA: Blackwell.

———. (2002c). 'Television and Religious Identity in India'. In F. D. Ginsburg, L. Abu-Lughod and B. Larkin (Eds), *Media Worlds: Anthropology on New Terrain* (pp. 134–151). Berkeley: University of California Press.

Mazzarella, W. (2003). *Shoveling Smoke: Advertising and Globalization in Contemporary India*. Durham, NC: Duke University Press.

———. (2005). 'Middle Class', published as part of Rachel Dwyer (Ed.), South Asia Keywords, an online encyclopedia maintained by SOAS. Retrieved from, http://anthropology.uchicago.edu/docs/mazz_middleclass.pdf

McCarthy, C. (1998). 'Living with Anxiety: Race and the Renarration of White Identity in Contemporary Popular Culture', *Journal of Communication Inquiry*, 22(4): 354–65.

McDaniel, D. (2002). *Electronic Tigers of South East Asia: The Politics of Media, Technology, and National Development*. Ames, IA: Iowa State University Press.

———. (1998). 'Unintended Consequences: Media Policy in Asia'. In A. Goonasekera and D. Holaday (Eds), *Asian Communication Handbook 1998* (pp. 241–250). Singapore: AMIC.

McGuire, J., & Reeves, G. (2003). 'The Bhartiya Janata Party, Ayodhaya, and the Rise of Populist Politics in India'. In G. Mazzoleni, J. Stewart and B. Horsfield (Eds), *The Media and Neo-Populism: A Contemporary Comparative Analysis* (pp. 95–121). Westport, CT: Praeger.

McLuhan, M. (1964). *Understanding Media: The Extensions of Man*. New York: McGraw-Hill Book Company.

McRobbie, A. (2009). *The Aftermath of Feminism: Gender, Culture, and Social Change*. London: Sage.

Mehta, S. (1992). *The Eternal Web: Hindu-Muslim Relations*. New Delhi: Cosmo Publications.

Mendelson, A. L. & Papacharissi, Z. (2011). 'Look at Us: Collective Narcissism in College Students Facebook Photo Galleries'. In Z. Papacharissi (Ed.), *A Networked Self: Identity, Community, and Culture on Social Network Sites* (pp. 251–73). New York: Routledge.

Menon, S. (2004, January 12). 'Mad Cow Disease of Self-Consumption'. *Outlook*. Retrieved May 24, 2008 from, http://www.outlookindia.com/full. asp?fodname=20040112&fname=QSadanand+Menon+(F)&sid=1

Metcalf, B. D. (1995). 'Too Little and Too Much: Reflections on Muslims in the History of India', *The Journal of Asian Studies*, 54(4): 951–67.

Meyer, M. (2003). '"It's me. I'm it": Defining Adolescent Sexual Identity Through Relational Dialectics in Dawson's Creek', *Communication Quarterly*, 51(3): 262–76.

Meyrowitz, J. (1985). *No Sense of Place: The Impact of Electronic Media on Social Behavior*. New York: Oxford University Press.

Mies, M. (1982). *The Lace Makers of Narsapur: Indian Housewives' Produce for the World Market*. London: Zed Press.

Miller, B. S. (1991). 'Contending Narratives: Political Life of the Indian Epics', *The Journal of Asian Studies*, 5(4): 783–92.

Mishra, P. (2006, July 6). 'The Myth of New India'. *The New York Times*. Retrieved from, http://www.nytimes.com

Mitra, A. (1992). '"Mahabharat" on Doordarshan: The Articulation of Television and Popular Culture in India'. *Dissertation Abstracts International*, 53(07): 2147A.

———. (1993). *Television and Popular Culture in India: A Study of the Mahabharat*. New Delhi: Sage.

Mitter, S., Fernandez, G. & Varghese, S. (2004). *On the Threshold of Informalization: Women Call Center Workers in India*. Retrieved May 24, 2008, from http://www.wiego.org/publications/Chains%20of%20Fortune%20Chapters/Mitter%20Fernandez%20Varghese%20Women%20Call%20Centre%20Workers%20in%20India.pdf

Mohanty, C. T. (1991/2012). 'Under the Western Eyes: Feminist Scholarship and Colonial Discourses'. In M. G. Durham and D. M. Kellner (Eds), *Media and Cultural Studies: Keyworks* (pp. 347–64). Maldan, MA.: Willey-Blackwell.

Mongia, P. (1996). 'Introduction'. In P. Mongia (Ed.), *Contemporary Postcolonial Theory* (pp. 1–18). London: Arnold.

Morley, D. & Brunsdon, C. (1978/1999). *The Nationwide Television Studies*. London: Routledge.

Mufti, A. R. (2000). 'A Greater Story-Writer Than God: Genre, Gender, and Minority in Late Colonial India', In P. Chatterjee and P. Jeganathan (Eds), *Subaltern Studies XI: Community, Gender and Violence* (pp.1–37). New York: Columbia University Press

Mulvey, L. (1996). *Fetishism and Curiosity*. Bloomington: Indiana University Press.

Munni Begum performs in Delhi. (2008, January 7). *The Times of India*. Retrieved from, http://timesofindia.indiatimes.com

Munshi, S. (1998). 'Wife/mother/daughter-in-law: Multiple *Avatars* of Home-maker in 1990s Indian advertising', *Media, Culture & Society*, 20, 573–91.

Murphy, P. D. (1999). 'Media Cultural Studies' Uncomfortable Embrace of Ethnography'. *Journal of Communication Inquiry*, 23 (3): 205–21.

Murty, N. (2007, September 10). Guest Edit: Time for *Chak De*, India. *The Times of India*. Retrieved from, http://timesofindia.indiatimes.com

Nandy, A. (1998). 'Indian Popular Cinema as a Slum's Eye View of Politics'. In A. Nandy (Ed.), *The Secret Politics of our Desires: Innocence, Culpability, and Indian Popular Cinema* (pp. 1–19). New York: Zed Books.

Narayan, K. (1993). 'How Native Is a "Native" Anthropologist?' *American Anthropologist*, 95, 671–86.

New-age terrorist is a techie to boot (2007, July 10). *The Times of India*, p. A13.

Ninan, S. (1995). *Through the Magic Window: Television and Change in India*. New Delhi: Penguin Books.

———. (1998). 'Transforming Television in India'. In E. E. Dennis and R.W. Snyder (Eds), *Media and Democracy* (pp. 43–51). New Brunswick, NJ: Transaction Publishers.

Niranjana, T. (1992). *Siting Translation: History, Post-Structuralism and the Colonial Context*. Berkley: University of California Press.

Ohm, B. (2010). 'Forgetting to Remember: The Privatization of the Public, the Economisation of Hindutava and the Medialisation of Genocide'. In S. Banaji (Ed.), *South Asian Media Cultures: Audiences, Representations, Contexts* (pp. 123–43). New York: Anthem Press.

Olson, C. (2005). 'Politics, Power, Discourse and Representation: A Critical Look at Said and Some of His Children'. *Method & Theory in the Study of Religion*, 17, 317–36.

Omvedt, G. (1994). *Dalits and the Democratic Revolution*. New Delhi: Sage Publications.

Opposition stalls house: Stop count of Muslims in forces. (2006, February 17). *Indian Express*. Retrieved January 25, 2007 from, Lexis-Nexis database.

Ortner, S. B. (1991). 'Reading America: Preliminary Notes on Class and Culture'. In R. G. Fox (Ed.), *Recapturing Anthropology: Working in the Present* (pp. 163–90). Santa Fe: School of American Research Press.

Oza, R. (1999). 'Contentious Bodies: Globalization, Sexuality and the Politics of Culture in India'. *Dissertation Abstracts International*, 61 (07): 2862A.

———. (2001). 'Showcasing India: Gender, Geography, and Globalization'. *Signs*, 26(3): 1067–95.

———. (2006). *The Making of Neoliberal India: Nationalism, Gender, and the Paradoxes of Globalization*. New York: Routledge.

Pai, S. (2001). 'From Harijans to Dalits: Identity Formation, Political Consciousness and Electoral Mobilization of Dalits in Uttar Pradesh'. In G. Shah (Ed.), *Dalit Society and State*, volume 2 (pp. 258–87). New Delhi: Sage Publications.

———. (2002). *Dalit Assertion and the Unfinished Democratic Revolution: The Bahujan Samaj Party in Uttar Pradesh*. New Delhi: Sage Publications.

Pandey, G. (1990). *The Construction of Communalism in Colonial North India*. New York: Oxford University Press.

———. (1997). 'In Defense of the Fragment: Writing about Hindu-Muslim Riots in India Today'. In R. Guha (Ed.), *A Subaltern Studies Reader, 1986-1995* (pp. 1–34). Minneapolis: University of Minnesota Press.

———. (2001). *Remembering Partition: Violence, Nationalism, and History in India*. Cambridge, MA: Cambridge University Press.

———. (2006). *Routine Violence: Nations, Fragments, Histories*. Stanford, CA: Stanford University Press.

———. (2006). 'The Time of Dalit Conversion', *Economic and Political Weekly*, 41(18): 1779–88.

Papastergiadis, N. (2005). 'Hybridity and Ambivalence: Places and Flows in Contemporary Art and Culture', *Theory, Culture & Society*, 22(39): 39–64.

Parameswaran, R. (2001). 'Feminist Media Ethnography in India: Exploring Power, Gender, and Culture in the Field', *Qualitative Inquiry*, 7(1), 69–103.

———. (2004a). 'Global Queens, National Celebrities: Tales of Feminine Triumph in Post-liberalization India', *Critical Studies in Media Communication*, 21(4): 346–70.

———. (2004b). 'Spectacles of Gender and Globalization: Mapping Miss World Event Space in the News'. *The Communication Review*, 7: 371–406.

Parry, B. (1987). 'Problems in Current Theories of Colonial Discourse', *Oxford Literary Review*, 9(1–2): 27–58.

Peer, B. (2007, May/June). 'Style over Substance: Despite India's Media Boom, its Journalism is Shrinking', *Columbia Journalism Review*, 24–25.

Police posts set fire in mob fury (2007, September 23). *The Times of India*. Retrieved September 24, 2007 from http://timesofindia.indiatimes.com/ Delhi_mob_torches_police_posts/articleshow/2394270.cms

Pollock, S. (1993). 'Ramayan and Political Imagination in India', *The Journal of Asian Studies*, 52(2): 261–97.

PM trying to fool Muslims with Quotas Talks BJP. (2006, November 3). *Indian Express*. Retrieved January 25, 2007 from, Lexis-Nexis database.

Pratyush (2007, September 23). 40 Injured in Mob Violence in Delhi, one Policeman in Coma. Message posted to http://www.instablogs.com/,

archived at http://pratyush.instablogs.com/entry/40-injured-in-mob-vio-
lence-in-delhi-one-policeman-in-coma/

Press Trust of India. (2005, October 30). Delhi Blasts: 22 Detained for
Questioning. *Rediff India Abroad*. Retrieved January, 25, 2007 from, http://
ia.rediff.com/news/2005/oct/30delhi6.htm

PricewaterhouseCoopers. (2006). *The Indian Entertainment and Media Industry:
Unraveling the Potential*. New Delhi: FICCI.

Prison is only place where Muslims are over-represented (2006, October 28).
Indian Express. Retrieved January 25, 2007 from, Lexis-Nexis database.

Punathambekar, A. (2005). 'Bollywood in the Indian-American Diaspora:
Mediating a Transitive Logic of Cultural Citizenship', *International Journal
of Cultural Studies*, 8(2): 151–73.

Punwani, J. (2012). 'Framed by the State', *Economic & Political Weekly*, 47(41):
10–12.

Radway, J. A. (1984/1991). *Reading the Romance: Women, Patriarchy, and
Popular Literature*. Chapel Hill, NC: The University of North Carolina Press.

Ragusa, A. T. (2005). 'Social Change and the Corporate Construction of Gay
Markets in the New York Times' advertising business news'. *Media, Culture
& Society*, 27(5): 653–76.

Raja, M. C. (2006, July/August). 'India and the Balance of Power', *Foreign
Affairs*, 85(4): 17–32.

Rajagopal, A. (1992). 'Uses of the Past: The Televisual Broadcast of an Ancient
Epic and Its Reception in Indian Society'. *Dissertation Abstracts International*,
53(10): 3681A.

———. (1999). 'Thinking about the New Indian Middle Class: Gender,
Advertising, and Politics in an Age of Globalization'. In R. Sunder Rajan
(Ed.), *Signposts: Gender Issues in Post-Independence India* (pp. 57–99). New
Brunswick, NJ: Rutgers University Press.

———. (2001). *Politics after Television*. New York: Cambridge University Press.

Rajagopal, S. S. (2003). 'Ethnic Identity and Cultural Conflict in the Cinema of
the South Asian Diaspora', *Journal of Communication Inquiry*, 27(1): 49–66.

Raley, A. B. & Lucas, J. L. (2006). 'Stereotype or Success? Prime-time Television's
Portrayal of Gay Male, Lesbian, and Bisexual Characters', *Journal of
Homosexuality*, 51(2): 19–37.

Rao, A. (1999/2001). 'Understanding Sirsagaon: Notes towards Conceptualizing
the Role of Law, Caste and Gender in a case of "Atrocity."' In R. Sunder
Rajan (Ed.), *Signposts: Gender Issues in Post-independence India* (pp. 205–49).
New Brunswick, NJ: Rutgers University Press.

Ravindran, S. (2008, June 2). Swiggin' Janes. *Outlook*. Retrieved May 24, 2008
from, http://www.outlookindia.com/full.asp?fodname=20080602&fname=
Cover+Story&sid=1

Rosaldo, R. (2005). 'Foreword'. In N. Garcia Canclini (Author), *Hybrid Cultures: Strategies for Entering and Leaving Modernity*. Minneapolis: University of Minnesota Press.

Roy, Arundhati. (1999). 'The Greater Common Good'. *Outlook*. Retrived May 24, 2008 from, http://www.outlookindia.com/full.asp?fodname=19990524&fname=narmada&sid=1

———. (2008, February 4). 'Listening to Grasshoppers: Genocide, Denial and Celebration', *Outlook*. Retrieved May 24, 2008 from, http://www.outlookindia.com

Roy, S. (1979). *Status of Muslim Women in North India*. Delhi: B.R. Publishing Corporation.

Runkie, S. (2005). The Beauty Obsession. *Manushi*, 145. Retrieved May 24, 2008 from, http://www.indiatogether.org/manushi/issue145/lovely.htm

Rushdie, S. (1999). *The Ground beneath Her Feet*. New York: Henry Holt.

———. (2004). 'Yes, this is about Islam'. In F. J. Lechner and J. Boli (Eds), *The Globalization Reader* (pp. 357–59). Malden, MA: Blackwell Publishing.

———. (2005). *Shalimar the Clown*. New York: Random House.

———. (2008). *The Enchantress of Florence*. New York: Random House.

Saberwal, S. (1996). *Roots of Crisis: Interpreting Contemporary Indian Society*. New Delhi: Sage Publications.

———. (1986). *India, the Roots of Crisis*. New Delhi: Oxford University Press.

Sachar Committee. (2006, November). *Social, Economic and Educational Status of the Muslim Community of India*. New Delhi: Government of India.

Said, E. W. (1979). *Orientalism*. New York: Vintage Books.

Samad, Y. (1998). 'Media and Muslim Identity: Intersections of Generation and Gender'. *The European Journal of Social Sciences*, 11(4): 425–38.

Samuel, G. & Rozario, S. (2010). 'Contesting Science for Islam: The Media as a Source of Revisionist Knowledge in the Lives of Young Bangladeshis'. *Contemporary South Asia*, 18(4): 427–41.

Sanjay, B. P. (2008). 'Legal Aid to the Jamia Accused and Media Intervention'. *The Hoot*. Retrieved from, http://www.thehoot.org/web/home/searchdetail.php?sid=3354&bg

Sardar, Z. (1996). 'Beyond Development: An Islamic Perspective'. *European Journal of Development Research*, 8(2): 36.

Sarkar, S. (2002). 'The Decline of the Subaltern in Subaltern Studies'. In D. Ludden (Ed.), *Reading Subaltern Studies: Critical History, Contested Meaning and the Globalization of South Asia* (pp. 400–29). London: Anthem.

Schulz, W. (2004). 'Reconsidering Mediatization as an Analytical Concept', *European Journal of Communication*, 19(1), 87-101.

Sen, A. (2006). *Identity and Violence. The Illusion of Destiny*. New York: W. W. Norton & Company.

Separate and Unequal. (2006, November 18). *Indian Express*. Retrieved January 25, 2007 from, Lexis-Nexis database.

Shani, O. (2007). *Communalism, Caste and Hindu Nationalism: The Violence in Gujarat*. Cambridge: Cambridge University Press.

———. (2011). 'The Politics of Communalism and Caste'. In I. Clark-Decès (Ed.), *A Companion to the Anthropology of India* (pp. 297–312). Malden, MA: Wiley-Blackwell.

Shankar, V. (2004, January 12). 'Teflon-coated Bubble Wrap Cocoons'. *Outlook India*. Retrieved May 24, 2008 from, http://www.outlookindia.com

Sharma, D. (2005). 'Agriculture: The Missing Dimension'. In N. Rajan (Ed.), *Practicing Journalism: Values, Constrains, Implications* (pp. 134–147). New Delhi: Sage Publications.

Sharma, K. (2005). 'Urban Reporting: Citizens and "Others"'. In N. Rajan (Ed.), *Practicing Journalism: Values, Constrains, Implications* (pp. 148–52). New Delhi: Sage Publications.

Sharpe, J. (2005). 'Gender, Nation, and Globalization in Monsoon Wedding and Diwale Dulhania Le Jayenge'. *Meridians: Feminism, Race, Transnationalism*, 6(1): 58–81.

Shirky, C. (2012, June). 'How the Internet Will (one day) Transform Government'. Retrieved from, http://www.ted.com/talks/clay_shirky_how_the_internet_will_one_day_transform_government.html

Shome, R. (2006). 'Thinking through the Diaspora: Call centers, India, and a New Politics of Hybridity', *International Journal of Cultural Studies*, 9(1): 105–24.

Siddiqui, A. (2005). 'Panchayati Raj and Women in Kerala: The Case of Muslims'. In Z. Hasan & R. Menon (Eds), *In a Minority: Essays on Muslim Women in India* (pp. 284–309). New Delhi: Oxford University Press.

Silverstone, R. (2005). 'Mediation and Communication'. In C. Calhoun, C. Rojek and B. Turner (Eds), *The International Handbook of Sociology* (pp. 188–207). Sage: London.

Singh, K. (1994). 'The Constitution and Muslim Personal Law'. In Z. Hasan (Ed.), *Forging Identities: Gender, Communities, and the State in India* (pp. 96–107). Boulder: Westview Press.

Sinha, S. K. (2004, January, 12). 'Age of the "Zippie"'. *Outlook India*. Retrieved May 24, 2008 from, http://www.outlookindia.com

Sivaramakrishnan, K. & Agrawal. A. (2003). 'Regional Modernities in Stories and Practices of Development'. In K. Sivaramakrishnan and A. Agrawal (Eds), *Regional Modernities: The Cultural Politics of Development in India* (pp. 1–61). Stanford: Stanford University Press.

Spear, P. (1970). *The History of India: Volume II*. Baltimore, MD: Penguin Books.

Spivak, G. (1985). 'Subaltern Studies: Deconstructing Historiography'. In R. Guha (Ed.), *Subaltern Studies: Writings on South Asian History and Society, volume 4* (pp. 330–63). Delhi: Oxford University Press.

———. (1995). 'Can the Subaltern Speak?' In B. Ashcroft, G. Griffiths and H. Tiffin (Eds), *The Post-Colonial Studies Reader* (pp. 24–9). New York: Routledge.

Spivak, G. (1999a). *A Critique of Postcolonial Reason: Toward a History of the Vanishing Present*. Cambridge, MA: Harvard University Press.

———. (1999b). 'The New Subaltern: A Silent Interview'. In V. Chaturvedi (Ed.), *Mapping Subaltern Studies and the Postcolonial* (pp. 341–49). London: Verso.

———. (2000). 'Discussion: An Afterword on the New Subaltern'. In P. Chatterjee and P. Jeganathan (Eds), *Subaltern Studies XI: Community, Gender and Violence* (pp. 305–34). New York: Columbia University Press.

Spivak, G., & Guha, R. (Eds). (1988). *Selected Subaltern Studies*. New York: Oxford University Press.

Stern, S. (2004). 'Expressions of Identity Online: Prominent Features and Gender Differences in Adolescents' World Wide Web Home Pages', *Journal of Broadcasting and Electronic Media*, 48(2): 218–43.

Sudipta, K. (2005). 'An Outline of Revisionist Theory of Modernity'. *European Journal of Sociology*, 46(3): 497–526.

Sultana, N. (2006, September). 'Your Terrorist, My Indian: Are Indian Muslims Second-Class Citizens in a Secular Democracy?' *Hardnews*. Retrieved January 25, 2007 from, http://www.hardnewsmedia.com/2006/08/564

Sunder Rajan, R. (1993). *Real and Imagined Women: Gender, Culture and Postcolonialism*. London: Routledge.

———. (1999/2001). 'Introduction'. In R. Sunder Rajan (Ed.), *Signposts: Gender Issues in Post-Independence India* (pp. 1–16). New Brunswick, NJ: Rutgers University Press.

Swami, P. (2007, July 8). 'Shattered Certitudes and New Realities: Efforts Need to be Made to Explore the Ideological Landscape in which the Karnataka Jihadis Moved On'. *The Hindu, Sunday*, p. A10.

Tambiah, S. J. (1990). 'Reflections on Communal Violence in South Asia'. *The Journal of Asian Studies*, 49(4): 741–60.

Targeting Youth an Investment in India: E&Y. (2007, June 8). *Indian Express*. Retrieved July 20, 2008 from, http://www.expressindia.com/news/fullstory. php?newsid=87876

Taylor, C. (2000). 'Modernity and Difference'. In P. Gilroy, L. Grossberg and A. McRobbie (Eds), *Without Guarantees: In Honour of Stuart Hall* (pp. 364–74). London:Verso.

———. (2002). 'Modern Social Imaginaries'. *Public Cultures*, 14(1): 91–124.

Tharu. S. (1999/2001). 'The Impossible Subject: Caste and Desire in the Scene of the Family'. In R. Sunder Rajan (Ed.), *Signposts: Gender Issues in Post-Independence India* (pp. 188–205). New Brunswick, NJ: Rutgers University Press.

The Great Indian Hope Trick. (2006, February 25). *Economist*, 378(8466) 29–31.

Thussu, D. K. (2007). 'The 'Murdochization' of News? The case of Star TV in India'. *Media, Culture & Society*, 29(4): 593–611.

Tilak, S. G (2012, September 25). *Delhi Police Accused of Framing Suspects*. Retrieved September 26, 2012 from, http://www.aljazeera.com/indepth/features/2012/09/20129248127364613.html

Timmons, H. (2007, December 13). 'India, a Stirring Giant, is the New Place to See and be Seen'. *The New York Times*. Retrieved from http://www.nytimes.com

Turner, V. (1969/1977). *The Ritual Process: Structure and Anti-Structure*. Ithica, NY: Cornell University Press.

———. (1974). *Dramas, Fields, and Metaphors: Symbolic Action in Human Society*. Ithaca, NY: Cornell University Press.

Van Nieuwkerk, K. (2004). 'Veils and Wooden Clogs Don't Go Together.' *Journal of Anthropology*, 69(2): 229–46.

Varma, P. K. (2004). *Being Indian: Inside the Real India*. London: William Heinemann.

———. (1998). *The Great Indian Middleclass*. New Delhi: Viking Publishers.

Varshney, A. (2002). *Ethnic Conflict and Civic Life: Hindus and Muslims in India*. New Haven, CT: Yale University Press.

Vatuk, S. (2008). 'Islamic Feminism in India: Indian Muslim Women Activists and the Reform of Muslim Personal Law'. *Modern Asian Studies*, 42(2/3): 489–518.

———. (2005). 'Muslim Women and Personal Law'. In Z. Hasan & R. Menon (Eds), *In a Minority: Essays on Muslim Women in India* (pp. 18–68). New Delhi: Oxford University Press.

VHP to oppose quota for Muslims. (2006, November 5). *Hindustan Times*. Retrieved January 25, 2007 from, Lexis-Nexis database.

Victims of bias, Muslims at bottom of social barrel. (2006, April 18). *Indian Express*. Retrieved January 25, 2007 from, Lexis-Nexis database.

Virtual champions. (2006, June 3). *Economist*, 379(8480): 4–6.

Wafa, A. W. & Gall, C. (2008, April 22). 'Afghan Ministry Bans the Broadcast of 5 Foreign Soap Operas'. *The New York Times*. Retrieved May 26, 2008 from, http://www.nytimes.com/2008/04/22/world/asia/22soaps.html?partner=rssnyt&emc=rss

Waldan, A. (2003, October 20). 'Sizzling Economy Revitalizes India'. *The New York Times*, Retrieved May 26, 2008 from, http://www.nytimes.com

Weekly Box Office Review. (2007, October 13). Retrieved from, http://bolly-wood-buzz.com/news/2044/weekly-box-office-review.html

Weiner, M. (1997). 'India's Minorities: Who are they? What do they want?' In P. Chatterjee (Ed.), *The State and Politics in India*, (pp. 459–96). Delhi: Oxford University Press.

Wells, D. R. (1998). *Consumerism and the Movement of Housewives into Wage Work*. Brookfield, VT: Ashgate Publishing Company.

Werner, J. F. (2006). 'How Women are Using Television to Domesticate Globalization: A Case Study on the Reception and Consumption of Telenovelas in Senegal'. *Visual Anthropology*, 19(5): 443–72.

Williams, P. (2011). 'Hindu-Muslim Relations and the "War on Terror"', In I. Clark-Decès (Ed.), *A Companion to the Anthropology of India*, pp. 241–259. Malden, MA: Wiley-Blackwell.

Willis P. (1990). *Common Culture: Symbolic Work at Play in the Everyday Cultures of the Young*. Boulder: WestView Press.

———. (2000). *The Ethnographic Imagination*. Malden: Blackwell.

Wolf, M. (1992). *A Thrice Told Tale: Feminism, Postmodernism, And Ethnographic Responsibility*. Stanford: Stanford University Press.

Yin, J. (2005). 'Constructing the Other: A Critical Reading of the Joy Luck Club'. *The Howard Journal of Communications*, 16, 149–75.

Zacharias, U. (2000). 'The Question of the Author: Television and Cultural Politics in the Time of the Ramayan'. *Dissertation Abstracts International*, 61 (07), 2507A. (UMI No. 9980427).

Zakaria, F. (2006, March). 'India Rising'. *Newsweek*, 147(10): 32–42.

Zengottia de, T. (2005). *Mediated: How the Media Shapes Your World and the Way You Live in it*. New York: Bloomsbury.

Zizeck, S. (1997). 'Multiculturalism, or the Cultural Logic of Multinational Capitalism'. *New Left Review*. 225.

INDEX

Index

ABOUT THE AUTHOR

Tabassum Ruhi Khan is Assistant Professor in the Department of Media and Cultural Studies at the University of California, Riverside. She received her PhD from Ohio University and a masters degree from Syracuse University.

She teaches courses analysing intersections of media and popular culture within neoliberal globalized contexts with a strong focus on political economy of media.

Her research interests include minority and marginalized identities in interconnected and mediated worlds suffused with possibilities for participation and assertion of citizenship rights. Specifically, she focuses on emerging minority Muslim identity in globalized India.

She is also a filmmaker, and has previously worked as a producer and channel manager with the Discovery Channels International, National Geographic Channel, and STAR TV.